Vicious Games

Anthropology, Culture and Society

Series Editors:
Jamie Cross, University of Edinburgh,
Christina Garsten, Stockholm University
and
Joshua O. Reno, Binghamton University

Recent titles:

The Limits to Citizen Power:
Participatory Democracy and the
Entanglements of the State
VICTOR ALBERT

The Heritage Machine:
Fetishism and Domination
in Maragateria, Spain
PABLO ALONSO GONZÁLEZ

Becoming Arab in London:
Performativity and the Undoing of Identity
RAMY M. K. ALY

Anthropologies of Value
EDITED BY LUIS FERNANDO ANGOSTO-
FERRANDEZ AND GEIR HENNING
PRESTERUDSTUEN

Ethnicity and Nationalism:
Anthropological Perspectives
Third Edition
THOMAS HYLLAND ERIKSEN

Fredrik Barth:
An Intellectual Biography
THOMAS HYLLAND ERIKSEN

Small Places, Large Issues:
An Introduction to Social
and Cultural Anthropology
Fourth Edition
THOMAS HYLLAND ERIKSEN

What is Anthropology?
Second Edition
THOMAS HYLLAND ERIKSEN

Deepening Divides:
How Territorial Borders and Social
Boundaries Delineate our World
EDITED BY DIDIER FASSIN

At the Heart of the State:
The Moral World of Institutions
DIDIER FASSIN, ET AL.

Anthropology and Development:
Challenges for the Twenty-first Century
KATY GARDNER AND DAVID LEWIS

Children of the Welfare State:
Civilising Practices in Schools,
Childcare and Families
LAURA GILLIAM AND EVA GULLØV

Faith and Charity:
Religion and Humanitarian Assistance
in West Africa
EDITED BY MARIE NATHALIE LEBLANC
AND LOUIS AUDET GOSSELIN

Private Oceans:
The Enclosure and Marketisation
of the Seas
FIONA MCCORMACK

The Rise of Nerd Politics:
Digital Activism and Political Change
JOHN POSTILL

Base Encounters:
The US Armed Forces in South Korea
ELISABETH SCHOBER

Ground Down by Growth:
Tribe, Caste, Class and Inequality in
Twenty-First-Century India
ALPA SHAH, JENS LERCHE, ET AL

When Protest Becomes Crime:
Politics and Law in Liberal Democracies
CAROLIJN TERWINDT

Race and Ethnicity in Latin America
Second Edition
PETER WADE

Vicious Games

Capitalism and Gambling

Rebecca Cassidy

First published 2020 by Pluto Press
345 Archway Road, London N6 5AA

www.plutobooks.com

British Library Cataloguing in Publication Data
A catalogue record for this book is available from the British Library

ISBN   978 0 7453 4038 8   Hardback
ISBN   978 0 7453 4039 5   Paperback
ISBN   978 1 7868 0586 7   PDF eBook
ISBN   978 1 7868 0588 1   Kindle eBook
ISBN   978 1 7868 0587 4   EPUB eBook

This book is printed on paper suitable for recycling and made from fully managed and sustained forest sources. Logging, pulping and manufacturing processes are expected to conform to the environmental standards of the country of origin.

Typeset by Stanford DTP Services, Northampton, England

Contents

Series Preface	vi
Acknowledgements	vii
Introduction	1
1 Gambling's New Deal	21
2 Raffles: Gambling for Good	40
3 The Birth of the Betting Shop	57
4 The Rise of the Machines	73
5 The Responsible Gambling Myth	91
6 The Bookmaker's Lament	109
7 Online in Gibraltar	127
8 The Regulation Game	153
Conclusions	174
Notes	188
References	196
Index	214

Series Preface

As people around the world confront the inequality and injustice of new forms of oppression, as well as the impacts of human life on planetary ecosystems, this book series asks what anthropology can contribute to the crises and challenges of the twenty-first century. Our goal is to establish a distinctive anthropological contribution to debates and discussions that are often dominated by politics and economics. What is sorely lacking, and what anthropological methods can provide, is an appreciation of the human condition.

We publish works that draw inspiration from traditions of ethnographic research and anthropological analysis to address power and social change while keeping the struggles and stories of human beings' centre stage. We welcome books that set out to make anthropology matter, bringing classic anthropological concerns with exchange, difference, belief, kinship and the material world into engagement with contemporary environmental change, capitalist economy and forms of inequality. We publish work from all traditions of anthropology, combining theoretical debate with empirical evidence to demonstrate the unique contribution anthropology can make to understanding the contemporary world.

Jamie Cross, Christina Garsten and Joshua O. Reno

Acknowledgements

This book is the culmination of many years of fieldwork and it would be impossible, in a brief note, to acknowledge everyone who has played a part in its production. On the other hand, not everyone who contributed to this book would wish to be recognised for their input. So I begin by expressing my appreciation to everyone who has spoken to me or written to me about gambling over the past fifteen years. Every conversation in the margins of a conference or in a betting shop was valuable and helped to inform my understanding of gambling and politics, perhaps not always in the ways intended by my interlocutors.

My greatest debt is to the many gamblers who shared their experiences with me, and made me question the powerful narrative that gambling is a leisure activity, the equivalent of going bowling or to the cinema. I am particularly indebted to those who spoke to me about gambling harm. To take time to speak with a researcher while dealing with the utter misery that gambling addiction can inflict upon individuals and their families is an act of great generosity. I hope that hearing about their experiences will inspire more people to accept that gambling addiction is an illness and that the harm caused by gambling is everyone's responsibility. In striking contrast to other fields where patient and public participation is considered absolutely essential, the views of experts by experience have not informed gambling policy and research in the UK. I hope that this situation is about to change, largely thanks to the efforts of charities including Gambling With Lives.

I would also like to thank everyone in the gambling industry who took the time to speak with me, particularly the small number of bosses who allowed me to work in their offices and interview their staff. I will continue to attempt to persuade the UK Department of Digital, Culture, Media and Sport (the department lead on gambling at the time of writing) that access to industry data and environments, provided as a condition of licensing, is the only way to ensure that policy makers receive the evidence they need to inform their decision making. Without access to data, gambling research will continue to be speculative and the industry will remain largely unaccountable for its actions.

I have decided not to thank any colleagues by name simply because this may not assist them in negotiating access to other secretive, profitable worlds. I hope that by thanking everyone who has argued for greater accountability, transparency and independence in research (including gambling), I include many of the people who have helped to create this book. Thanks also to my fellow anthropologists, at Goldsmiths and elsewhere, who continue to sustain me with their ideas, passion and collegiality: returning to anthropology after a long stint in the field always feels like coming home.

Introduction

It's all a game: money, gambling, the City, politics. It's all the same. It just happens that the game we play is particularly vicious. (Senior bookie, London)

This book is about the global expansion of commercial gambling which has taken place since the early 1980s. It uses data gathered during long-term field research to understand how this growth has been underwritten by corporations, policy makers and academics eager to benefit from the profits of gambling. It describes the central role that the betting industry and policy makers in the UK have played in this process, and shows that the impact of reframing gambling, from a potential source of crime to a legitimate leisure activity, has been felt much further afield. It tells this story through the everyday lives of gambling industry professionals and their customers.

I have been interested in gambling since 1999 when I began fieldwork in Newmarket, the famous headquarters of British horse racing (Cassidy 2002). As a stable lass on a struggling racing yard, I would gallop horses on the heath in the early mornings, before spending the afternoons, half asleep, in the 'bookies'. There I could meet with friends, watch 'our' horses race, and sometimes place the odd bet. It was cheaper (if slightly dirtier and smokier) than the pub. At the time, gambling was a relatively low-profile activity: casinos were not allowed to advertise, betting shop windows were blacked out, online gambling was more pipe dream than reality. All this changed in 2007 when a new Gambling Act came into force in the UK, setting into motion a number of related processes, some of them intended (the growth of the online industry), others unanticipated (the clustering of betting shops on high streets). For an anthropologist, this change opened up important questions about British society, including how ideas about risk and reward were changing and being shaped by the growth of gambling.

Although we are beginning to learn about the impact these changes are having on people who gamble, less is known about the 'black box' of the gambling industry. In this book I focus primarily on the people who produce gambling, including members of the various industries, regulators and politicians. The industry is (in their words) 'secretive, litigious and extremely well-funded' (North American casino executive, speaking in 2012). The soundtrack of my research is punctuated with slamming doors, the dialling tone and most of all ... silence. Gambling executives are quite open about deliberately avoiding engagement with independent academics in order to prevent them from conducting research. As one explained when I interviewed him in 2013, 'You just sit tight and hope that the research looks somewhere else. I would ignore your emails, then be really apologetic and upfront if I saw you again. Polite, but with no intention of ever, ever coming through for you.' Unsurprisingly, negotiating access to gambling environments takes a long time, and usually ends in failure. After all, why would gambling corporations want academics to find out how their business works?

So how did I manage to get people to talk to me? Sheer persistence, and playing the long game produced some exceptional opportunities. For example, an offhand remark to a neighbour during a boisterous betting industry conference yielded access to a chain of betting shops. The man sitting next to me turned out to be the CEO of a small up-and-coming bookmakers and, as soon as he learned that his rivals had turned down my requests for access, he welcomed me on board – he thought that my work might disrupt his competitors: 'My enemy's enemy is my friend', he said, with the belligerence for which he is well known. It is also important to understand that while, from the outside, the gambling industry may appear exploitative and greedy, insiders do not feel the need to constantly defend themselves against criticism – they are among friends and have created particular ways of understanding the world, and their place in it, as I will show. Once I was inside this world, my presence was infrequently questioned, and people were often surprisingly candid.

If I sometimes struggled to get into gambling worlds, at other times, becoming assimilated was a problem. During long periods of fieldwork in betting shops, for example, I had to remind my colleagues that I was a professional anthropologist and not a cashier looking to fast-track a career in retail. At a cocktail party in Tokyo a lawyer representing a casino operator told me that if I chose to write the social responsibility policy for his client then I would 'never need to work again'. I reminded him that I am interested in commercial innovation and the arguments which underpin gambling expansion including 'responsible gambling' and he put his fingers in his ears and said 'La la la! Not listening!'

Over a period of almost twenty years, I have been able to conduct fieldwork at racetracks in the UK and USA, betting shops and social gaming studios in London, casinos in Las Vegas, pachinko parlours and card rooms in Japan, mobile casino operators in Gibraltar and casinos and VIP rooms in Macau. These conventional ethnographic encounters have been supplemented by more disparate experiences at conferences all over the world, where the industry gets together to express a collective, dysfunctional identity described quite accurately by one of its members as, 'like a particularly fascist and sexist version of the worst type of '80s banker'.

Not surprisingly, the gambling industry is a diverse group and I will not attempt to provide an exhaustive categorisation of their differences as though these map easily onto different sectors or jurisdictions. Having said that, some of the toughest people I spoke with were bookmakers in the UK and casino representatives in Australia. I have been shouted at and patronised, sprayed with crumbs, talked over, mansplained and blanked by lots of (mostly) men, some of whom are in very powerful positions in their organisations. Scattered among this group were interesting and accomplished people, a few of whom were deeply depressed about working in gambling. 'I hate this business. It's turned my soul black and made my hair fall out', one emailed me when I failed to turn up at a conference, 'When are you coming?' He continued, 'You are the only person who makes this whole fucking thing bearable.' There were also incredibly smart people, one or two with a conscience.

I will explain more about this variation in later chapters, but it's helpful to understand from the start that while commercial gambling is normally represented in public by bubbly and enthusiastic (often female) endorsers of 'responsible' or 'safer' gambling, when going about their normal business, the companies involved are far less squeamish. Equally, not all bookmakers or casino executives have horns and a tail. They offered several different explanations for being involved in a business which harms people and is stigmatised and (in some places) associated with organised crime. Many of the people I worked with had in the past described themselves as 'accountants' or (at least until the financial crisis in 2008) 'bankers'. More recent recruits often described themselves as working in 'technology'. Some of them had not told their extended family that they worked in gambling: in one case a casino manager's occupation had remained hidden from his wife's parents for over thirty years. Like people everywhere, gambling executives are able to accommodate apparent paradoxes in their lives, including being loving fathers and husbands, with selling harmful products. Many do this by embracing the idea that gambling is harmless fun for most people, most of the time, and creates jobs and income for society, an idea that I will explore in detail in this book. More broadly, they do it by embracing principles which are culturally and historically distinctive, but presented as natural facts – for example, the idea that connections between individuals are secondary rather than primary facts. For many people working in the gambling industry, like the politicians on whom they depend to produce supportive policies, people are individuals, responsible only for themselves, a curious idea with a distinctive and recent history (Sahlins 2008).

As well as the people who produce and sell gambling, I have also spent a lot of time with the people who create gambling policies and regulation. In the UK and Europe, politicians were unanimous that responsibility for gambling is a poisoned chalice, or in the words of one former minister, 'shit on your shoe'. They described themselves as obliged to do business with the gambling industries, at the same time as managing headlines about problem gamblers and their families. A conventional way to approach this problem has been to present their policy-making activities as 'evidence based', and their decisions as apolitical. I discuss the consequences of this framing, and its origins, in chapter 1.

As well as working with the industry and policy makers, I wanted to find out what frontline workers in the UK thought about gambling and how they made sense of their jobs. I trained as a cashier and assistant manager, and worked in betting shops as an unpaid cashier for two different companies. I learned the difference between Yankies, Trixies and Round Robins, how to calculate bets in the event of a power cut, and how to tell if someone is trying to cheat by using a slow count or dodgy handwriting. I write about these experiences in chapter 3.

Between 2012 and 2017, to complement my knowledge of betting shop punters, I worked with ordinary people, including people who did not gamble, and attended meetings of local groups in London and the south-east of England ranging from middle-class poker-playing golfers to social gaming 'Yummy Mummies'. I consumed a lot of tea and cake with seniors, learned about archery, the history of clowning and hearing dogs for the deaf. I gave talks to groups of businessmen, ladies who lunch, anglers and cricket teams. I handed out surveys, questionnaires and diaries. I created discussion groups and held 'surgeries' for gamblers and non-gamblers. I ran raffles and collected for tombola. I went to race nights, bingo nights, point-to-points, fetes and fairs of every kind, celebrating dogs, apples and the end of the First World War. I stopped people on streets in Kent villages and on commuter trains in what is known as 'the stockbroker belt' to ask them about gambling. I interviewed more than two hundred people and trawled through the Mass Observation archives in Brighton. I was delighted when, at a beetle drive in my own village, a woman named Rose took me to one side and told me that a cousin of a friend in a neighbouring county had been to a talk given by a woman who was interested in gambling, did I want her to try to put us in touch? 'That was me!' I told Rose, who was a bit disappointed.

Outside the UK I have hung out with gamblers, racehorse trainers, breeders and jockeys in Kentucky, Kyrgyzstan, Georgia, Mongolia, India and Hong Kong. I have worked with professional gamblers in Hong Kong and Singapore, pachinko players in Tokyo, bingo hotshots in Ohio, slots slaves in Las Vegas and gone on junkets with would-be card sharks in Macau. In Gibraltar I accompanied people to work at three different companies and interviewed over a hundred policy makers and workers. I've spent time on trading floors, watched markets for football matches being made by bookmakers, and organised focus groups with betting shop punters in London.

The purpose of this flurry of activity was to expose myself to all kinds of gambling and to use a variety of methods and approaches to find out what a range of people think about it, the extent of their involvement in it, and how they think things have changed recently. Unlike a prevalence study, which counts the numbers of people who gamble, how much and how often, the intention is not to produce a snapshot of gambling, but to drill down into particular places and some of the practices found there. These 'thicker' descriptions of gambling provide data that complements more generic survey findings. The book is part of a qualitative turn that is taking place in gambling research, towards a more grounded perspective and a more critical approach which places the experiences of gamblers and their families at the centre of the analysis and also pays attention to the inequalities that gambling creates and reinforces including those of class, race and gender (Cassidy et al. 2013; Nicoll 2013, 2019; Schüll 2012).

The book is explicitly comparative and draws on data from a range of contexts and jurisdictions. This approach, central to anthropology, disrupts the idea that the organisation of gambling in any one place or time is natural or inevitable. Simply looking elsewhere and seeing how things are different can undermine 'conventional wisdom', raising new questions and opening up fresh perspectives. Unlike lab-based psychology experiments, I embrace the confusing and messy circumstances in which gambling takes place. Whether someone is betting on an illegal dog fight in Deptford, or on baccarat in a casino in Macau, is, to me, a significant and interesting part of the data, rather than 'noise' to be controlled for, or 'written out' of my account. Unlike psychologists, I am not seeking to make generalised observations about gambling behaviour or indeed gamblers. On the contrary, I am trying to problematise categories and ideas that have become entrenched and powerful, and to show how their manifestation is a significant part of the process of legitimising commercial gambling.

All of my fieldwork took place openly, and in accordance with the ethical guidelines of the Association of Social Anthropologists of the UK. Participants were invited to provide written or verbal consent after I had explained the nature of my project. In order to protect the privacy of my research participants, and in keeping with their wishes, all names have been changed in the text. Where research participants shared stories which might cause them to be identified, I have changed details in their narratives in order to protect their anonymity. As for all anthropologists, the safety and privacy of my participants is my priority and takes precedence over any other concerns. In the course of my fieldwork, I have been privileged to speak with many people who have personal experience of gambling harm, and their views and priorities have shaped this book. The historical lack of input from 'experts by experience' in gambling research and policy making is a weakness that must be addressed.

The research was funded by a few different sources. The first grant I received to work on gambling came from a joint venture between the Economic and Social Research Council, a non-departmental public body funded by the UK government, and the Responsibility in Gambling Trust (RiGT, now called GambleAware) a charity supported by voluntary contributions from the gambling industry to pay for research, education and treatment of problem gambling (Cassidy 2012a). When I shared my findings with the RiGT I was told that I could not speak in public about them without first receiving written clearance. This injunction is far from unusual: charities, quangos and government departments all over the world with responsibility for funding gambling research routinely impose conditions on academic freedoms. However, as a young, naïve researcher, the experience had a profound effect on me and on the direction of my work. I decided that, in future, I would not seek funding from sources that were directly linked to gambling profits, and that I would pay greater attention to the process of producing evidence about gambling in general (Cassidy et al. 2013).[1] In 2010 I received a four-year award from the European Research Council (ERC) to use anthropology to explore the expansion of commercial gambling (ERC 2015).[2] This support enabled me to take a very broad approach to gambling, without any fear of interference.

How much gambling is there?

Although gambling sometimes appears to be everywhere, on our televisions and phones, our streets, and on the shirts of sports stars, it is very difficult to get an accurate estimate of exactly how much of it there is, because of the paucity of available data and the vested interests of those doing the counting. In 2015, Morgan Stanley estimated that the global gambling market was worth $423 billion, and would grow to $635 billion by 2022. According to their report, land-based casinos were the largest sector, accounting for 35% of revenue, followed by lotteries at 29%, with 'other gambling', such as sports betting and pari-mutuel racing at 28% and online gambling at $37 billion or 9% (Morgan Stanley 2015). To give a sense of the scale of the industry, according to *Bloomberg*, in 2017 casinos were the twelfth largest industry globally, just ahead of Chemicals and Coal Mining (*Bloomberg* 2016). How is this money distributed geographically? According to Forbes: of the $146 billion from land-based casinos, US commercial and 'tribal' operations[3] took in $67 billion or 46%, Asia and Australia casinos $61 billion or 42%, and the rest of the world $18 billion or 12% (Cohen 2015).

There is little doubt that regulated gambling has grown rapidly in the past four decades, all over the world. However, estimates of the rate, extent and distribution of this growth vary considerably, depending on the inclinations of the source. The many ways in which the profits generated by gambling are measured (including the most common, gross gambling revenue [GGR], which is broadly defined as the amount wagered minus the winnings returned to players) vary between jurisdictions and companies and are sometimes closely guarded commercial secrets. Furthermore, private companies are not under the same obligations to publish data as their public rivals. The data gathered by regulators is often incomplete, or incomparable across jurisdictions, or lags behind technology and new markets. As it catches up and includes new categories of gambling in its returns, comparisons become increasingly difficult. To complicate matters further, the precise methodologies used to gather data are often missing from reports. Meaningful comparisons through time or across space are therefore virtually impossible.[4]

The result of this is that gambling statistics are brought into existence and acquire lives of their own. The fact that predictions of growth in particular markets or sectors are often pitches is ignored, and even established companies have had to radically alter figures in the face of disappointing results. In 2015, for example, Morgan Stanley reduced their projection of the size of the US online industry in 2020 down from $5 billion to $2.7 billion (Pempus 2015). My approach to this patchwork of rhetorical data has been to triangulate where possible, and to maintain the link between various estimates and their sources, which sounds elementary, but is not something that always happens. In 2014, for example, National Basketball Association (NBA) Commissioner Adam Silver wrote to the *New York Times*, arguing for the legalisation of sports betting in the US on the basis that the illegal market was worth $400 billion (Silver 2014). A journalist for *Slate* magazine traced the origin of this figure to a 'guesstimate' by a member of Congress, and has described how, 'a statistic that may well have been made up on the spot was sealed into history' (Weissmann 2014), becoming a key number in subsequent changes to legislation, even after its origins had been questioned. This is typical of the way in which statistics function in gambling policy and research.

Different approaches to gambling regulation

Although the growth of commercial gambling is a global phenomenon, this growth is uneven and the businesses on which it is based vary wildly. In Macau, for example, 'King of Gambling' Stanley Ho held the monopoly on licensed gambling for over 70 years until the American Sands Corporation (the largest casino company in the world) was granted a licence in 2004. Macau, the only place in greater China where casino gambling is legal, gradually became the largest market for gambling in the world, peaking at $45 billion gross gaming revenue in 2013, before declining after a crackdown on 'graft' (corruption) in China (Ge 2016). Despite the slowdown in growth, Macau still outstrips Las Vegas by some distance: in 2017 gross gaming revenue in Macau was $33 billion, compared to $7.09 billion in Las Vegas (*Casino News Daily* 2018).

Although electronic gaming machines have been the drivers of growth in the US and Australia, this is not always the case (Schüll 2013). For example, the most popular game in Macau, by a huge margin, is baccarat (accounting for $29.2 billion of revenue in 2017), played at tables, with live dealers. In complete contrast, the majority of revenue in Las Vegas ($3.64 billion in 2017) is generated by slot machines (*Casino News Daily* 2018). However, it is Japan, not the US, which has the highest number of gambling machines per head in the world, even though 'gambling' (apart from betting on horse, boat and cycle racing) is, technically, illegal (Ziolkowski 2016). Pachinko, a noisy variety of pinball played in distinctive 'parlours' on streets in Japanese suburbs, is fast and immersive, just like slots in Vegas and pokies in Australia. However, unlike pokies and slots, it is defined as 'entertainment' on the basis that any winnings must be collected from a kiosk located outside the parlour. After many years of lobbying by North American companies, Japan is in the process of licensing its first resort casino in Osaka (Wilson and Saito 2018). However, online gambling, with the exception of betting on horse races, bicycle races, motorcycle races and motorboat races operated by the Japanese government or municipal bodies, remains strictly illegal.

It is also important to remember that while gambling is growing rapidly in many places, in others it is totally or partially prohibited. As well as in the majority of the US, sports betting is illegal in India, Pakistan and China, three of the largest gambling markets in the world. Needless to say, gambling takes place in these countries, sometimes feverishly and often in distinctive and interesting formats (Puri 2014). However, the focus of this book is the regulated industry and the governmental logics that underpin legality. Gambling is also banned in most Muslim countries and in some of them, including Brunei and the United Arab Emirates, this ban is rigorously enforced. Canada and several countries in Scandinavia take a different approach altogether, granting the state a monopoly on regulated gambling and either supplying the market themselves or contracting out that opportunity to private companies. Australians spend the most per person on gambling, and do so with a mixture of commercial and local, charitable organisations (Economist Daily Chart 2017). These differences in definitions, tastes and practices are a product of distinctive social histories and proclivities, including shifts in regulation, as I will explain.

London leads the way

The best place to appreciate the scale and diversity of the global gambling industry is at the International Casino Exhibition (ICE), the largest commercial gambling conference in the world, which takes place every

February at the Excel Centre in London. ICE is international, innovative, dynamic, aggressively liberal, and sexist: the ideal place to reflect on London's role in the global expansion of gambling. As a sensory experience, ICE rivals a Tokyo pachinko parlour. It is deafening, overwhelming and relentless, as hundreds of exhibitors attempt to make their product stand out from the other roulette wheels, casino chairs or automatic card shufflers. Purveyors of the latest slot machines command the largest marketing budgets and produce some spectacular effects. In 2017 an Isle of Man-based software provider launched a new game 'Jurassic Park World' from a specially constructed dinosaur bar complete with 'dinosaur eggs, mosquitoes preserved in amber' and 'a mammoth 5m × 5m shark-eating Mosasaurus, a replica of the genetically modified reptile from the Late Cretaceous period' (Press Releases 2017). The previous year the same company constructed a 'cryolab' to showcase their pioneering work in Virtual Reality (VR) roulette. However, they were upstaged by Endorphina's regular Twerk Slot, as promoted by Di Baddest, a group of 'glamorous dancers'. The treatment and representation of women at ICE attracted criticism in 2018, but in 2019 it was business as usual, a reflection of the unapologetic sexism that exists within some sections of the industry (Davies and Marsh 2018). For example, in the midst of the row in 2018, I asked an executive what he thought about feminism and he responded: 'much like Health and Safety. An affront to our way of life. Equal rights? Who wants to see a bloke walking around with his tits out?'

ICE is also important because, unlike the Global Gaming Expo (G2E), its North American counterpart which is held in Las Vegas each year, it draws exhibitors from every jurisdiction in the world, and from every sector of the industry including bingo, casino, lottery, mobile, online, social gaming, and sports betting. G2E is huge and showy but comparatively parochial, and emphasises the elements that complete the so-called 'bricks and mortar' industry in the US: lotteries, slots and 'hospitality' (specifically: 'food and beverage' a category of huge importance in the US, which is non-existent at gambling events in the UK).

Despite a recent ruling by the Supreme Court, online gambling remains illegal in the majority of the US, and strongly vilified in some quarters (Katz 2019). High-profile campaigns against legalisation include the powerful Coalition to Stop Internet Gambling (CSIG) funded by casino owner Sheldon Adelson, CEO of the Las Vegas Sands Corporation (Ho 2016). The situation in Macau is similar: at a conference in 2016 I was puzzled by the small audiences in the main sessions: an insider from an online sports betting company based in the Philippines explained that the real conference was taking place in private, in hotel rooms and restaurants. Executives from companies operating in the so-called 'grey' and illegal markets of Asia did not want to risk being photographed by the police at the conference as had apparently happened the previous year.[5]

Senior executives in the US told me that their businesses are currently around fifteen years behind the UK in terms of innovation, regulation and knowledge. In stark contrast, the UK is the largest regulated market for online gambling in the world (GamblingCompliance 2018), and corporations are already comfortable exploiting the intersections of gambling and gaming, betting in-play, social gaming, Bitcoin, financial trading and spread betting, betting exchanges, e-sports and, most profitably, mobile gambling. In the US, while the implications of the Supreme Court ruling in 2018 remain unclear, they are still focused on finding new players and different attractions to replace the income generated by 'grinders', the older generation of casino customer who have kept the industry afloat and are now dying off: 'We are still looking at cheap food and booze while you guys have cornered the market on phones and online' explained one Las Vegas executive in 2017. The contrasting experiences offered by gambling expos shows that the expansion of commercial gambling is shaped by local and regional politics. This diversity, and the paradoxes and inconsistencies that produce it, show that while commercial gambling has an affinity with late capitalism, there is nothing inevitable about its expansion, or fixed about the form that expansion might take.

The natural history of gambling

The expansion of gambling is often presented by policy makers as the inevitable result of a combination of changes in attitudes, desires and technology, which are associated with progress towards a broadly neoliberal version of modernity in which markets provide solutions to economic and social challenges. In relation to gambling, these arguments take several different, not totally consistent, forms. The first suggests that risk taking, including gambling, is part of human nature and therefore universal. These arguments have a long history. In 1870 Steinmetz suggested that gambling was 'a universal thing' (1870: 4) and in 1901 Thomas described 'The gaming instinct' as something which is 'born in all normal persons' as an 'expression of a powerful reflex fixed far back in animal experience' (1901: 760).

More recently, Zheng and Wan write that, 'Gambling is a universal phenomenon in human societies' (2013: 2). Conjuring images from Coolidge's series *Dogs Playing Poker*, historian David Schwartz has suggested that, 'The gambling impulse even predates humanity.' 'A variety of animals', he argues, 'embrace risk for a chance at a reward' (Schwartz 2006: 5). The ethnographic record suggests that, unless one broadens the definition of gambling to include all playful or risky behaviour, in many places and times, including Melanesia, people did not gamble (Binde 2005; Pickles 2014). Nevertheless, assertions of the universality of gambling by researchers are ubiquitous: 'Gambling is universal, occurring in some form or another in most societies over time' (Breen 2008: 137). The idea that gambling is a natural-cultural phenomenon (universal, with diverse local forms) enables some authors to describe its emergence as a biological, rather than historical process: 'Gambling is a universal phenomenon ... virtually every culture has *evolved* some way of letting its members stake something of value on an event of uncertain outcome' (Abt et al. 1985: 7). Even those one might expect to resist these narratives are responsible for repeating them: 'Gambling is just like eucalyptus oil – it's natural', is an unusual analogy, more surprising for being made by the chairman of the Australian Churches Gambling Taskforce (quoted in Australian Associated Press 2014). Less surprisingly, the gambling industry uses these arguments to naturalise their existence and present their activities as responsive and reactive: they are fulfilling, rather than creating demand for popular products. The Compliance Department of a large corporation once wrote to me asking me to provide evidence that gambling 'is natural' adding, 'We have proof that it is already, but we want an up to date reference from you.' I asked how it would be used. 'It shows gambling's part of life.' He told me, 'We want to use it in a submission [to the government].'

The second inevitability argument is that 'gambling is part of our culture: it is natural *here, for us.*' In other words, 'Risk-taking is a distinctively American value' (Hurt 2005: 372). Or, as Findlay wrote in *People of Chance*, 'Las Vegas represents a link between America's frontier past and the contemporary values of the Sunbelt culture' (1986: 1). In the UK, the Culture, Media and Sport Committee in the House of Commons noted that, 'Gambling has been a part of British culture for many hundreds of years' (House of Commons Culture Media and Sport Committee 2012a: 3), echoing the view that 'gambling has long been knitted into the culture of the English' (Pitt 2012: 2) and making the proclivity to gamble a marker of national or regional identity. Clapson (1989: i) has described how, when commercial gambling was expanding rapidly between 1853 and 1960 to disparage gambling was to be 'un-English'. A similar argument was made during a public debate about betting shop closures that I attended in east London in 2013. Discussing the perceived clustering of betting shops in a street nearby, the manager of one of the shops told a local council member:

> You can't tell a bloke that he can't have a bet! It's the right of every Englishman to have a bet! What next? Ascot won't be Royal? The Grand National will be steeplechase number 59! Do me a favour! You may as well have surrendered to the Germans all them years ago as tell a man he can't have a bet.

The same argument has been made by the gambling industry in Australia, where opposition to commercial expansion has been presented as 'un-Australian' (Australian Associated Press 2011).

The third argument suggests that the distribution of gambling is the expression of biological characteristics. For example, 'We can't prove this but most likely [Asian immigrants] have some kind of biological predisposition to gambling in general, in life' (Fong, quoted in Louie 2014). Although not exclusively,[6] this argument is applied most often to Chinese gamblers, who may also be given extraordinary physical attributes: 'Gambling industry sources said Chinese players exhibit some unusual characteristics. One is the size of their bets. Another is the ability to play without sleep' (Pomfret 2002). Genetic explanations for gambling are also growing in popularity, for example, 'Researchers [at the Chinese University of Hong Kong] suspect that the Chinese love of gambling may also have a genetic component and are keen to begin blood tests on local gambling addicts' (Rennie 2001). These kinds of argument can have dire political consequences. For example, the Chinese community in London are eager to conduct an urgent discussion about the harm caused by gambling in their community. However, they have found it extremely difficult to gain any purchase against the idea that to be Chinese is to gamble. As the head of one community organisation explained to me in 2014: 'The Asian gambler is a figure brought into existence only in relation to the commercial gambling industry. Until then, this man is a brother, a husband, or a son. Once he becomes an Asian gambler all is lost. After all, who can fight one's essential character?'

In what follows I bracket conventional arguments about the inevitability of gambling expansion and instead focus on its stuttering and uneven reality. I use fieldwork with industry executives, gamblers and politicians to unpack expansion as a social phenomenon that has been manufactured (and can therefore be submitted to critical analysis and intervention) rather than a natural (and therefore inevitable) consequence of changes in tastes, attitudes and technology.

My primary focus is the UK, reflecting its role as a centre for the international industry, and informed by my fieldwork in Europe, Asia and North America. Other social scientists have described the expansion of gambling in particular jurisdictions, including the Netherlands (Kingma 2008), Canada (Cosgrave and Klassen 2009), the US (Schüll 2012), Australia (Nicoll 2019) and South Africa (Sallaz 2009). These important contributions show that gambling does not sweep all before it, nor does it expand in the same way in every place. My contribution is to attempt to show how the gambling industry has also developed an international dimension, which helps it to expand across borders. Gambling expansion is an achievement, not an unintended consequence of 'modernity' or economic growth. Nor is it the natural expression of an evolutionary advantage – the hunter gatherer's willingness to take risks. The unnatural history of gambling is far more diverse and interesting.

The cost of gambling expansion

The gambling industry has become increasingly powerful since the 1980s, particularly in the UK, US and Australia, where global corporations command vast budgets for lobbying and advertising. As a regressive form of taxation, gambling extracts wealth from some of our poorest communities (Kohler 2016). Furthermore, recent research shows that gambling is taking its toll on everyone, whether they gamble or not. In New Zealand, for example, the total burden of harms occurring to gamblers has been estimated as 'greater than common health conditions (such as diabetes and arthritis) and approaching the level of anxiety and depressive disorders' (Browne et al. 2017: 199). Problems with gambling are also associated with elevated rates of suicidal thoughts, and attempted and completed suicide: a recent study in Sweden found that people with a gambling disorder were fifteen times more likely to commit suicide compared to the general population (Karlsson and Håkansson 2018).

Moreover, the harm caused by gambling is not restricted to people suffering from a gambling addiction. For every person who has a problem with gambling, an average of six other people are directly affected (Goodwin et al. 2017) whether that is a partner unable to afford shoes for their children, or an employer who is a victim of petty theft. More broadly, research has shown that in Victoria, Australia, the majority of harm produced by gambling (85%) comes from low- and moderate-risk gambling (Browne et al. 2016: 3), undermining the common misconception, carefully nurtured by the industry and policy makers, that the harm caused by gambling can be contained by focusing on the treatment of a small number of addicted individuals.

The scale of gambling harm in the UK has not been measured. However, recent data gathered by the Gambling Commission shows that more than 2 million people in the UK are either addicted to gambling or at risk of developing a problem (Conolly et al. 2017). In addition, 125,000 children in the UK are either problem gamblers, or at risk of developing problems with gambling (Gambling Commission 2018b). A recent study by the Institute for Public Policy Research (IPPR) estimated that problem gambling was costing the UK between £270 million and £1.17 billion a year (Thorley et al. 2016), although the huge range of this estimate has detracted from its impact on policy. No attempt was made by the UK government to assess the social and economic costs of gambling before the changes to the legislation and there are no plans to attempt to estimate their scale today, despite useful studies taking place in other jurisdictions. The impact that liberal gambling regimes will have on the future behaviour of young people is extremely difficult to predict, but evidence from tobacco, alcohol and junk food suggest that increased exposure to advertising is associated with greater risks of adult harm (Anderson et al. 2009; Hastings et al. 2003).

The majority of studies of gambling focus on its problematic consumption. Partly because of the challenges of studying such a closed and intimidating world, the production of gambling tends to be overlooked and gambling becomes, by definition, something that people do, rather than something that is manufactured and promoted. The effect of this lacuna is that the expansion of gambling appears inescapable: a natural fact, and therefore immune from criticism. 'Bookmakers are greedy!' I was told, when I asked people why they thought gambling was growing at such a rate. 'Because of the internet and smart phones' said others. These responses conceal more interesting structural explanations that can be accessed by working anthropologically, spending time alongside members of the gambling industry, and showing how they collaborate with politicians, lawyers, academics and others in order to produce and maintain profitable businesses.

The tobacco, alcohol and gambling industries have learned many important lessons from one another, routinely exchanging ideas and personnel. In 2019, for example, it was announced that Brigid Simmons, CEO of the British Beer and Pubs Association, would step down in order to lead the newly formed Betting and Gaming Council (Wood 2019). Researchers are beginning to do the same: investing in collaborative international and multidisciplinary networks which will form the basis of stronger and more confident interventions in public health in the future. They are also using new methods to explore not just the consumption of gambling but also its production, including participant observation, the hallmark of anthropological inquiry. Because it involves talking to people throughout a community, rather than relying on those responsible for presenting its public face, fieldwork can undermine established and powerful positions, replacing them with more interesting, less obvious alternatives. The gambling industry's presentations of self are generally bland and uninteresting, couched in terms of 'responsible' or 'safer' gambling and intended for public consumption. The everyday discussions which take place at work are far more enlightening and a better reflection of the attitudes and mechanisms which underpin the business.

The field of gambling studies developed alongside the regulated industry and is incapable of providing a critical perspective on the processes that enabled its development and ensure its future (Schüll 2012). Despite the perils of industry support, which are well understood in fields such as alcohol and tobacco, gambling research continues to be dependent on funds that are raised from gambling, including disordered gambling, whether through government levies or industry profits. As well as being mortally conflicted by its financial ties with those who profit from gambling, the lens of gambling studies is too tightly focused on individual consumers, who are often presented as mere bearers of harm or insufficiently disciplined subjects (Reith 2004). On the other hand, historical and political studies of gambling can sometimes stand too far back, away from the sticky floor of a betting shop in London, or the deafening racket of a pachinko parlour in Tokyo. Anthropology provides a solution to this methodological and political impasse by placing the experiences of people involved in producing, selling and promoting gambling at centre stage.

Plan of the book

This book is about the extraordinary synergy between commercial gambling and the ideology and philosophy of late capitalism. It is about the affinity between politicians who are determined to make the individual the primary unit of political importance, and gambling executives who argue that it is more important to allow people the opportunity to consume dangerous products than it is to safeguard public health. It shows how the freedom to choose became sovereign, and how attempts to limit the exposure of people to harmful products could be presented as an arrogant and patronising act of contempt. Under these conditions, good government came to mean 'light-touch regulation' – 'roll back the state' and let the markets decide. In order to flourish, commercial gambling depends on precisely these principles – an approach to life that is inherently, deliberately, asocial, a way of thinking about the collective as a drag on individual freedom. The success of this social project, undertaken by politicians and corporations, can be measured in tax revenue and company profits. The externalities – the harms caused by gambling – are to be managed at the individual level. According to this logic, individuals should control themselves, seek treatment and cultivate additional will power. The positions and ideals expressed by the industry and their defenders which I capture in this book may strike some readers as harsh or even inhuman. However, they are merely extensions of much more commonly accepted ideas which attract surprisingly little criticism. In this book I show how the belief that there are no collective duties, only individual rights, helped the gambling industry to get where it is today.

In the first chapter of the book I use interviews to provide a new perspective on the changes to gambling legislation which have taken place in the UK since the 1980s. Working for such a long period of time in this relatively small field allowed me to gain access to many of the people who contributed to this process, including bookies, consultants, lobbyists, politicians and casino company executives. The purpose of the chapter is to show that the current phase of growth is not just a spontaneous reaction to changes in consumer demand caused by new products which are in turn made possible by new technology. On the contrary, it has been carefully manufactured and sustained by explicit policies pursued by successive governments. I also want to undermine the idea that fixed odds betting terminals (FOBTs), for example, were forged in the white heat of innovation created by the bookmakers. In practice, and according to the people involved, the betting revolution was 'more of a casserole than a stir fry'. It took place over a long period of time and was led by politicians and other market makers, including, but not exclusively, the industry itself.

In the second chapter I focus on raffles, a ubiquitous form of gambling which has been virtually ignored by researchers. Everyday games like tombola, lotteries and drawing lots undermine the idea that gambling can have a single definition or function. My fieldwork shows that, on the contrary, we are inconsistent about what we think constitutes gambling, as well as which kinds are helpful or harmful. By using an anthropological approach I'm also arguing for the value of comparison. It makes no sense to try to search for the essence of gambling. Its meaning and appeal is predicated on the way in which it is inserted into and changed by a particular society. The chapter is also intended to illustrate that gambling can be redistributive, and is not inherently anti-social. Again, the social function of gambling, whether it increases or reduces inequality, for example, depends on how it articulates with the wider system of which it is a part, hence the importance of anthropological studies of particular activities, objects, products and processes.

Chapter 3 describes a popular form of gambling in the UK: betting on horses and sports in purpose built high street shops. It describes the origins of betting shops in the UK, their distinctive ambience, and how they became working-class, masculine spaces. In the 1960s, when betting shops were legalised, laws were designed to allow the industry to accommodate existing demand, without stimulating any additional growth. The shops changed radically as a result of deregulation in the 1990s and in 2005 a new Gambling Act removed the demand principle altogether and re-categorised bookmaking as part of the leisure industry. The chapter is based on the testimony of betting shop managers and customers who experienced these changes at first hand.

For decades, the services provided by betting shops were similar to those offered by bookies working illegally in factories, chip shops and homes a century earlier: bets on live horse and dog racing, and an annual calendar dominated by Classic races, big handicaps and the Grand National. Few in the traditional betting industry thought that a machine showing casino games based on dumb luck could replace the painstaking study of form that took place in 'turf accountants'. But by 2006, FOBTs were making more profit than betting over the counter on horses and dogs, halting the demise of high street bookies and providing a lightning rod for public opposition towards the expansion of gambling in the UK. Chapter 4 uses fieldwork at the headquarters of a leading UK bookmaker and in betting shops in London to ask: 'How are niches for new products discovered and exploited?' and specifically: 'Where did these machines come from?', 'How did they manage to capture such a large part of the betting market in the UK so quickly?' And, 'Why did it take so long to get rid of them?'

Responsible gambling programmes are produced and promoted by trade organisations and operators as an essential part of the 'compliance' process that preserves self-regulation and delays the imposition of meaningful harm reduction measures. In chapter 5 I describe how abstract codes are produced and compare them with the embodied ethics which govern daily interactions in betting shops in London. I describe the violence that my colleagues and I experienced while working in betting shops, and use interviews with managers to reflect on its causes. In this context, codes operate to deepen structural inequalities between workers and their managers. The chapter shows that in this space, 'social responsibility' is an aspect of public relations, necessary to legitimate gambling profits.

At the same time as FOBTs transformed betting shops in the UK, the focus of so-called 'remote' gambling was shifting from the telephone to the internet. In chapter 6 I describe the view from the trading floor of a major UK bookmaker as the internet takes over from traditional ways of making prices or odds. Using fieldwork with traders and odds compilers, I show how new kinds of betting, including through exchanges, and in-play, transformed the rhythm of gambling and the place of trust in relationships between bookies and punters. The purpose of the chapter is to show how different products and processes generate moral economies and how these are embodied, sustained and defended. The chapter uses fieldwork to evoke the existential challenge faced by bookmakers used to trading on their knowledge when confronted by geeks armed with algorithms who knew nothing about racehorses or jockeys.

Gibraltar has played a key role in the transformation of online gambling, from a criminal subsidiary of the porn industry, to a legitimate offshore business supplied by licensed, listed companies. Chapter 7 uses fieldwork with casinos and sportsbooks to describe how online gambling was partially and perhaps temporarily domesticated in Gibraltar, showing how the embodied practices of producing and consuming gambling are transmitted and occasionally resisted, and how different approaches to customer service reproduce divergent ideas about the social role of gambling and the responsibilities of 'providers'. It describes how 'social responsibility' is shaped by the transition from physical customers to anonymous 'account holders', including those who are given the ominous title of 'VIP'.

In chapter 8 I use data gathered at conferences and during interviews with regulators, politicians and operators to see how the scripts which constitute gambling's facts are produced and maintained. The gambling community attends conferences to network and strategise, establishing shared understandings of political shifts and their potential impact on business. In this chapter I focus on the gambling industry's response to the aftermath of the financial crisis. As governments attempted to find new sources of revenue, the gambling industry circled overhead, eager to profit from the rush to capitalise national assets. In the final chapter of the book I describe 'responsible gambling', its origins and the ways that it fits with and is an expression of other neoliberal policies, including gambling deregulation.

1

Gambling's New Deal

We have … set out a new deal for the British gambling industry. It will take away unnecessary, outdated restrictions that stop the gambling industry from operating and marketing itself on the same basis as any other legitimate leisure industry. (Tessa Jowell, Secretary of State for Culture, Media and Sport 2002)

In the final decades of the twentieth century an attempt was made to transform gambling in the UK from an activity that was tolerated, to a business to be encouraged. A new way of thinking about gambling became normative among some politicians and parts of the industry even though it was not widely supported by the public. A survey by the Office of National Statistics in 2002, the year in which Tessa Jowell was describing gambling as an increasingly mainstream leisure activity, showed that 80% of people had not changed their attitude to gambling over the last ten years, 15% said it was more negative, and 6% said their attitude was more positive (Gambling Review Body 2001: 239).[1]

This chapter explores the background to these changes, and their relative success. It sets out the most important events in the transformation as interpreted by the people involved: bookmakers, casino operators and politicians. Its broader purpose is to shine a light on the ways in which gambling can be partially and perhaps temporarily, domesticated. Gambling legislation has also been rewritten since the 1980s in Australia, South Africa, the Netherlands, Canada, New Zealand and, more recently, in Singapore, each driven by different priorities and with different outcomes. The US remains resolutely undecided about gambling – casinos and poker are relatively acceptable while sports betting and online gambling continue to be controversial (Katz 2019). Japan has been deliberately inconsistent – tolerating a multibillion dollar pachinko industry (Chan 2018) while claiming to ban gambling (with the exceptions of betting on horse racing, and a few other sports). In 2018 casinos were finally legalised in Japan after years of lobbying from American companies. The new casinos will be subject to strict conditions, and must be part of a wider entertainment complex – the so-called 'resort' model pioneered in Las Vegas and reinterpreted in Singapore (Kyodo 2016). The UK is an interesting case because it was the most comprehensive attempt to create an open market for gambling at a time when most other jurisdictions were taking a far more cautious approach.

Until the 1990s, the supply of gambling in the UK was limited to fulfilling existing demand in order to inhibit the development of an illegal industry. Advertising was banned, membership rules prevented people from entering casinos on a whim, and betting shop windows were blacked out, creating their unique, some might say 'seedy' atmosphere. In the 1990s a completely new approach was embraced, culminating in one of the most striking examples of New Labour's commitment to using market solutions to answer social questions, an approach described by Tony Judt (1998) as 'opportunism with a human face'. Some of those responsible for the policy, including David Blunkett and Harriet Harman, have since admitted that they got it wrong (Woodcock 2012; Press Association 2012). The purpose of this chapter is to better understand how discussions about gambling were shaped and reframed and, crucially, to assess the lasting impact of these changes on gambling in the UK and elsewhere.

Despite the best efforts of its promoters, gambling has been even less successful than other financial services in decoupling itself from moral questions about the relationship between risk and reward. It also has historical and ongoing relationships with the grey and black economies.[2] For these reasons, the positions taken by those involved in gambling tend to be articulated with particular force and urgency. In this chapter I use interviews with policy makers, politicians and gambling executives to capture the partial transformation of the gambling industry from a pariah to a partner in 'UK plc'. I show how the industry and successive governments attempted to reframe gambling, from a tolerated working-class habit to a rational expression of individual economic choice. By 'reframing' I mean the attempt to set the terms on which meaningful discussions about gambling could take place and to embed this framework in legislation (Preda 2009; Rose 1999). I start by describing how gambling was recast in 2001, from a potential source of crime managed by the Home Office, to a leisure activity which is the responsibility of the Department for Culture, Media and Sport, dubbed 'the Ministry of Fun' by David Mellor, its first Secretary of State (Brown 2001).

Setting the scene

In a speech to a conference of media bigwigs in January, Tessa Jowell set out her theory of governance. '*People often ask me: what is the purpose of government?*' she said. Then she provided her own answer: '*[To] promote competition and regulate – if we have to – to protect the public, the consumer.*' (Born 2003)

When you look at gambling on TV and in the shops, the scratchcards and all that, not to mention every kind of gambling under the sun a click away on the phone in your pocket, it's hard to believe what my father did was illegal when he started. The exact same thing as companies on television and quoted on the stock market are doing today was illegal in his day and mine. A boy growing up today wouldn't have a clue that gambling was illegal not so long ago. (Bookmaker, south-east London, 2006)

The key events in the transformation of gambling in the UK took place over a relatively short period of time, initially under the Conservatives during the 1980s and 1990s and then under New Labour. When I asked bookmakers to describe how this process unfolded, several started by referring to Gilmour's Act in 1986. At that time gambling was covered by a variety of laws, including the 1968 Gaming Act, which the Gaming Board (responsible for regulating arcades, betting, bingo, casinos, slot machines and lotteries until it was replaced by the Gambling Commission in 2007), the gambling industry and politicians agreed were in need of updating. 'The law was, in this case, a massive ass', said one MP, talking to me in 2010. 'The new kinds of gambling that were coming through, online and in shops, were not a glint in even the most futuristic bookmaker's eye in the 1960s. [The laws] were hopeless.' Bookmakers and casino operators also felt that the rather apologetic way in which they were forced to conduct their business was out of step with what they referred to as 'the modern world'. As one casino operator said in 2001 when describing the changes taking place at the time:

You can't have the state telling you how to spend your money, looking down its nose at you, wagging its finger and saying, 'you bad, bad boy'. Fuck that. Times have changed and people want to be masters of their own destinies. They don't want to be told what to do by the state, the church, authorities like that. Money is king. In the '80s people had plenty and they were determined to spend it as they pleased.

At a time when the rest of Britain was booming, betting shops were still deliberately dingy, prevented by law from 'stimulating demand' and forced to have blinds across the doors and opaque windows to prevent people seeing the delights inside. Incredibly, even though racing had been televised for decades, televisions were still banned from the bookies, a fact which created the odd spectacle of customers trooping out of the shops to watch the races through the windows of television rental showrooms. Bookmakers claimed that this paternalist approach encouraged law breaking by illegal bookies who could operate outside heavy taxes and restrictive regulations. And so, in 1986, Gilmour's Act permitted betting shops to have televisions with screens of up to 30 inches and to serve hot drinks, biscuits and crisps (but not cakes). The carefully worded concessions preserved the idea that there should be no attempt to promote betting, but questioned whether it really was necessary to make punters leaving a shop feel as though they were leaving a brothel, as had apparently been the intention of the legislation in the 1960s.[3]

Gilmour's Act coincided with the 1986 Financial Services Act, the proximate cause of the sudden deregulation of financial services known as the Big Bang. It was based on similar principles: popular capitalism, of the kind championed by Margaret Thatcher (Elliott 2001) and the light-touch regulation favoured by Ronald Reagan and epitomised in the Garn–St. Germain Depository Institutions Act of 1982 (Krugman 2009). Televisions and biscuits may seem trivial but for the bookies they reflected a significant change in parliamentary attitudes towards their trade. Some of the veteran executives working in the UK gaming and betting industries began their careers in the 1950s when cash betting was illegal. They saw Gilmour's Act as a moment when 'grudging tolerance' was replaced by an admission that bookmaking was, at least potentially, a respectable business:

This was an important time for us, without doubt. Other people look at the lottery [in 1994], but this was really the beginning because it was a principle conceded as much as anything. The idea that the bookies could be a comfortable place and a place where you could spend leisure time. That admitted us into the ranks of the cinemas and dance halls from your porn shops and strip clubs. We crossed the aisle then.

Despite the change, betting shops and casinos were still not allowed to advertise, or even list themselves in the 'Yellow Pages', the retail telephone directory, until 1999 (*BBC News* 1999). The creation of the National Lottery in 1994 produced the odd situation in which one kind of gambling could, with the blessing of the government, be vigorously and expensively promoted in a high-profile campaign featuring a gigantic hand coming out of the sky, godlike, to inform potential customers that 'It could be you!' at a time when all the others could not so much as tell potential customers of their existence.[4]

The National Lottery

Gambling got short shrift from Margaret Thatcher, who was, by disposition and upbringing, suspicious of merriment. As she told one interviewer, 'For us, it was rather a sin to enjoy yourself by entertainment. Life was not to enjoy ourselves. Life was to work and do things' (Filby 2013). The National Lottery was ushered in by John Major, who describes his role in the process in an article entitled, apparently without irony, 'How I gave hope to the poor' (Major 1999). He recalls that when he told the cabinet of his plan to include it in the 1992 manifesto, he was greeted by 'a roomful of raised eyebrows and doubtful faces'. Major placed opposition to his plan into two camps: the first included Liverpool MPs anxious about the fortunes of the football pools and bishops and Conservatives concerned about the morality of state-sanctioned gambling. To Major, these objections were valid. But what made him 'more determined than ever' to proceed with a national lottery was the 'paternalist nonsense' coming from 'Labour and Liberal benches as well as from Tories': 'In short, they thought the poor needed protection from themselves ... People don't have to buy Lottery tickets. But I see no good reason why they shouldn't be given the opportunity to do so' (Major 1999).[5]

The betting industry was slow to react to the National Lottery, but eventually realised that it was both a threat and an opportunity. A report in 1995 by the Henley Centre, commissioned by the Association of British Bookmakers (ABB), the bookmakers' trade association, painted a bleak future for the industry, suggesting that the lottery would force the closure of 2000 shops and the resultant loss of at least 6500 jobs. They used these contentious figures to argue strongly for a reduction in betting duty which had been in place since 1966 and in 1995 was set at 7.75% (Smurthwaite 2000). With the National Lottery threatening to steal their customers, bookmakers began to argue that these deductions made the industry uncompetitive and encouraged illegal betting.

Simultaneously, in 1997, Victor Chandler moved his operations to Gibraltar, where he could accept bets by telephone and pay much less tax (Doward 1999, 2000). Other firms followed and in 2000, alarmed by the loss of revenue from betting duty and lobbied by friends of racing in Parliament, the government commissioned a review of betting taxation (Paton et al. 2002). In October 2001, betting (and by extension, the racing industry, which depends on a levy on betting turnover to subsidise prize money) faced several huge challenges. As well as competition entering the market from offshore bases, established operators were moving offshore in order to avoid paying taxation, including the levy. Second, Betfair, the betting exchange which allowed punters to bet directly with each other rather than via a bookmaker, was gaining ground and taking custom away from traditional, poorer value bookmakers.[6] Finally, an outbreak of foot and mouth disease meant that horses could not travel to compete at racecourses, which are spread across the country, causing the cancellation of race meetings and severely curtailing the volume of 'betting product'. Punters prefer races with large numbers of runners, and have favourite racecourses – foot and mouth played havoc with the established form on which many punters base their decisions.

In 2001, under pressure from both the betting industry and the racing establishment, both of which include influential individuals, the Chancellor replaced betting duty with a tax on gross profits based on the net revenue of bookmakers (Paton et al. 2004). In return, the bookmakers agreed to abolish all charges on bets and to repatriate their operations. Some of the bookmakers who had moved offshore did indeed return (temporarily) and, one year later, HM Customs and Excise (2002) reported turnover as having increased by 35–40%. The amount staked in betting shops jumped to £45 billion, having been stable at £7 billion throughout the 1990s (HM Customs and Excise 2002). William Hill's profits increased from £32.4 million in 2002 to £170.8 million in 2003 (Bolger 2004). Victor Chandler chose not to return, his spokesman saying that:

> The proposed 15% tax on gross profits is simply another 'stealth tax'. Regrettably, this looks like a hollow victory for the punters, as they will continue to pay – only this time they won't realise it. (Quoted by *BBC Sport* 2001)

A year later the effects of the new fiscal and regulatory regime were being felt by the gambling industry: times were good. Ladbrokes posted a 22% increase in profits, William Hill reported a 32% rise and was listed on the stock market, in an offer that was oversubscribed ten times over (Cummings 2002). Mark Blandford, chair of SportingBet, at the time the world's largest internet-based betting service told the BBC that, 'The UK is setting out its stall to become the gambling capital of the world' (Cummings 2002). In an academic paper that assessed the impact of the change, supporters of the shift praised the UK government's decision to 'base its betting taxation policy on economic criteria', adding that, 'this contrasts significantly with the approach taken by other countries such as the USA and Australia, where an assessment of the social costs of gambling has played a much more important role in the consideration of policies regarding betting activity' (Paton et al. 2002: F312).

In retrospect, the National Lottery was one of the best things that ever happened to the UK gambling industry, as a consultant told me in 2006:

> The lottery was a Trojan horse for us. The government went from meeting unstimulated demand for gambling to promoting it. That put them in a new position. In 1992 they were facing challenges from the EU [European Union] over gambling laws and they also were beginning to realise that direct taxation was much more controversial than raising money through a lottery. Happy days. Once the lottery was in place the cat was out of the bag.

Or, as Graham Sharpe, Public Relations Manager for bookmaker William Hill put it, 'Once the John Major government officially sanctioned gambling, in the form of the National Lottery, they couldn't go on pretending that betting should be frowned upon' (quoted in Hey 2001).

Modernisation in action: Budd

Bookmakers and casinos continued to secure incremental concessions from the Conservative government under the Deregulation and Contracting Out Act 1994, but the so-called 'demand principle', which allowed suppliers to meet existing demand but prohibited them from stimulating additional demand, held fast until the election of New Labour. A review of gambling was announced by Jack Straw in 1999 and the economist and former special adviser to the Thatcher administration, Alan Budd, was chosen as its chair. Budd's approach to regulation echoed that of the Conservatives and New Labour: 'The case for regulating gambling has to be justified. Our proposals generally move in the direction of allowing greater freedom for the individual to gamble' (quoted in Travis 2001).

The *Gambling Review Report* (Gambling Review Body 2001), widely referred to as the Budd Report, is the high water mark of gambling deregulation. It advocated the abolition of the demand principle and in doing so changed the ground rules of gambling legislation. A cap on the number of machines in a large casino with more than 80 tables? Why? Similarly, the committee could see no justification for limiting the number of casinos or betting shops in a particular area. Surely these were matters for markets to decide. On the other hand, citing the Office for National Statistics survey which showed that 80% of people interviewed had not changed their views about gambling in the past ten years, the Budd Report recognised that:

> attitudes about the acceptability and seriousness of the various forms of gambling do not lead us to believe that there is a public desire for unrestricted access to gambling ... we interpret the survey data as encouragement for our view that there should be a cautious approach to relaxing the controls on gambling. (Gambling Review Body 2001: 72)

This caution was particularly evident in concerns about gambling in non-specialised environments (called 'ambient' gambling), about the potential proliferation of small casinos and 'machine sheds', and children gambling. The report called for a ban on machines in taxi cab offices and cafes, recommended a minimum floor area of 2000 square feet (and a ratio of eight machines to every table) in small casinos, and called for limited stakes and cash-only prizes on the gaming machines located in seaside arcades that were, for historical reasons, played legally by children. It was also notable for its localism. The Budd Report advocated giving local authorities 'the power to institute a blanket ban on all, or particular types of, gambling premises in a specified area' (Gambling Review Body 2001: 5), one of the few suggestions that was not taken up in legislation.

A Safe Bet for Success: *morally neutral gambling laws?*

The government responded to Budd in a report called *A Safe Bet for Success*, which adopted 167 out of his 176 recommendations, predicted that expenditure on gambling would increase by £500 million per annum under the new regime and stated that, 'the law should be morally neutral to gambling' (DCMS 2002: 29).[7] *Safe Bet* endorsed the three regulatory objectives which Budd had adopted from the Gaming Board: keeping crime out of gambling, fairness to the punter, and protecting the vulnerable. It also added another:

> We ... want to see a successful gambling industry, one that is able to respond rapidly and effectively to technological and customer-led developments in both the domestic and global marketplace building on its existing reputation for quality and integrity and in the process increasing its already important contribution to the UK economy. (DCMS 2002: 1)

This objective was reinforced by the publication by DCMS in 2003 of *The Future Regulation of Remote Gambling* which set out the government's 'desire to see Britain become a world leader in the field of online gambling' (DCMS 2003: para. 133).

When the Gambling Bill was unleashed on an unsuspecting public in 2004 all hell broke loose in the tabloids (Douglas 2004). The press focused on the admission, made in passing, that, 'Almost all of the evidence we have received points to the fact that this legislation would increase the number of people in the United Kingdom with a gambling problem' (Tempest 2004). This was contrary to Tessa Jowell's statement earlier in the year that she did 'not accept that the Bill will lead to an increase in problem gambling' (Joint Committee on the Draft Gambling Bill 2003–4). *Daily Mail* readers choked on their cornflakes. Despite the fact that the bill had cross-party support, the *Daily Mail*'s campaign, to 'Kill the Gambling Bill' was backed by politicians across the board, including Roy Hattersley, who contributed a column denouncing New Labour for 'Betraying the values my party stood for' (Hattersley 2004). Tessa Jowell was depicted as fighting for her political career as the Gambling Bill, once trumpeted, was gradually watered down. First, the number of casinos was limited to 24 (eight of each category of small, large and 'resort'), then, before the general election in 2005, the number of resort casinos was reduced from eight to one.

Giving evidence to the Culture, Media and Sport Committee in January 2012, Richard Caborn, former Minister for Sport and Tourism, explained the last-minute changes to the bill by saying, 'Not to overstate it, there were two things. The first was that you've got a campaign run by a national newspaper, *The Daily Mail*. The second thing was that you were coming up to an election in 2005. That was the reality of it' (House of Commons Culture, Media and Sport Committee 2012b: Ev107). The bill eventually received Royal Assent in April 2005. The possibility of Las Vegas-style casinos all over the UK, then just in Blackpool, then (surprisingly) in Manchester (*BBC News* 2007), eventually fizzled out when Gordon Brown, another party leader with a Methodist background, came into power in 2007 and unceremoniously vetoed the plan (Quinn and Wilson 2007).[8] 'We were resigned to it by then', a gambling executive close to the process explained in 2013, 'Brown had form – his last budget was a bastard for gambling. He had put his cards on the table.'

Gambling has gone into and out of favour in the past. This phase of deregulation was distinctive because it was characterised as 'modernisation', defined as progress towards a market-driven solution, which was presented as apolitical and explicitly 'morally neutral'. At the Betting Show in 2006, Conservative MP and chair of the Draft Gambling Bill Joint Committee John Greenway, told the audience that, 'When the whole Budd process started what we were trying to do was to take the politics out of this issue altogether … and we thought we had taken a lot of the politics out of it.' This idea of progress and its defence by gambling expansionists is an example of the 'mundane processes' that Mitchell has argued 'create the appearance of a world fundamentally divided into state and society or state and economy' (1991: 95). The effect of this separation is to make the economy animate and to grant it a character and an internal coherence and energy. Conceived of in this way, the economy is placed outside society and therefore beyond criticism. In the case of gambling, the separation between the economy and society was performed explicitly, and with particular conviction, precisely because it is prone to slippages and recombinations which are then captured in headlines in the *Daily Mail* about otherwise ordinary people stealing from their employers in order to continue gambling (see, for example, Witherow 2018). When politics and markets converge and cannot be held apart, as is the case with gambling, the threat is not simply to profitable opportunities but to the foundational categorical distinctions which underpin capitalism.

Conservative with a small 'c'

The Budd Report captured the deregulating Zeitgeist. How did the gambling industry contribute and respond to these changes? The industry is highly heterogeneous: how did the various sectors adopt, adapt and resist new ways of conceptualising gambling? In the aftermath of the Budd Report, some bookmakers expressed surprise at its far-reaching conclusions. They had been accustomed to a certain kind of treatment by parliamentarians and civil servants. Old hands said that they were 'about as popular as a fart in a space suit' before the 1990s. Another that, 'as soon as you say you're from gambling the door shuts in your face'. After the Budd Report they found that 'market talk' as they called it, was far more welcome than 'the old rag and bone man act of coming cap in hand to ask about a bit off this and a bit off that':

> We went up there for one day to give evidence sometime in the late '90s and I'm not kidding it changed me for life. I went up there talking about very modest changes and I found myself being coached by the men there doing the questioning to talk about wealth creation and jobs. It was surreal. We knew that the wind had changed. We started to talk to real lawyers. Lawyers from outside gambling who thought outside the box, built you a new box and sold it to you, no expense spared.

Another bookmaker described how the Budd Report marked a significant turning point in the identity of the industry, and in the way it presented itself to government:

> before Budd … knowing our place, keeping in our place, being very grateful for any favours, taking them racing, taking them to a casino, seeing their credit was good, all the things we did for them, but we were servants, servile to them, subordinate … we knew how to play a particular role and pre-Budd the role to play was to say 'yes sir', 'no sir', 'thank you very much sir'. That changed when the market makers came and told us we could have gambling not because we'd behaved and kept the mob out of it, but by right, as entrepreneurs and businessmen. It was a very pleasant surprise.

According to bookmakers, significant support for an open market for gambling came from the Better Regulation Task Force (BRTF) a powerful quango created in 1997 'to advise the Government on action to ensure that regulation and its enforcement are proportionate, accountable, consistent, transparent and targeted' (quoted in House of Lords 2004). In their submission to the review, these unpaid, government-appointed advisers

(Weir 1999), or 'market makers', as bookmakers called them, dared to say things which the industry did not, including:

> We do not think that the issue of problem gambling should influence the nature of gambling regulation; however the industry has a social responsibility to ensure that it contributes to measures to help problem gamblers. (BRTF quoted in Gambling Review Body 2001: 9)

And:

> Regulatory measures may be required to ensure that vulnerable consumers are not targeted specifically by the gambling industry. However, government regulation should not have the effect of preventing mature consumers from exercising their right to spend their money as they see fit. We would urge you to consider self-regulation, such as a code of practice endorsed by the industry. (BRTF quoted in Gambling Review Body 2001: 9)

Even Budd blanched at the BRTF recommendations: 'Our proposals do increase the freedom of adults to gamble how, where and when they might wish but they do not go as far as implied by the submission of the Better Regulation Task Force' (Gambling Review Body 2001: 9). Subsequent policy makers were less reticent.

The Conservatives under Thatcher and Major had advocated 'better regulation'. Under New Labour the government became increasingly attracted to 'risk-tolerant' deregulation, including of gambling (Dodds 2006). Some executives were taken aback. Despite the free market credentials of many, they were on unfamiliar territory:

> We were astonished to be honest. It went far beyond what we had hoped for. Even though most of us were Conservative voters, and bookies at that, we also felt a little bit worried that it had gone too far! It was a funny old feeling. We got the report, took it to the pub for a few drinks, couldn't believe it, and then we got into a massive row about casinos. We were three old timers sitting there on what should have been the best or the most profitable or promising change in our industry for a generation and two of us were singing from the old Methodist hymn sheet! We'd pushed at the door and the whole house fell over. That's how it felt. (Bookmaker)

Members of the casino industry also commented on the strange political alliances that animated the changes:

> Most of us were swashbuckling liberals. Or at least we were for professional purposes. In practice we were probably a bit old-fashioned, a bit socially conservative, small and large 'c', compared to New Labour, and we formed an odd little group. Let's just say we didn't hang out. Bookmakers and casinos aren't natural bedfellows to start with. Then you combine dyed-in-the-wool Thatcherites, which is what most of us gambling lot were, with gung-ho Blairites, and you get a very odd little group. Quite a lot of potential for misunderstandings and dislike, but we all had our reasons to get it done. (Casino executive)

The *Daily Mail* and other opponents of the Gambling Act concentrated primarily on the increase in the numbers of casino licences, and especially the proposal for a 'resort' casino which was to be larger than anything ever seen before in the UK. Changes to the betting industry, including the end of the demand principle and the legal recognition of fixed odds betting terminals (FOBTs), both of which proved to be highly significant, went relatively unscrutinised. The resort casino was the headline grabber.

According to insiders, the Act created winners and losers, exacerbated existing divisions within the industry and created new ones:

> The roots of the animosity between casinos and bookmakers lies in the Act. Before that we had different briefs. They had their customers and I had mine. The difference was once the Act came along and more was on offer we all got greedy. It was all about machines. We had machines: consolation for the lottery, and what a consolation! I'd give up betting tomorrow if I could and just have machines. But the casinos got battered. They asked for too much, they came very close to getting it but they ended up with less than they bargained for. We did pretty well, we stayed just below the radar which was even more important. (Bookmaker)

The antipathy between bookmakers and the casino industry is particularly obvious in the exchanges between the ABB and both the British Amusement Catering Trade Association (BACTA) and the National Casino Forum (NCF). Briefing and lobbying against competing sectors in the industry is common. One politician, speaking in 2006, described being 'held to ransom by one group or another. It's war, literally war. They hate each other.' A casino executive offered me money to conduct research into 'those bloody machines in betting shops' on several occasions, saying: 'just tell me what you need and we can do it. Whatever you need.' In 2012 MP John Penrose, Minister for Tourism and Heritage (a brief which, at the time, included gambling) explained in the House of Commons that he could not 'start twiddling' with machine regulations

> without everybody else in the industry making the same argument. You've only got to listen to, 'BACTA is concerned about B2 machines in high street bookies', 'High street bookies are concerned about BACTA's members' and vice versa. The moment we change one thing, they will all come knocking on your door. If you have done it for one, why wouldn't you do it for another? (House of Commons Culture, Media and Sport Committee 2012b)

Innovation anyone?

The government presented deregulation as freeing the industry from unwarranted restrictions in order to nurture innovations which were being stifled by arcane laws. In practice, according to those who were part of the process, innovation was scarce:

> Gambling was enterprised up by the government. Once that happened Labour found themselves defending a policy and a principle that the industry hadn't asked for initially but would fight tooth and nail for once it was on offer. The public didn't want it. So why defend it? Because it was a matter of principle – it fell apart around them. (Conservative MP)

According to industry insiders, the highly traditional bookmaking industry was particularly lacking in innovation, for significant structural reasons. The legal industry that had emerged during the 1960s had gradually changed from a large number of independent operators to an oligopoly, dominated by three main providers, who maintained their advantage through market dominance, brand recognition and the high cost of entering the market:

> Bookmakers do not innovate for at least three reasons. One: they are flush with cash. Two: they are planned economies. It takes three to five

years to change the pens in the shops. Last: they are run by dinosaurs. They were presented with an opportunity. They practically fell over it. (Online gambling executive, 2013)

In keeping with this Jurassic approach, terrestrial bookmakers saw online gambling as a threat, rather than an opportunity, for a surprisingly long time. In January 2000 the chief executive of a major UK bookmaker gave a speech at an industry event which drew a memorable analogy between the online betting industry and Luke Skywalker:

> This country, with its well-regulated, highly respected betting industry, has a unique opportunity to simultaneously protect and grow its core home market, the betting shops, and emerge as a world leader for sports betting, an exporter of bets, and an earner of foreign currency. Negative legislation would kill that possibility and seriously weaken the home market. The UK can either become a major centre for e-commerce business or a Luddite casualty of a new and dynamic era. The brat from outer space is only a threat if we treat him as one. He also has the potential to be the greatest opportunity of all time to change things for the better, for everyone. (Field notes 2000)

A sector analyst who had been involved in every stage of deregulation told me that it was impossible to exaggerate the role that politicians played. The industry itself was 'risk averse' and 'passive', 'an industry to which change happened, rather than an initiator of change':

> You can hardly say that telephone and internet gambling represent innovation by the industry. They were just things that came along. The large bookmakers were terrible at innovation. Totally risk averse. For years they treated new media as additional channels. Like a shop on a computer or a phone, basically. They completely failed to see the potential of new media. The innovation came from New Labour and it was to create markets for gambling, reduce taxation and recategorise it as leisure. The bookies just saw the way the wind was blowing and went along with it. (Senior analyst, London 2006)

According to this respected commentator, having tripped over this opportunity, bookmakers were the quickest to adopt and adapt the new frame as well as the least damaged by the increased scrutiny produced by the Gambling Act. The casino industry, by contrast, had had its inner workings exposed and found wanting. The behaviour of lobbyists and politicians made great headlines, for example when John Prescott visited Philip Anschutz, owner of the London Dome and one of the bidders for the super casino, on his ranch in Colorado, and was presented with: 'cowboy boots, a belt, buckle and spurs, a pair of Stetson blue jeans and a leather notebook, worth a total of \$1,354 (£737)' (Sherwell and Hennessy 2006). Casinos were on the back foot. Bookmakers emerged with FOBTs in shops, and the unlimited potential of online gambling.

Maintenance work

Financial workers may evince an ethical framework that underpins their work: 'the democratization of credit' (Appel 2014) for example, or the provision of liquidity for entrepreneurial activity. Gambling executives have no such obvious public good to invoke. 'We live in the jungles of self-interest, not the hanging gardens of academia', as one British executive put it to me. How do politicians and gambling executives in the UK seek to maintain a particular framework for public discussions about gambling?

The most common response to criticism of gambling is a kind of weary exasperation, as I discovered when I pressed MPs who had supported the Gambling Act. 'Look,' one said, followed by a long pause and a hard stare:

> I didn't come into politics to liberalise gambling, I can tell you that. If it hadn't been us it would have been the other buggers. It was business. It was coming. We dealt with it. It's not a question of right or wrong. We did what we had to do. There was no alternative.

The underlying logic is both an argument for a familiar image of modernity (where commerce or 'business' and society are separate) against the primitive (where these functions are inappropriately combined or blurred) and also for a particular kind of temporality in which progress towards this superior state is inevitable and welcome. Failure to support gambling expansion is presented as a categorical mistake, a failure of understanding, or a lack of sophistication. Arguments such as these draw on familiar imagery and arguments which present political processes as ideologically empty: so, for example, to use markets to determine the availability of gambling is 'morally neutral', to support self-regulation is to 'take the politics out of gambling regulation'. The effect is to make rational opposition almost impossible.

This way of thinking about gambling permeates mundane interactions as well as formal statements and is consistently gendered. At gambling conferences and meetings, executives regularly presented opposition to gambling as an inappropriate and emotional response to what was simply a business like any other:

> Women often become very emotive when they talk about gambling. They lose touch with reality. They don't understand that gambling is fun and harmless for almost everyone. The people with problems get a disproportionate amount of attention. Problem gambling gets blown up out of all proportion and people get hysterical. It's a terrible way to make policy. (Senior executive, 2006)

Many of the industry or quasi-academic events I attended featured large groups of men and small knots of women, often treatment providers, regulators, civil servants and academics. On one memorable occasion a female academic and I were seated for a 'working lunch' with the secretaries brought along as a 'treat' by their bookmaker bosses, forming a table of women alongside eleven tables of men who stood up and told sexist jokes about one another. On another, a bookmaker addressed me before taking a seat at a conference about women and problem gambling. It was after lunch and he had been drinking: 'You aren't one of the hair shirts are you?' he asked, 'I just want to sit here and be left alone. Will you do me the great honour of waking me up when it's going home time? Thanks love.' A former bookmaker who is now a consultant explained 'how these things are run', as follows:

> We are on our best behaviour. A woman do-gooder wheels out some poor bastard who has done his nuts on the machines. We listen like good boys, take our medicine. It's just got to be done, but it does get a bit old. It's a ritual. Right up your street. Sometimes we do get sick of their bullshit though.

'Why did gambling grow in the UK?' I asked a former MP now working in the gambling industry. He repeated my question, as we ate lunch in a restaurant in London, looked at me quizzically, and said, 'Well, it was because of technology. The old fogey attitude wouldn't wash anymore, now that everyone was at it. You needn't worry about all that! Don't worry your pretty little head about it!'

The greatest threat to the right to gamble freely is the Nanny State, a villain I encountered on many occasions, including nine times during a ten-minute speech given by a solicitor who provides advice to the gambling and leisure industries. The speech also included a graphic description of the casino industry as having been placed 'on the naughty step'. Objections to gambling are also often presented as evidence of class prejudice. As a Gambling Commission official told me in 2011, 'I file most objections to gambling under middle-class cant.' Or, as gambling consultant, secretary of the Parliamentary All Party Betting and Gaming Group and former Special Adviser to the Culture, Media and Sport Select Committee Inquiry into the Gambling Act 2005 Steve Donoughue said in 2013: 'there's a party going on that the killjoys don't understand' (in Bennett 2013). To deprive others of their right to gamble is to be a middle-class nag: 'Most of the people moaning about gambling haven't got a clue what they're on about. Nimby nonsense' (Bookmaker 2009). Or, as Tessa Jowell put it in 2004:

> There's a whiff of snobbery in some of the opposition to new casinos: people who think they should remain the preserve of the rich; others that find them gaudy and in poor taste; others that don't want the big investment that will come from the United States. They are entitled to those views, but they are not entitled to force them on others. (Quoted by Kite 2004)

According to this argument, familiar from the history of alcohol and tobacco policy, to oppose the expansion of gambling is to threaten the freedom of the individual to behave as they please.

The new deal

The 'modernisation' of gambling in the UK began in parallel with privatisation and the deregulation of the financial services during the 1980s and 1990s. These processes emphasised the responsibility of the individual to become a consumer of risky products rather than subject to collective forms of risk management provided by the state. Ironically, it was the launch of the National Lottery in 1994 which encouraged the transformation of gambling in the UK from an industry which was to be tolerated to one which embodied many aspects of the new, riskier economy. Not because it reflected a wholesale change in attitudes towards gambling (the majority of the UK population remained resolutely ambivalent about gambling), but because it created an opportunity for the gambling industry to argue for wider regulatory changes on the basis that it was hypocritical of the state to encourage one form of gambling while restricting another. Gambling deregulation after 1997 was the apotheosis of the New Labour commitment to free people to forge their identity through their choices as consumers, in an example of what Nikolas Rose (1999) might describe as government through the 'powers of freedom'.

The 2008 financial crisis reopened perennial questions about the morality of capitalism, and particularly the inequalities it creates and depends upon. Works by Thomas Piketty (2014) and David Graeber (2011) have reached wide audiences and their insights have been taken up by popular movements and entered mainstream political debate. Distinctions which held fast despite earlier crises, including between gambling and speculation, markets and society, are being questioned once again (Appel 2014). The crisis of 2008 also prompted a re-examination of the social role of banking, and of the value of new ways of profiting from contingency. These questions invoke wider political frameworks, particularly the trade-off between individual freedom and collective responsibilities.

A central feature of gambling deregulation has been to force diverse positions onto a single continuum. Deontological disagreements have been replaced by utilitarian calculations: cost–benefit analyses of 'social harms' set against 'commercial benefits'. Those who continue to stand outside this metric   particularly those who oppose the expansion of gambling on principle, are presented as primitives: peddlers of myths which must be busted by trade organisations and MPs patrolling the modern. And yet, despite their best efforts, gambling regularly produces headlines which puncture this separation and show that gambling can produce a kind of misery which is blind to class or gender. These inconvenient truths detract from the well-worn stories told by the industry, sympathetic politicians and compromised researchers which is that gambling is good clean fun for the majority of people and anyone who says anything different is ignorant, old-fashioned, or a freedom-hating Nanny Stater. In the next chapter I describe what bookmakers did with their new-found freedoms, including lifting betting shops out of the shadows, both literally and figuratively.

2

Raffles: Gambling for Good

A line of parked cars leads to a building behind a school on a wet and windy November night. It resembles many of the other church halls, club rooms and scout huts that I have visited during my fieldwork. Red brick, Victorian architecture, peeling paint and a quiet hum of evening activity. The uncurtained windows are lit up and inside I can see several women carrying trays of cakes and biscuits from a kitchen ante room into a larger room full of chairs and tables and more women. The perimeters of the room are lined with computers – we are in the sixth form annexe of the local school. The double doors are held awkwardly open by a plastic chair. I push my way through them and head for the bathroom, base camp for my assault on the latest meeting of the Women's Institute (WI). After calming my windswept hair, I tag along behind two women who have come to the meeting together. 'I'm guessing that this is the WI,' I say and they laugh and reply, 'It's a wild leap but you could be onto something!'

Together we enter the overheated damp classroom and are met with upturned faces and greetings. 'Hi there, you must be Rebecca,' says Ann, who is sitting at a table facing the entrance with the essential equipment of WI secretaries everywhere: a list of names, some pens and an empty sweet tin containing a small sum of money. Before I can reply she continues, 'Marjory has told us all about you. When you wrote an email to her it came through to all of us you see. Marjory is a bit under the weather today so she's not coming tonight, but you'll see her next time.' 'Great!' I say. 'Raffle ticket?' says a woman to my right, who is clutching a half-empty, pink book of numbered tickets. The question mark is silent: this is not so much an invitation as a statement. 'A pound each or three pounds for a strip [of five].' The three of us reach obediently for our purses without a murmur.

The raffle ticket ambush is a technique that I have come to know well during my trip through the lesser known gambling dens of Kent. 'Strike early, before they've got their coats off,' a hardened pusher tells me at a village fete. 'That's the best chance you have of catching them off guard.

And you'll be surprised by how many people'll take a strip if you ask them in front of other people.' Her techniques have been honed by chuggers and doorstep hawkers. In this woman's opinion, 'if you can't sell raffle tickets you can't sell anything,' she says, 'It's like standing in front of someone and asking them whether they are a good person or a selfish sod.' 'What are the two most predictable facts of country and suburban life in Britain?' a man in a tweed three-piece asks me at a local dog show. I shrug my shoulders and invite him to tell me. 'Tax and bloody raffles,' he says.

The women I came in with each buy a ticket each and I do the same. We exchange a sympathetic look as we move past the saleswoman (who I gradually come to understand has been assigned that role due to her fearlessness and direct manner). 'We all do it,' says the first woman. 'It's expected, isn't it?' says the second. 'Absolutely,' I say and take a seat. We make small talk until the meeting begins and I am invited to introduce myself and to explain why I am at the meeting – to recruit volunteers to be interviewed as part of my project on gambling. Ann responds to my small speech by saying that although no one in this group gambles we might be able to find a husband who goes racing or has been to Las Vegas. I clutch my raffle ticket and try not to smile.

What counts as gambling today?

Three national prevalence surveys have been conducted in the UK, in 1999/2000, 2006/7 and 2009/10. The two most recent included questions about attitudes to gambling.[1] We know from these surveys that attitudes towards gambling are generally negative. On both occasions, a large majority of respondents felt that gambling was, on balance, not good for families and communities, that there were already too many opportunities to gamble, and that gambling should not be encouraged. On the other hand, most people believed that gambling should be permitted and that it was up to the individual to decide whether or not to gamble.[2] Attitudes had become 'slightly, but significantly' (Orford 2012) more positive between the two surveys, perhaps due to increased exposure to gambling advertising on television and online. According to Jim Orford, a psychologist who has studied gambling in the UK for many years, and a member of the team responsible for the prevalence studies, 'suspicious attitudes towards gambling have long acted as a restraining mechanism, but one whose power is being eroded' (Orford 2012).

In 2012 questions about gambling were included in the Health Survey for England (HSE) and the Scottish Health Survey. Three reports based on data from these surveys have been produced, covering the period between 2014 and 2017 (Wardle et al. 2014). In 2017 attitudes towards gambling were more negative than in 2016: 80% of people thought that there were too many opportunities to gamble (up 2% from 2016) and 71% thought that gambling was dangerous for family life (up 2% from 2016); 64% of respondents thought that people should have the right to gamble 'whenever they want', a reduction of 3% since 2016 (Gambling Commission 2018a: 49). The increase in negative attitudes towards gambling is coincident with high-profile campaigns focused on both fixed odds betting terminals (FOBTs) in betting shops and intrusive gambling advertising, particularly on television during live sports. It is possible that the erosion of suspicion noted by Orford, and perhaps influenced by increased exposure to gambling, has abated.

In this chapter I provide a different kind of picture of gambling using data gathered from community groups in Kent and London. The methods I use are deliberately open-ended and less prescriptive than surveys. Given time and space to reflect, many people I spoke with often began by turning the questions round to me, asking, 'What do you mean by gambling?' These interventions encouraged me to include questions about deliberately taking risks that don't always fit with the formal or accepted definitions of gambling including buying Premium Bonds, stock market investment, taking out credit cards and payday loans. In general, when allowed to speculate about the nature and meaning of commercial gambling many participants describe it as one aspect of a broader trend: the increasing tolerance of cultivating uncertainty in order to create wealth.

Raffles are not usually considered in discussions of gambling in the UK, and the Gambling Commission doesn't gather information about them.[3] However, based on my experiences in London and the south-east, the volume of money redistributed through raffles each year, throughout the country, is considerable. These multitudinous exchanges of small sums of money are ubiquitous and form a significant part of the gambling culture of the country. They give meaning to more squarely commercial forms of gambling, sometimes as a counterpoint and sometimes as part of a single continuum. They are an interesting place to start to think about the meanings of risky, profitable exchanges and how these change over time, because they are so thoroughly embedded in our communities.

More than fifty local groups helped with my research. Some welcomed me without showing any particular interest in what I was doing. Those with more of the trappings of formal organisation, including membership secretaries and appointed leaders, were occasionally more hesitant to admit me, often indicating that the group didn't do any gambling and showing some reluctance to be associated with gambling in any way. In part, this reflects the diverse and fluid understandings of what constitutes gambling in the UK. It also reflects a general reticence about gambling, which is reflected in surveys and took a number of different forms when I was negotiating access. Members of a local history society, for example, were happy to be asked to consider how gambling might have changed in the town, but they were less comfortable about the possibility of members being asked about their own activities. A member of a school committee explained that they would not be able to help me because they knew nothing about gambling, saying, as Marjory had of the WI, 'I don't gamble and there are no gamblers in our group.' Every group I attended used uncertainty to redistribute money or goods, whether for enjoyment or to raise funds, through prize draws, sponsorship, raffles, tombola, sweepstakes, football pools, rounds of golf, flipping coins, card games, bingo, dominoes or bridge. Every group included people who bought raffle tickets, played the National Lottery, bought Premium Bonds and laid bets on the Grand National while answering 'no' to the question, 'Do you gamble?'

The question 'Are you a gambler?' is provocative and therefore interesting, but is not a good measure of people's involvement in gambling activities, for reasons that were carefully explained to me by Rose, a retired pharmacist:

Asking someone 'Are you a gambler?' is not quite like asking them 'Are you a paedophile?' but it's not far off! The connotations of gambling are negative, but it's not just that. It's that you are asking someone to accept the label; in a way you are asking 'Does gambling define you?' So, that is why we have collected all of these negative responses which then go on to be qualified by saying, 'Well, I do the lottery or the bingo.'

Albert, a retired schoolmaster, also spoke about the images that this question provoked for him:

When I hear someone say that they are a gambler, which I must say I never would have until we started working with you on this project,

I have an image of a gunslinger in a Western saloon! After that what springs to mind is some poor soul in a bookies paying out his last pennies on a three-legged horse! It's just not a description that you would offer of yourself, is it? The way I understand it is this. You imagine being asked, 'Are you a father?' I am and I am happy to call myself that, so I say 'yes' and you tick the box. 'Am I a gambler?' Yes, I am, but I don't want to describe myself as such. I'm not a gambler but I do gamble. It's about how we see ourselves, that question.

For others, the perception of what counts as gambling meant that it was entirely possible for them to participate in raffles, the National Lottery, and even to bet on the Grand National, without 'gambling'. The lingering associations of the 'disreputable' verb 'to gamble' is conjured at the start of the 1947 Mass Observation report into gambling. The (unidentified) authors describe how 'Words often carry with them from history subtle insinuations which their acknowledged current meaning does not support' (Anonymous 1947: 2). Differences of opinion about what counts as gambling are helpfully quantified in the report:

> When we asked people whether or not they went in for gambling or betting at all, 49% said they did not. But when we asked another similar sample whether they had put money on pools, dogs, horses, cards, raffles or newspaper competitions, only 14% said they had not. (Anonymous 1947: 2)

In the 1940s, the question of whether or not buying a raffle ticket was gambling, or not, produced a mixed reaction:

> when we asked people whether or not they considered buying a ticket in a raffle to be gambling, 38% said they thought it was; 44% that it wasn't; and most of the rest thought it depended on whether or not the raffle was being conducted in a good cause – thus introducing yet another factor, the motives of those promoting the 'game of chance', as a criterion of whether the players may properly be called gamblers. (Anonymous 1947: 2)

The figures I gathered in Kent in 2016 were quite similar. Of 268 people, 40% said that they did not gamble. Ten per cent clarified that they did not participate in any of the forms of gambling listed, including the National

Lottery and raffles; thus 30% claimed not to gamble but participated in one or more activities that are included in the prevalence study. Forty-six per cent of people thought that raffles were gambling, 38% that they were not, many on the basis that it was in aid of a good cause. Money, motivation, the balance between luck and chance, and timing were all used to distinguish between gambling and other kinds of games or risk taking, saying, for example:

> Raffles aren't gambling because you don't win money.

> Raffles aren't gambling because you aren't doing it to win money or prizes. You're just giving a donation and if you win so be it.

> The lottery isn't gambling because it isn't skill.

> The lottery isn't gambling because you buy a ticket in advance.

These were common ideas, and the fact that they do not fit neatly with the Gambling Commission's definition of gambling ('gambling is defined as betting, gaming or participating in a lottery … Raffles, tombolas and sweepstakes are all types of lottery') does not mean that they are misguided, but that the meaning of 'gambling' is nebulous and imperfectly captured by formal definitions. Indeed, the British are not alone in being uncertain about what is, and is not, gambling. Recent studies have found that only 16.9% of North American adults thought that raffles or buying fundraising tickets constituted gambling (Williams et al. 2017). The same studies found that only 52.5% of those asked thought that betting on sports was gambling, echoing the sentiments of numerous UK bettors, one of whom told me, 'I don't gamble and I disagree with gambling in principle, but I do like a bet.' The various ways in which people make decisions about what is and is not gambling, and the value that they place on these activities, is part of an important discussion about ways of making and distributing wealth. Rose suggested that gambling was one of a group of activities which used risk to create wealth:

> Is payday loans gambling? These bankers? Could that be considered gambling? I certainly think so. At the heart of it is the way you make money. Do you use money to make money? Or do you make things with value or sell your work? It seems ever more likely these days that you

will be encouraged to find a way to make money from money, often money you don't have. Look at the young people encouraged to take out credit cards when they start university so that they can get a credit rating later on. It seems like madness to me to see taking out a credit card as an indication that someone is a good bet for a mortgage. Quite the opposite I would have thought. (Rose, 70s)

Another of my participants, Ivan, a retired bank manager, brought his own professional expertise to bear on his consideration of the connections between gambling and other financial services:

I regard it as a criminal act when the powerful [with money] prey upon the weak [mentally, financially] with lies and false claims [same thing]. I had a very 'interesting' conversation when a financial adviser could not 'hear' my opinion that investing in stocks and shares was gambling. He did not agree that every transaction should have a 'betting tax' levied on it. (Ivan, 60s)

In practice, as I shall show, raffles often demonstrate the redistributive capacities of gambling and the use of uncertainty to increase equality. They are exempt from many of the criticisms that are levelled at 'harder' forms of gambling, most often described as taking place in banks, casinos, online or in betting shops.

'The Trolley' and other raffles

Next time you are asked to buy a raffle ticket, contain yourself and apply an anthropological perspective to the rules of the game. Even the most elementary forms of raffling can reveal interesting details about a group. 'The Trolley', for example, a raffle I encountered weekly at a meeting of retired residents of sheltered housing, incorporates complex rules and is divided into rounds and longer sets. As such, it resembles the redistributive games played by the Inuit in the 1970s (Riches 1975) and the Hadza in the 1960s (Woodburn 1982). In both cases, gambling redistributed scarce essentials (food, bullets) thereby reducing inequalities in wealth or hunting prowess. The Hadza live in north central Tanzania and continue to forage and hunt: unlike the communities around them, they have not settled or taken up pastoralism. They are famously egalitarian and the games of chance that they play ensure that surplus resources are immediately redistributed. Observing these games, the anthropologist James Woodburn was struck by the fact that, 'a game based on a desire to win and, in a sense, to accumulate should operate so directly against the possibility of systematic accumulation. Its levelling effect is very powerful' (1982: 444). A similar phenomenon was observed by Jane Goodale (1987) among indigenous Australians in the 1980s: gambling produced a more equitable distribution of cash from wages and pensions. In total contrast, Clifford Geertz (1973) famously described betting on cock fighting in Bali as a macho dramatisation of social hierarchy. Gambling reveals where power lies in a society, or, as Geertz famously put it: 'As much of America surfaces in a ball park, on a golf links, at a race track, or around a poker table, much of Bali surfaces in a cock ring. For it is only apparently cocks that are fighting there. Actually, it is men' (1973: 417).

A world away from the violence and competition of the cockfight, the trolley sits to one side of the entrance to the large, airy community centre, accumulating a variety of 'bits and bobs', one from each person, as the group assembles. A tin of sardines, three Penguin biscuits lashed together with an elastic band, a purse still in its packaging, a set of three small tubes of hand cream, a photo album with a brightly coloured cover, a bar of milk chocolate and a packet of Hobnob biscuits. There are 53 people in the room, sitting in five groups around circular tables, chatting. The organisers sit at the table nearest to the kitchen: four women – Vicky, a young professional from Age Concern, Jean, a retired lady who bakes the delicious cakes we have every other week, and two volunteers from the village, Lisa and Mary, both retired. The majority (50) of the members are women. The seniors attending have all paid a pound 'sub' (a commonly used abbreviation of 'subscription'), which is collected by Vicky, Lisa and Mary. In return they are given a raffle ticket. The duplicate tickets are folded up into equal, tiny squares and placed in a bowl. Once everyone has arrived and is sitting comfortably Vicky begins to draw out tickets and call out the numbers. As their number is called each 'winner' exclaims and holds their ticket aloft and, because mobility is an issue for many, Mary wheels the trolley to them. They choose something, usually with advice from their neighbour about what looks nice, what they like, and perhaps a joke or two. Vicky draws tickets until there is nothing left on the trolley. We all wait patiently and pay attention to see who gets what. It is the way we start every meeting, whatever else we do, whether it's a beetle drive, quiz, dominoes, or biscuit decorating.

The Trolley is the opening ritual for our little group; it is about sharing and expressing surprise and pleasure for ourselves and each other. The goods that we take from the trolley are, anthropologically speaking, gifts. They are anonymised – we drop our contribution as we come through the door, and so it is not always possible to trace back who has given what, to whom – however quite often winners shout out something affirming like, 'This is a lovely photo album! Is this yours Sheila? Are you sure? It seems too nice to take! Do you not want it?' Sheila approves the choice by saying, 'It's my daughter's Pat. You are welcome to it! I don't have any photos to put into it, it's just collecting dust. If you've got some nice snaps you can put in it then you take it my love.' Pat is delighted with her album and the approval of its donor. It even has a story to follow up later as she asks Sheila, 'Has your daughter been to visit then Sheila?' Sometimes, after the Trolley, a secondary series of swaps may take place as people with more favourable draws offer to swap with people who have been left until late. 'Come on Margaret, I'll have those sardines and you can have my Cadburys. I know you don't like fish and I'm not that bothered about chocolate.'

This chance-based shunting around of small, inessential items creates a collective identity. We constitute the group by holding a ticket and by holding a ticket we forge a relation to the group. This much is unavoidable, and the distribution that ensues is democratic – made according to chance and therefore fair. In addition, optional, short-term dyadic relations are created between donors who choose to identify with their goods and those who choose them, or those who swap. This can create links between people who are not well known to each other, or cement and maintain existing friendships. In this case uncertainty enhances fairness and equality.

The carbohydrate of fundraising

Raffles are ubiquitous in south-east England: during fieldwork I bought 342 tickets, including for meat in pubs, plants at horticultural society meetings, cakes at WIs, booze at Rotary Club dinners, and balls at golf clubs. Like the Trolley, raffles reflect, create and lubricate relationships. The first event to be attended by a new parent, a social evening with the bridge club, or the church fete: all are eased by the routine participation in a raffle. I participated in raffles at school fetes, Elvis tribute nights, pumpkin-carving competitions, jumble sales, exhibitions of contemporary art, cheese board suppers, annual quiz nights and pantomimes. As Penny, a serial raffle organiser explains:

Raffles are like potatoes, they go with everything. They are the carbo-
hydrate of fundraising. If you imagine your event as a plate you've got
your overall theme – this year we're doing the Wild West. Then you've
got your protein. In our case that's the mechanical bull. Absolutely
hilarious and worth every penny, but might actually operate at a loss.
What it will do is attract a crowd, that's the theory anyway. Then you
have your veggies, which are: face painting, bric-a-brac, stocks, coconut
shy, whack a rat, those bendy wire things, that lot. But raffles are your
carbs. (Penny, 30s)

In discussions about gambling, raffles are often presented as fundraising mechanisms and emphasis is placed on their production, management
and outcomes. These present their own challenges, including the difficulty of securing good prizes, and ensuring that people turn up in order to
buy tickets. As Theresa, organiser of a school fete explains:

We always run a raffle, it keeps us going really and that way we don't
have to charge a membership fee or subs or what have you which not
everyone might be able to afford. Everyone always buys a ticket. We've
had some good prizes in the past: a trip away one time, a Hoover I can
think of quite a few good prizes. (Theresa, 30s)

For some organisers, the point is not to win but rather to keep goods
circulating. As a male newcomer suggested, with his tongue in his cheek:
'Raffles are a way of shifting the contents of your spare room into someone
else's' (Paul, 30s). Veterans of the scene like Geoff endorsed this view and
reported extreme cases:

Raffles keep detritus circulating and at the same time generate income
for good causes. I've quite often seen something I put into one of our
raffles reappear. Sometimes on more than one occasion. Once I took
photographs of every item in our raffle [17 items] and about a quarter
reappeared next time. I spoke to the secretary about it and he said that
as long as it didn't put people off buying tickets it didn't matter. We
still sold about a hundred tickets, so you could argue that the content
is less important than the collective principle that raffles depend on.
(Geoff, 50s)

Like Paul, people often stressed the redistributive rather than extractive function of raffles, reflecting first on their social function, and only secondarily on the experiences of consumers or players. Even then, the motivation to participate was often to contribute to the cause rather than secure any of the prizes. For example, I asked 206 people why they were buying a raffle ticket at a large event in Kent. Just under two-thirds responded that they were buying a ticket because it was for a good cause. Typical responses included:

> Oh well, it's a good cause isn't it, you come along to these things and you are expected to support the school. No, I didn't see the prizes yet. Anything good? (Woman, 20s)

> I always buy a raffle ticket. It's the only kind of gamble, if you like, that I allow myself, because it's for a good cause. If I win I take the prize to the charity shop, or give it to another raffle. My parents were Methodists you see, so I'm not really keen on gambling. (Woman, 50s)

Forty people mentioned the opportunity to win a prize:

> You never know I might get lucky, and I fancy that Hoover. (Woman, 60s)

> I just thought that dish looked nice and if I win that's what I'll choose. Knowing my luck I'll probably end up with nothing. Doesn't matter! (Woman, 70s)

Twenty-six mentioned that it was expected and many of these had no idea about the causes or the prizes. Not all of them were willing participants, for example:

> Raffles are an indirect tax on parents. One of many. I don't know what it's in aid of. It's not relevant. I assume it's something to do with the school, is it? Who knows? It's expected and at this point I've stopped asking. (Man, 40s)

> I automatically buy a raffle ticket. More out of habit than anything. I don't really stop to think about it, but now you've asked me, it's brought me up short a bit! I suppose it's perhaps a sense of obligation to make a

contribution in a way that is recognised and accepted. Raffles are good things aren't they. They help out the community. (Man, 60s)

Only six people mentioned the excitement they experienced when taking part in raffles.

My heart beats a bit faster when they make the draw and you're looking at your numbers and you might hear it and your heart jumps, but you can't be sure so you read it again and you don't trust your eyes because your heart is just leaping, but you read it a third time and there it is. You've got the winning ticket! Up your hand goes, and people are pleased for you and you get to pick a prize or maybe something is set aside for you and it might be a lovely plant or a box of chocs, but the lovely thing is that you've got a surprise. (Woman, 70s)

One woman described a particular kind of winner's anxiety:

When they are making the draw I say a little prayer that I'm not going to win something and that if I do it's something small and easily recycled, so I guess you could say that yes, I experience some accelerated heart rate, but it's more dread than excitement. (Woman, 50s)

The rules of raffling: not winning too often

Like other social interactions, raffles are shot through with rules about how to win, and how winners and losers should behave. The Trolley creates and reinforces equality. On my first visit to the group I declined a prize, feeling uncomfortable about taking even very limited resources from people who appeared to have less than me. The next week Mary, one of the organisers, encouraged me a little more strongly than she had in the first week, making it clear that by not accepting my 'present' I had highlighted inequality and thereby caused discomfort, 'Come on Rebecca. You've brought something for the Trolley like everyone else, so you must have a present, like everyone else.'

Raffle etiquette is often aimed at preserving parity. It's inevitable that there will be winners and losers, but those fortunes should be shared among the group, even when chance dictates that this is not always the case. As Deirdre, a member of the local history group, explained:

It's not good to win too often. You don't want to be greedy, so one month I remember I was very lucky, and I won first prize two weeks in a row, well blow me but the ticket came out a third time. We'd all had a good laugh the second week, you know, people had said, 'Goodness me Deirdre, what a lovely surprise! You lucky thing! You must go and buy a lottery ticket today!' and things like that, but I wasn't sure that people would think it … fair if I won a third week straight, so I just kept quiet and held onto my ticket, put it in my purse later and made sure I hid it. They thought the ticket had been lost and drew again and my friend Sylvia won, which was lucky too, so you never know, these things have a way of coming right. (Deirdre, 70s)

The careful management of outcomes, a layer placed upon the brute operations of chance, was mentioned frequently, and suggests that an ideal distribution could be envisaged. This ideal includes a sense of spreading the benefits throughout the group, and also distinguishes between those who organise and those who attend. As Liz, fundraiser for Guide Dogs for the Blind explained:

If you've bought a strip and you win twice you pick something small the second time. You don't want to be the kind of person who takes something nice both times and leaves nothing for anyone else. Everyone here would do that, if they won a second time. Pick something small, a gesture, like. Or they might just say, 'Draw again Jean, I'm happy with what I've got.' If my ticket gets drawn I pick something small because I'm an organiser. It all evens out that way and people can enjoy themselves. (Liz, 30s)

Discussions of how raffle prizes are collected and donated also provoke important distinctions between different kinds of giving in which good causes are balanced against one another, some proving more deserving than others according to calculations that are sometimes highly individualised, sometimes quite generalisable. In many of the local communities where I worked regular participants in the raffling economy had built up repositories of gifts and had complex ranking systems which helped them to determine the next move for any particular object. These collections accumulate in spare rooms or garages. As Liz explained when she welcomed me to her house:

Welcome to my grotto, or as my husband calls it my 'tombola crapola'. What do you need? I've got vases, table mats, glasses, table cloths, toys, games, puzzles, tea towels, picnic hampers, ice skates, roller skates, oven mitts, aprons, pasta makers, cookie cutters, you name it. Anything edible I put in that corner. I try to use it before the sell by date or I give it to the kids or my parents-in-law. (Liz, 30s)

Note that what might be acceptable as a gift to children or parents (out-of-date food) was not seen as a potential raffle prize. Ice skates and roller skates were a surprise, and sit uneasily alongside the more conventional prizes of smaller items which were conventionally thought of as appealing to women. Although most of the raffle hoarders I encountered were women, a few men also accumulated these kinds of gifts. Brian, a postman, described how objects moved through the room and through a ranking system for gifts, from presents for people in hospital, to raffle prizes, to the boot sale, to the final resting place of almost all raffled objects: the dump:

This room seems to have been taken over by the raffle really, plus you always need something handy at short notice if someone needs a prize or a pressie for someone in hospital. Yes, I suppose there is a lot of stuff in here. I should have a clear out at some point, and take it to the dump or a boot sale. Most of it I've won at raffles. Some of it I don't even know where it came from. (Brian, 60s)

Clear-outs can also generate value. An event I attended in December 2012 invited children to the raffle room in a village house where they paid £2 to choose a gift for their parents from the pile inside. The gift was then wrapped, ready for Christmas day. As Penny, the organiser, explained, 'It's a relief to shift so much of it in one swoop and a lot of the kids looked really pleased to find something for their mum or dad. I think I would do it again. Every so often you have to refresh your stock. And we raised £112 for Cancer Research, so that's good.'

Raffles were disproportionately organised and supported by women, who dominated many of the community groups including the WI, but also school groups, amateur dramatics and support groups for older people. This dominance was less marked among Parent Teacher Associations and sporting or hobby-based groups such as photography clubs, bridge clubs, cricket or golf clubs. Although men were organisers and supporters of raffles, they also offered some of the strongest criticisms of them, as Ralf, an accountant and self-confessed raffle refusenik told me:

> Raffles are one of the most grindingly pointless parts of country life. They keep the little women busy, collecting all of this garbage from one another, and they are too stupid to see that it would be simpler to just make a donation. Or you see otherwise sane women spending hours baking cakes to raffle for pennies when the ingredients and the oven have probably cost them much more and you think 'What the hell is going on here?' It's difficult not to see it as some kind of care in the community. I refuse to have any part of this nonsense. (Ralf, 40s)

Ralf has missed what is important: the much broader challenge of how to create relations and bind people together. Raffling is part of this process, along with other unnecessary acts of kindness which also fall outside the rudimentary cost–benefit analysis he describes, including checking on elderly neighbours when it's cold, picking up litter in communal spaces and so on. A different criticism arose from the idea that raffles are in fact *too* self-interested, as retired bank manager Ivan suggested:

> I don't buy raffle tickets and I think they shouldn't be used so much. Why? If you want something you buy it. If you want to support a cause make a donation. It's not honest to buy a ticket for something, to get something for it. A donation is freely given, without any expectation of a return. A raffle reduces things to self-interest. What's wrong with just giving? If that's what you want to do. But people won't, you see. (Ivan, 60s)

If raffles are an annoyance to these two men, for quite different reasons, for others they are unacceptable, often because of particular religious or moral beliefs. Because it is such an everyday practice, *not* participating in raffles can sometimes be received as a kind of anti-social behaviour, as retired farm worker Nigel (70s) explained, 'I never gamble. Not even raffles unless I'm forced to. I'm religious you see. I'm dead against it.' A similar position was put forward by retired school teacher David:

> I find it very hard at bowls matches so have to come to terms with the notion that I have to pay an extra £1 match fee rather than embarrass

my club, team mates and opponents by having to explain that I dislike all forms of gambling including raffles. (David, 60s)

David's wife, Glenda, confirmed that, 'I do not buy raffle tickets and I'm made to feel very mean when I refuse.'

Barely gambling

'What is gambling?' is an open question. Some respondents felt very strongly that lotteries, including raffles and tombola, were gambling. The more common view was that these activities were 'barely', 'nominally' or 'just about' gambling. 'Not gambling' could also include playing bingo in a community hall or pub, cards for pennies with friends, golf for pounds. Less frequently, it included betting on horses ('only the big races', or 'only the National') and playing cards in a casino ('but only for fun'). Activities that always counted as gambling included playing FOBTs in betting shops and online gambling. These contentious categorisations were based on motivation, the amount of money spent and the regularity with which they were undertaken. It was context (including the intentions of players), rather than any essential logic, which distinguished 'gambling' from 'not gambling'. Sweepstakes and raffles are predicated on relationships, create obligations and generate their own etiquette. Betting and scratch cards were described as atomising.

According to the Gambling Commission, playing the National Lottery is the most popular form of gambling in the UK (Gambling Commission 2018a). However, more than half of my participants claimed that they played 'rarely' while only 30% played each week or more often. Raffles were not exactly 'more popular', but rather, less easily avoided. Raffles and tombola were mechanisms for sustaining community life. The quintessential, ordinary scenes of gambling in the UK are the tombola at a school fete, a raffle in a community hall, the office sweepstake and a round of bingo in an old people's home. The function of these activities is to create enjoyment and cohesion at the same time as raising funds, but not profits. For many of my participants, their value lay not in the prizes won, or even the money raised, but in the connections made, as Brian explained:

If you are active in the community you end up getting all kinds of weird and wonderful things and you can hardly say, 'No thanks, I've already got six or seven at home' when someone tells you you've won an electronic pepper grinder or a doorstop shaped as a gaggle of geese. This room contains a lot of goodwill. It's a shrine to our better instincts, to share and make good. You see badminton sets and bad art. I see twenty years of giving and taking. (Brian, 60s)

Brian's description captures the essence of raffling, and the lack of emphasis placed upon the objects themselves: 'bad art and badminton sets', compared to the value, both monetary and social, created by their 'giving and taking'.

Raffles reveal what people value about uncertainty (the capacity for fairness, redistribution, support for good causes, the possibility of a big win), and when they become more cautious (when people are duped, or if players spend too much time or money). They show that there is nothing intrinsically anti-social about gambling. Like trade and all exchanges, gambling is generative and social – it creates and alters relations, offering them up to uncertainty and allowing them to fall where they will. It upsets existing orders: it can level, or even liberate. Where problems arise it is due to the ways in which gambling is separated off from other kinds of exchange, in order to be inserted into them. Under these circumstances, gambling acts to solidify and nurture particular distributions of resources, including those that are highly unequal. In these cases, the role of gambling is not to redistribute scarce resources where storage is challenging, as among the Inuit or Hadza, but to exacerbate and reinforce inequality, contrary to its nature, and despite its liberating potential.

3
The Birth of the Betting Shop

If a woman came to the door I'd say, 'What's up love? Lost your way?' I don't want a woman in here putting the men off. Mostly they're looking for their old man. If he moves fast enough I hide him out the back! (John, 65-year-old betting shop manager)

In the next three chapters I focus on betting shops. How did we come to have betting shops on British high streets? What are they like? Who uses them? What are people doing in there? I've been a betting shop habitué since I began fieldwork in Newmarket in the 1990s. Then, they were good places to go and hang out with fellow lads and lasses, keep out of the bad weather, have a bet and see how 'our' horses ran. I continued to spend time in bookies, enjoying the non-conformist atmosphere and risking the disapproval of my middle-class mother, until I trained and worked as an unpaid cashier with two different firms of bookmakers in London in order to see what life was like on the other side of the counter.

As well as visiting hundreds of betting shops in the UK I have also spent time in similar outlets in the United States (where they are given the tantalising title of 'off-track betting parlours'), Holland, Spain, Germany, Sweden, Singapore and Hong Kong. With the exception of Singapore, where they were like a dentist's waiting room, betting shops reflect (and to some extent subvert) accepted behaviour outside. They are spaces where people who cannot afford to spend their time in pubs, cafes and museums can hang out, meet friends, be left in peace and maybe hope to win some money, at least in the short term. They are often extensions of street life in a way that the majority of retail outlets are not, and the activities that take place in them encompass, but also surpass betting, as I will show.

Betting shops were legalised in the UK in 1961 but betting on horses has been part of working-class life for much longer. Both betting shops and racecourses give licence to carnivalesque behaviour: they are liminal spaces where distinctions are temporarily, and conditionally, suspended.

Oliver Cromwell banned racing in 1654 not because he was a Puritanical killjoy, but because he was afraid of the revolutionary potential of large gatherings of men on fast horses – the failed Jacobite rebellion in 1715 rallied at Dilston races (Nash 2013). The racecourse was a place for ideas to be shared in a space which was difficult to control.

Betting on horses initially took place between owners, on two horse races or 'matches', until the eighteenth century when contests with more runners and commercial bookmaking developed alongside one another (Huggins 2000). During the nineteenth century racing consumed the whole country and vast crowds would walk from London each June to attend the Derby at Epsom (Huggins 2000). The racecourse became a 'super cosmopolis' where 'Princes and rogues mingled in the world of wagering' (Sidney 1976: 18). William Powell Frith's 'Derby Day', produced during the 1850s and apparently Queen Victoria's favourite painting, captures this era well and depicts cheating thimble riggers, a pickpocket stealing a gold watch from a well-dressed man, a beggar eyeing up a splendid picnic, child tumblers and sex workers. A horse race is taking place somewhere in the background.

In the twentieth century, the popularity of betting raised concern among Christian socialists and led to legislation intended to limit betting in cash, the favoured medium of working-class punters. The legislation was unpopular and ineffective and in 1961 betting shops were licensed (Miers 2004). Held back by laws designed to prevent them from 'stimulating demand', they changed surprisingly little until the creation of the National Lottery in 1994. Tax changes in 2001 and the Gambling Act 2005 brought in new products, including the infamous fixed odds betting terminals (FOBTs), the focus of the next chapter.

Today, there are 8423 betting shops in Britain, alongside 650 bingo premises, 152 casinos, 1639 arcades and 60 racecourses (Gambling Commission 2019a). 'Non-remote betting' remains popular and generates almost a quarter (22.1% or £3.2 billion) of the overall total of £14.5 billion gross gambling yield (GGY)[1] in the UK, slightly more than the National Lottery (£3 billion, 20.6%) but less than the largest, and only growing sector: 'remote' gambling, which includes online bingo, casino and betting. Between October 2017 and September 2018, online gambling generated £5.6 billion GGY, up 2.9% from the previous year and accounting for 38.8% of total GGY in the UK overall, an increase of 1.2 % from the previous year (Gambling Commission 2019a: 3). The casino industry accounts for a relatively modest £1.1 billion or 7.4% of the overall total, arcades £421.6 million, or 2.9% (Gambling Commission 2019a: 3).

Licensed betting offices (LBOs), known colloquially as 'betting shops' or 'bookies', are found on the high streets of most towns in the UK, with roughly a quarter of the total located within the M25, the London orbital road. For many years, Ladbrokes, Coral and William Hill (known as the Big Three) slugged it out for dominance, with smaller companies trailing in their wake until they were joined by BetFred to make the Big Four. In 2016 Ladbrokes and Gala Coral merged. The new company was acquired by online gambling giant GVC in 2018, in a set of deals which epitomises recent activity in the sector, illustrating both the value of brand and economies of scale, and also the dominance of online gambling over retail, or 'bricks and mortar' investments (*BBC News* 2017). After this shake up, William Hill (2282 shops, 27% of total), Ladbrokes (1849 shops, 22% of total), BetFred (1644 shops, 20% of total) and Gala Coral (1540 shops, 18% of total) account for 87% of the market, the rest of which is made up of small groups or single shops run by so-called 'independents' (Gambling Commission 2019b: 18). The firm with the most shops, William Hill, is listed on the London Stock Exchange and in 2018 generated profits of £1.6 billion, £150.3 million of which came from betting shops (William Hill 2019).

Despite the ubiquity of betting shops, and the large sums of money that they generate, many people in the UK have never been inside one: a great deal of business comes from mostly male, mostly working-class 'regulars'. For the majority of people in the UK, betting shops are invisible, and what goes on in them a complete mystery. I begin the chapter by describing the illegal trade that betting shops replaced, 60 years ago, before describing how they have changed, based on the stories of those who were there to see them gain legality, if not respectability.

'Decent, honest men'

The amount of illegal betting taking place at any time is virtually impossible to quantify, and the literature is dotted with guesses that vary widely, and reflect the priorities of the source. However, two Royal Commissions (in 1932–3 and 1949–51) marshalled a range of evidence which suggested that gambling, and particularly betting in cash, grew rapidly during the twentieth century. The 1932 Royal Commission on betting and gaming claimed that:

total turnover on gambling today is probably at least as great as at any recent date, and much greater than it was at the beginning of the century ... a larger proportion of the turnover than at any previous time is represented by relatively small bets from the poorer classes of the community. (Rowlatt 1933: 58)

Throughout the era of illegal betting, working-class punters gave their bets to agents, known as 'runners', who visited homes and places of work, returning any winnings the next day (Chinn 2004: 145). Bets were collected in 'clock bags', their locks controlled by a timer, reducing opportunities for runners to tamper with bets. Unlike other kinds of gambling including 'pitch and toss' and cards, betting on horses appears to have been popular with women as well as men. A report written in 1926 claimed, for example, that more than half of the women in one poor district in Liverpool had the 'betting habit' (quoted by Huggins 2003: 75). The volume and the involvement of women may have been exaggerated by those who wanted action to be taken against illegal betting, but the range of evidence certainly suggests that betting was popular and taking place on the streets, and inside factories, chip shops and newsagents (Chinn 2004: 124).

Laying a bet with an illegal bookie implies some degree of trust and historians have argued that these men were often popular characters providing a welcome local service. As Chinn (2004) points out, in the definitive social history of street betting: dishonest bookies would soon go bust. Contemporary sources, including the 1923 Select Committee on Betting Duty, suggested that, 'the nature of the business requires that it must be carried out with scrupulous honesty'. Police witnesses confirmed this impression, one saying that bookmakers were 'exceedingly honest' and he had 'never heard a complaint of dishonesty' (Huggins 2003: 77). In 1932 the Chief Constable of Manchester admitted that street bookies were 'rather good to some of the poorer about them' (quoted in Huggins 2003: 77). These impressions were confirmed by people I spoke with who had bet with or worked illegally as bookmakers, including Eric, a 65-year-old betting shop manager whom I interviewed in December 2008. Eric had worked in betting since he was 16:

Local bookies were honest men and well respected in the local community and did a hell of a lot of good. If someone didn't come in they'd go round and check they were all right. If they heard someone was on their uppers, they'd bung them a few quid. If someone had passed away they'd put half a quid towards a funeral or pay for a funeral. If you can have an illegal person as a pillar of the community then these men were. Of course you did have the odd one who ran off because he couldn't pay up.

While respecting someone was one thing, several of the older punters I interviewed told me how they took this a step farther, protecting their local bookie by taking it in turns to go to the magistrates in order to be fined on his behalf:

> We'd take it in turns to go down the court and get done for it. Me and my brothers and all my friends would take it in turns. Turn up there, and it never went on your record or nothing, you know, you couldn't get a mark on your character, and the beak would say, 'Are you whoever?' And you'd take off your hat, and say 'Yes, your honour' all solemn, and he'd say 'Were you taking bets at such and such a place and such and such a time?' and you'd say 'Yes sir'. He'd say 'Guilty', fined so much. You'd pay your fine and get home and Harry [the bookie] would pay up and you were all right to do it a few times after that then it would be someone else's turn. (Trevor, retired tug boat driver, south-east London)

These stories support the claims made by Chinn (2004), that this trade was circulatory as well as extractive. Undoubtedly, some of my participants were exaggerating the differences between the benevolent community bookmakers of the post-war era ('decent, honest men, every one of them') and the modern corporations that replaced them ('money-grabbing toe-rags'). Nevertheless, their argument was sound: the value and function of betting depended on the wider system of which it was a part. Eric and John, for example, argued that in order to understand working-class betting before 1961 I needed to be mindful of the post-war depression:

> People gambled because they were desperate. They thought to themselves, 'How am I going to get myself out of this hole?' or 'How am I going to get my suit out of the pawn shop in time for my daughter's wedding?'

They explained how betting created the opportunity for short-term gains (as well as losses) and that occasional gains provided a welcome variation from a low and fixed weekly income:

When I first started work I would get £6 a week. £2.50 would go to my mum for board and keep. £1.50 for fares and I'd be left with £2. Now some weeks I would buy a packet of fags and a couple of pints, and find a girl to take out if I'm lucky. Another week I'd have a bet, and if it won I'd live like a lord, steak dinner and wine, and if not, I'd sit and read a book!

For John and Eric, betting during the 1950s with a local bookmaker fitted comfortably into their household economy: gains and stakes were limited, horse and dog racing were familiar sports and the payment of bills took precedence over betting since credit was, unlike today, either prohibitively expensive or completely inaccessible to someone of their means.

Dingy by decree

The 1932/3 Royal Commission chaired by Sir Sidney Rowlatt marked a turning point in Establishment attitudes towards gambling. Rejecting the Methodist argument that gambling was intrinsically harmful, or indeed 'wrong', it concluded that it should be restricted only where it could be shown to 'have serious social consequences if not checked' (Rowlatt 1933). The 1951 Royal Commission on Betting, Gaming and Lotteries (known as the Willink Commission after its Chair) embellished this position, saying that:

> we can find no support for the belief that [it brings] harm either to the character of those who take part in it, or to their family circle and the community generally. It is in immoderate gambling that the dangers lie … It is the concern of the State that gambling, like other indulgences such as drinking of alcoholic liquor, should be kept within reasonable bounds, but this does not imply that there is anything inherently wrong in it. (Willink 1951: 45)

The Willink Commission led directly to the Betting and Gaming Bill which was introduced in October 1959 and received Royal Assent in July 1960. It was based on the principle of 'unstimulated demand', which would underpin gambling regulation until 2005. Betting shops were to be legalised in order to accommodate the existing demand for betting on horses in cash, which would otherwise lead to illegal bookmaking. This was not a wholehearted embrace of gambling; indeed, the discussion in

Parliament was marked by both principled opposition and a pragmatic acknowledgement that it was already taking place in defiance of the law.

After 1961, betting shops opened at a rate of 100 a week, and six months after they were legalised there were 10,000 (Hey 2008). In 1963 the *London Evening Standard*, concerned by the number of shops, asked, 'Why have the English become gambling mad?' (8 January), anticipating the headlines that would appear in the *Daily Mail* during discussions of the Gambling Act 2005 and, more recently, in relation to the large amounts of money spent on FOBTs. By 1966 there were 16,000 betting shop licences in Britain, and Labour Prime Minister Jim Callaghan introduced the first betting tax (Rock 2001).

For the next 30 years, betting shops were strange and ambivalent spaces, invisible, but in full view. The compromise was described by Under-Secretary for the Home Office Dennis Vospers in 1960:

> the betting office should be a place of business. It should, therefore, have adequate facilities for the conduct of the business. We should not, on the other hand, go to the other extreme advocated by one or two of my hon. Friends, to the extent that people would be attracted to the place who would not otherwise go there for the purpose of betting. For that reason, we have consistently opposed the introduction of radio and television. (*Hansard* 1960)

Despite the fact that live television broadcasts of racing had taken place since the 1950s, betting shops were not allowed to have televisions, or to show live racing, until 1986. Results were broadcast over a tannoy and written on a blackboard by a 'board man'. Window and door screens made it impossible to see into the shops: chairs, toilets and the sale of refreshments were forbidden. As one punter said to me, with misty eyes, 'I remember when they brought pens in. That were a red letter day.' Bets were written on pieces of scrap paper, backs of envelopes, shopping lists, and could be very difficult to decipher, with the potential for ambiguity creating problems for shop managers, 'In them days we were accountants and diplomats,' as one manager explained:

> We were paid the same wage as a bank manager back then, and we were as respected; with that amount of cash lying about it was about integrity. Our role was to balance the books. Slips could be anything: pieces of paper, envelopes, fag packets. The cashier took the bets at the

counter. They would translate it [work out the stake]. After the race, I'd settle winning bets and the cashier would give the customer any winnings. (Jim, betting shop manager in London for 38 years, interviewed in September 2008)

The idea was that those who wanted to have a bet should be able to do so, but no-one should be enticed in, or encouraged to linger. As one manager said, 'they were modest in them days, very modest. We kept the place tidy, but we didn't have much to work with.' Women were not expected to frequent bookies and some managers wouldn't let them in:

It was one thing having a runner come round and pick up bets from me mum at home, but it was another thing her going off to a shop. Just wouldn't be done. Like going to the pub without me Dad. Just wouldn't be done in them days. (Eric)

Some of the first betting shops were simply converted rooms in shops and houses on the corners of working-class residential areas: a transitional phase between street betting and betting shops as urban commercial enterprises. Some of these shops had operated illegally before 1961 and, after licensing, were forced to remove furniture and cover windows in order to remain within the law. As Bob, a retired police officer told me:

We used to go to Coleman's on the way to the station. He had a house with his mother and he used the front room as his office. You could smoke, but you wouldn't want to get in the way of old Mrs Coleman. She'd soon put you straight if you dropped a butt or kicked the skirting. The room was warm and just had a counter, but you didn't linger, you just saw Fred and then hoped you'd be back next day to collect. I think Mrs Coleman hoped she never set eyes on you again.

On one slow afternoon when racing was cancelled due to bad weather, Bob took me to see the house where the Colemans, Fred and Mrs, had plied their trade many years earlier. As we stood in the rain and Bob reminisced about the past, an elderly man came to the door. It was the eponymous Fred, who ushered us inside. Although he was pushing 90, and a great-grandfather, Fred had clear ideas about the most important qualities a bookmaker must possess: 'integrity', he told me over tea and biscuits, 'and a strong right hook'.

Once legalised, betting on horses became more strongly gendered than it had been when it took place at home, on street corners, in factories and newsagents. Shops became notably masculine spaces (Cassidy 2014). The 1960 Act also legalised commercial bingo, and, as men frequented the dark, smoke-filled bookies, women headed for converted cinemas in search of a full house (Downs 2010). In 1968 sociologist Otto Newman described betting shops in London as working-class enclaves and betting on horses as a way to express local, working-class male identity (1968: 17). According to Newman, the enemy in this case was not the bookmaker, but 'Them' (1968: 24), that is, the massed anonymous forces of Power and Law (1968: 20). By the time I was spending large amounts of time in bookies attitudes had changed. The communalism of the independent bookies studied by Newman had not disappeared entirely – several small chains continued to provide a personalised service to loyal customers, but in general it had been replaced by an adversarial attitude towards the corporate chains and most punters now wanted to 'Beat the Bookie'.

The 1960 Act put betting shops in mothballs: they fell behind the rest of the comparatively cheerful high street shops, unable to advertise, hiding behind blacked out windows and doors. Bookies used various methods to get around the restrictions, 'We always had a policy of totty² behind the counter, and the blokes in the back doing the sums. Get the right girl on the counter and you could really turn around a shop that was struggling' (Len, bookmaker, 1950 to 1999, interviewed 2015). By the 1990s, many shops were extremely run down, including my local shop, where the televisions had long ceased working and the lino had worn away to reveal the filthy concrete floor. The development officer of the large chain which owned the shop explained that it was kept open for one profitable customer who had liver cancer. Refurbishment had been delayed and it was likely that on his death the shop would move to a new site.

The Big Three, the companies which came to dominate the land-based UK betting market, were well established before the legalisation of betting off-course in cash, and grew through acquisitions and mergers. Their oligopoly was protected by laws which limited the supply of gambling to one shop every quarter of a mile radius (a unique geography enforced by licensing hearings at local Magistrates Courts) and by the importance of trust in the name above the door at a time when gambling debts were not enforceable by law – something which would not change until the Gambling Act of 2005.

Each company entered the market slightly differently. William Hill had a credit betting office on Jermyn Street in London from 1934 and famously referred to licensed betting offices as 'a cancer on society' (Wood 1998). He didn't open his first until relatively late, in 1966. Ladbrokes was founded by Schwind and Pendleton in 1886. They had offices in the Strand and moved to Hanover Street in 1906. Ladbrokes was the most precocious and the first of the three to float, in 1967, at a value of £1 million, under the stewardship of their famous chairman Cyril Stein. Joe Coral, or Joseph Kagarlitski, born in Warsaw in 1904, came to the UK in 1912 and began bookmaking in 1926 (Wood 1998). The fourth member of the current 'Big Four', BetFred, is owned by Fred Done and his brother, Peter, and began as a single shop in Salford in 1967.

Racing and betting

Until the 1980s, horse racing accounted for between 80% and 90% of business in shops, as Ian, a 70-year-old punter who had spent time on both sides of the counter, explained:

> My generation grew up in the 60s to mid-70s when horse racing was the only thing you could bet on – it was what you were brought up on. We were fed a diet of ITV 7 [a multiple bet on seven races shown on ITV] on a Saturday afternoon. Before full-time work I worked at a bookies where we would listen to Radio 2 and scribble down results and settle the bets with Betty – the owner's wife. More like the Rover's Return than the modern betting shop. Customers were regulars, and locals. Bill, a printer for the *Daily Mail*, would work nights, sleep then put on 10 shillings to win five or six times per day. A local builder would go to the pub next door for lunch then do two races, £2 win each, next two races and a double. Angelo the Italian café owner from the corner. It was like that.

Significant changes began to take place during the 1990s due to the creation of the National Lottery and the development of tax-free betting with offshore operators, first through the telephone and then online. Feeling the pinch, the land-based gambling industry and its more acceptable dependent, the racing industry, began to lobby for change.

Betting and Racing (the capital 'R' denoting the institutionalised powers that be, including the Jockey Club and the British Horseracing

Board, now called the British Racing Authority) have a close but difficult relationship. No-one has captured it better than Jockey Club historian Richard Blackmore who wrote in 1891 that 'Betting is the manure to which the enormous crop of horseraces and racehorse breeding is to a large extent due' (1891: 349). Many of the trainers and breeders I worked for in Newmarket during the 1990s still held this view. They spoke passionately about the intrinsic value and beauty of the Sport of Kings and the duty of improving the breed of thoroughbred, and either looked down their noses at bookmakers and punters or were simply oblivious to them – they occupied completely separate worlds. In practice, the two worlds are symbiotic. Racing depends upon two main sources of income: wealthy owners paying monthly training fees, and prize money, which is subsidised by a levy, or hypothecated tax, raised on betting, most of it by working-class punters in betting shops.

When the National Lottery burst onto the scene Racing feared a drop in the levy and demanded protection. In 1993 the government allowed betting shops to open for the first time during summer evenings, during racing, in order to boost turnover. It also permitted racing on Sundays, previously a 'blank' day. In 1995 racing took place on twelve Sundays, with two fixtures each day, causing upheaval and consternation among the racing community, which had traditionally enjoyed a day off, and failing to produce much off-course turnover. The failure of increased opening hours to boost betting was blamed on the lottery.

In 1995 the Henley Centre report claimed that bookmakers' profits were 35% lower than they would have been without the lottery, causing a reduction of £6 million in the levy. According to the Association of British Bookmakers (ABB) (the major trade organisation representing the interests of bookmakers in the UK), government revenues had also fallen by £82 million and 400 betting shops had closed with a loss of 3400 jobs (ABB 2013a). In the House of Lords, peers echoed fears that had been voiced in the 1960s, that the regulated betting industry would no longer be profitable, resulting in the emergence of an illegal alternative.[3]

The Deregulation of Betting and Gaming Order 1996 removed many of the restrictions that had been placed on betting shops. For the first time, betting shops were allowed to provide machines called amusements with prizes (AWPs). These machines did not include any skill element and were common in pubs where they were called fruit machines. The initial aim of Racing (led by the British Horseracing Board) and the betting industry (led by the ABB) was to secure for shops the right to bet on the National

Lottery, in the same way that they could bet on the Irish Lottery. This right was never ceded and so the search for profitable products focused on the new machines: racing was on its way out.

From horses to numbers

Until the late 1990s, established betting industry wisdom held that the maximum number of events that a punter could consume each day was 40 and horse racing was king, accounting for the vast majority of business each day, as manager Chris explained in 2008:

> Twenty years ago there were only 28 betting opportunities a day, same as the number of virtual races in a day now. If there was bad weather, there could be 16 dog races. Between races you looked at the next race. Stakes were higher. Saturday mornings you used to get eight races at Hackney dogs. Popular bets would be doubles to eight, trebles to eight, forecasts. In the summer you'd have the last race from Hackney at 12.57 and then you'd have the horses at 2.00.

The rhythm of this day is relatively steady – there are gaps between each race, allowing for the possibility, at least, of reflection. Under these conditions, Chris claims that punters considered their next move, investing relatively more in those decisions than they do now that the number of events in each day has exploded, driven by a change in emphasis, from the quality of racing on offer during a day which ebbs and flows, to the number of events that can be packed into each hour of continuous activity (Cassidy 2012b).

The problem with horse racing as a betting medium is that it is extremely expensive to produce and depends on wealthy individuals prepared to spend a fortune maintaining fragile athletes which very rarely repay their investment. The economics of racehorse ownership are frightening and even the doyen of thoroughbred breeding, Tony Morris, likens purchasing a racehorse to buying a very expensive lottery ticket. The median price of a yearling racehorse sold at auction at Tattersalls in Newmarket in 2018 was 150,000 guineas (Tattersalls 2018). The Green Monkey, the most expensive racehorse ever sold at auction, for $16 million in 2006, failed to win a single race. Maintenance costs are relentless, and a slow, sick or injured horse costs as much to care for as a champion. In the UK, the Racehorse Owners Association suggests that it costs around £20,000 a year to train a racehorse whether it is a winner or (much more likely) a plodder, excluding entry fees, vet bills and insurance. For every £100 spent owners could expect a return, if that's the right word, of £21 on average (Beugge 2013). There are currently around 14,000 horses in training in the UK, paid for by more than 8000 owners at a net cost of over £475 million. Propping up this huge exercise in discretionary spending is the levy, the mechanism which links betting turnover to the production of racing, through prize money. Given its fraught business model, racing is constantly being presented as in crisis, or, as journalists like to say, 'entering the final furlong' (Thomas 2014).

In the 1990s, the expense of racing and its vulnerability to bad weather or 'blank days' prompted new recruits with backgrounds in retail rather than traditional bookmaking to ask previously unthinkable questions, including 'Why should we pay the horseracing levy?' Newcomers had learned from casinos that random number generators (RNGs) could produce unlimited numbers of 'events' at very low cost and that these events could be depicted in an endless variety of formats, including as horse and dog races or casino games, either on existing, multipurpose screens which were currently showing live racing, or on free-standing machines. These new entrants were unencumbered by knowledge about horse racing and the culture of betting. When I interviewed one senior executive at the Betting Show in 2007, for example, it was evident that he did not understand either odds or randomness (he spent some time trying to convince me that it was helpful for punters to see the history of spins on FOBTs because if the previous three spins had come up black then it was more likely that the next spin would be red). What was clear, however, was that he knew how to make money, as one of his colleagues explained:

> It was agreed for a long time that the maximum number of events you could have in an afternoon was 40 … it was just common knowledge. Then the new breed of director came in with no background in betting shops, from retail, and turned that on its head and said look at the average amount of time someone spends in a shop. Just a few minutes. So we should have as many events as possible, so there's always something they can bet on that minute. And on the other side of things, we should produce them ourselves. No more levy, no more doffing our cap to the racing set. Our own studios, our own products. That was a massive turning point in the industry. (Senior betting industry professional, mid-40s, interviewed March 2007)

The increase in the number of events each day was accompanied by the automation of 'translation' and 'settling' (the process of calculating the liabilities of each bet and calculating and paying out any winnings, respectively). The roll-out of electronic points of sale (EPOS) in the mid-1990s changed the role of shop manager, increased opportunities for surveillance and, as one manager put it, replaced trust in people with trust in machines:

> How does the song go? Things ain't what they used to be. That's for sure. Your word was your bond once, and that's gone out the window. Now you're disposable. Anyone can do this job. A trained monkey ... Pressing a few buttons. Used to be a very skilled, very knowledgeable job, and we looked up to the senior men. The red pen men,[4] you know, properly trained, but now there's no-one like that any more. The business is about meeting targets and selling new bets and keeping down costs. No personal responsibility any more, not for this company anyway. (Eric)

The rapidity of bet acceptance rose accordingly, and the skills required by cashiers and managers changed. The complex relationships that used to exist within the bookmakers, which were based on shared specialised knowledge of bets and of the horse and dog racing industries, were replaced by standardisation and the authority of the computer.

The final piece of this puzzle was the change to taxation which took place in 2001. Unshackled from the duty paid by punters on stakes or winnings, newcomers to the betting industry were free to invent alternatives to racing which could be produced cheaply, and in unlimited quantities, including virtual racing (an animated version of horse or dog racing based on randomly generated numbers, often referred to as 'cartoons' in shops), numbers games and, ultimately, roulette machines.

The racing establishment, including several journalists at the *Racing Post*, the daily racing newspaper in the UK, were appalled by these changes. Virtual horse racing was introduced to betting shops on 1 May 2002, and drew particularly strong criticism because it was closer to racing than other numbers products: 'I thought I had seen it all – Rapido, 49's, fruit machines, games machines – but no, virtual racing has arrived, taking the betting shop punter to new lows', wrote one. Several betting shop owners, including David Sainsbury of Grandstand Racing did not want to show virtual racing. A clipping I have saved from the letters page of the *Racing Post*, written by a bookmaker in 2002, captures their misgivings:

I would like to emphasise to you how ridiculous virtual racing is. It is worse than a bad joke, it is needless and it is embarrassing to me that I am seemingly endorsing it by showing it on my screens ... I desperately do not want this virtual racing in my shop.

In advocating a boycott, and suggesting that the person 'commentating' on the 'race' be tarred and feathered, *Racing Post* correspondent Paul Haigh described virtual racing as a 'loathsome, pathetic, disgraceful, execrable, rage-inducing slap in the face':

What is this abomination? It's a computerised 'race' on which betting is supposedly conducted. There is no 'form'; no reason to bet on one 'horse' rather than another; not even the pretence that anything at all is involved except the provision of an opportunity for mugs to hand over cash. This isn't animated roulette. It isn't even roulette. It is plain and simple trash. The big boss bookmakers will tell you it's just a bit of fun, 'ha, ha'. They'll be lying when they do. What 'virtual racing' really is, is a calculated insult to their customers: proof positive of their conviction that punters are idiots by definition who'd rather bet on anything than nothing. (Haigh 2002)

His outburst is typical of the anger directed at bets of these kinds by traditional horse race punters, who likened these activities (as well as playing the lottery, any form of numbers game, and bingo) to 'burning money'.

Racing journalists joined punters and betting shop managers in drawing a stark contrast between themselves and people they described as 'mugs' (Cassidy 2012b) and 'fruit machine freaks':

I'm not fundamentally opposed to the concept of virtual racing – except in the sense that I regard it as utter garbage for people who should find something better to do ... We know these games involve no skill whatever, and we agree that they aren't as good as proper racing, but I really can't muster the energy to worry too much about what fruit machine freaks do with their spare time and money. Mind you, that's not to say that we shouldn't look down our noses, ridicule them and be extremely patronising at every possible opportunity. (Thomas 2002)

Despite dire predictions, virtual racing took betting shops by storm, part of a wider shift from racing to numbers, from betting to gambling, and from risk taking to abandonment. This shift was precipitated by a change in taxation which was exploited by newcomers who had not worked in betting shops and therefore had no allegiance to horse racing, which struck them as an unaffordable and unnecessary luxury. The old guard held their tongues, put their tweed caps into storage, and took comfort in their soaring profits.

4

The Rise of the Machines

The powers that be are not happy. FOBTs [Fixed Odds Betting Terminals] are a very sore subject. I wouldn't mention them if I were you. They would rather you wrote about betting shops as community centres. That they would like, in fact, that they would pay for. They don't trust you. It's share prices at the end of the day. It just takes another 'crack cocaine' line to bugger it up. (Executive for a large bookmaker)

The current global expansion of gambling is characterised by two if not contradictory, at least contrasting trends – the continued profitability of electronic gaming machines (EGMs) and the emergence of online gambling. The constellation of arrangements that exist currently the culture clash between the gambling industries of Europe and the United States for example, or the recently lifted ban on casinos in Japan, is a reflection of political and social mores and not just different points on a line tracing the evolution of gambling from table games to machines, or from land-based to online gambling. In this chapter I elaborate on my argument that gambling markets flourish in regulatory spaces that are actively created and nurtured, rather than emerging spontaneously from 'modern' attitudes towards risk and profit. Although EGMs deliver experiences which appear to be inherently compelling, they also occupy specific niches in wider gambling ecologies, for historical, social and political reasons. Using fieldwork in betting shops and at the head office of a UK bookmaker I show how one of these niches, for FOBTs, was created and maintained.

What are EGMs?

EGMs are computers housed in wooden or plastic boxes, called 'cabinets', which offer server-based (networked) games to players seated in front of a video screen or screens. They have gradually replaced mechanical slot machines, including traditional 'one-armed bandits', as digital technology developed in the 1980s. The most lucrative forms include 'slots' in the US, 'pokies' or 'poker machines' in Australia, 'pachinko' and 'pachislots' in Japan, 'video lottery terminals' or 'VLTs' in Canada, the US and Europe, and 'FOBTs' in the UK. The most popular EGMs depict traditional casino games, including spinning reels, poker, blackjack and roulette – but they can, in principle, be used to show an infinite variety of animated events based on the outcomes of random number generators (RNGs), or, as for 'Instant Racing' in the US, the outcomes of actual events which took place in the past.[1] Spin speed, maximum stake and maximum prize vary widely, as do bonuses, return to player rates (the percentage of money staked that is paid back to players over time), the frequency of near misses, losses disguised as wins (celebrations that occur when players win less than they staked), responsible gambling messaging and so on. All of these differences potentially impact play, including harmful play.[2]

The regulations which govern the supply of EGMs also vary significantly, although most jurisdictions set limits on numbers and locations. In the US, slot machines are found primarily in purpose-built casinos, whereas in Australia, pokies are also found in pubs and clubs, a form of 'ambient' gambling which has contributed to a huge annual spend on gambling: the highest per person in the world (Keneally 2017). The ways in which EGMs are supplied or licensed are also highly variable. In the US and the UK, private companies own EGMs and are taxed on their income. In Australia, not-for-profit sports clubs own most of the pokies, and state and territory government rely increasingly on their income: in 2015–16, gambling revenue accounted for an average of 7.7% of state and territory taxation revenue (ACIL Allen Consulting et al. 2017: 58). In Canada, gambling is only legal when 'conducted and managed' by one of the ten provincial governments. In 2017–18 Ontario made $2.36 billion from gambling (Crawley 2017).

Anthropologist Natasha Schüll has used data gathered over 15 years in Las Vegas working with designers, executives and gamblers to show that EGMs are 'addictive by design' (Schüll 2012), showing how data gathered from the casino floor is used to adjust payout schedules in order to maximise 'Time on Device'. Games and environments are thereby attuned to players who want to enter a dissociative state described by one of Schüll's research participants as 'The Zone' (Schüll 2005). A similar phenomenon has been described in relation to the Australian pokie machine, suggesting that its attraction lies in its capacity to induce a fugue-like state for gamblers who crave a break from everyday life (Woolley and Livingstone 2009).

I found support for these observations everywhere in the world that I observed and engaged in machine play, from London to Tokyo, Singapore to Las Vegas. Users described the everyday banality of machine gambling, and play motivated and sustained by a search for the absence of desire. In Tokyo pachinko players explained that they had stressful jobs and that this helped them to unwind – six-hour sessions after work were not exceptional. In Las Vegas I worked with two middle-aged women who patiently played machines for eight hours each day before returning to their 'other jobs' as bar tenders. Their wins were usually moderate and always reinvested. They described their losses as 'drip, drip, drip. I'm feeding the casino even as it's killing me. It's a vampire!' It was a relief when, in Macau, I encountered gamblers who not only warned me about the machines, 'Fixed! All fixed!' but also appeared entirely capable of resisting their addictive potential. The casinos were full, the tables crowded with people three deep, but the machines were almost completely unused, not (yet) attuned to the market (Schüll 2013). Some players even rejected the idea that slot machines were gambling: 'these are for people for play games' one middle-aged man told me, 'Maybe for women or Americans. Not for gambling.' He waved his arm towards the crowded baccarat tables, then beamed back at me, coughing through the thick cigarette smoke: '*This* is gambling.'

Enter the FOBTs

When I first started fieldwork in betting shops in the late 1990s they were relatively quiet places, not dissimilar to public libraries. They could get raucous during significant events in the racing calendar like the Cheltenham Festival or the Grand National, but quiet contemplation was commonplace, particularly in the mornings. Most customers were older men, interested in horse racing, or, less often, dog racing. We would sit around talking about sport and politics and occasionally people would place bets. On Saturday afternoons, when the better racing took place, things would be more lively, people would increase the size of their bets on the basis that the form is stronger in better quality racing, and we would go through a similar, slightly more animated routine – plan bets, dispute, place bets, watch race, commiserate or congratulate, repeat. Sometimes there were disagreements brought in from the street, or caused by a perceived slight in the shop. Very occasionally there were fights, which were broken up by the manager, who occasionally barred troublemakers.

Our shop was near to a pub and we would combine these activities with a few drinks: sending someone next door to place our bets, usually a man named Jeff, a builder who was keen on the assistant manager, Tracy.

When machines arrived in our betting shop we paid them very little attention (Cassidy 2012b). Like virtual racing, they were gambling, not betting, and therefore nothing to do with us. 'Strictly mugs only' was the judgement made by Mark, a council worker on long-term sick leave. Led by the example of my colleagues, I ignored FOBTs, not even consciously dismissing them – like fruit machines in pubs they were a form of gambling that was simply invisible to me. However, I gradually became aware of changes in the shops. My field notes started to refer to strangers and new-comers, people without any knowledge of, or interest in racing, who came into the shops solely in order to play machines. Often these were young men, many of them recent migrants, playing the machines in groups, creating what one manager referred to as a 'two-state solution' in the shops: machine players on one side, traditional bettors on the other (Cassidy 2012b).

FOBTs can show several different games, but are predominantly used to play roulette. For the majority of my fieldwork they had a maximum permitted stake of £100 and each spin took 20 seconds, making them a relatively high stake, high-speed form of 'hard' gambling. Like EGMs in other jurisdictions including Australia and Canada, FOBTs are played by a disproportionate number of people who are classified either as problem gamblers or as at risk of developing problems with gambling (43% of FOBT players, according to the most recent Health Survey) (Wardle et al. 2014). FOBTs have also been implicated in several suicides, includ-ing those of Lee Murphy (Aitken 2015) and Ryan Myers (Belger 2016) in 2014. In May 2018, around 17 years after FOBTs were introduced to shops, the UK government announced that the £100 maximum stake would be reduced to £2 (DDCMS 2018a), news that was greeted with tremendous relief by pressure groups, gamblers and their families, a response that was moderated when it emerged that the ban would not take effect for two years (Davies 2018a). In November 2018, the announcement of a further delay by the chancellor, Philip Hammond, prompted the resignation of the Minister for Sport Tracey Crouch (Davies 2018b). Throughout their lifetime, FOBTs were hugely profitable for bookmakers: their rapid emer-gence marked a change in the nature of the betting shop, from a place where men went to bet in cash on live horse and dog racing, to somewhere people went to play roulette on a machine. In the next chapter I focus on the effect of FOBTs on betting shop staff and customers. In this chapter I go behind the scenes of a large corporation to explore their origins.

Pushing the boundaries

FOBTs were invented by business partners Walter Grubmuller, co-founder of Novomatic, an Austrian games machines manufacturer, and British betting shop manager Steve Frater. They were based on the 'amusements with prizes' (AWP) machines which were allowed into betting shops in 1996, as consolation for the creation of the National Lottery in 1994. As Frater said in 2013, 'The concept didn't start as a FOBT. It was about finding an alternative lottery product. The idea was to produce an automated numbers draw in our shops. It developed through the concept of taking the regulations and pushing the boundaries to the limit' (quoted in Pitt 2013). Betting shops are only allowed to take bets on events that take place off the premises. At the time, 'gaming', including playing roulette, was restricted to casinos, which were more stringently regulated: players had to become members, a process which took 24 hours, a delay intended to reduce impulsive play.

In 1996 Grubmuller and Frater bought two betting shops in London in order to test a new approach to machines. At the same time, the major companies were introducing 49s, a twice daily numbers draw, created to compete with the lottery. On a family holiday in Dubai, Grubmuller told Frater, 'I've got an idea and it's going to make us rich' (quoted in Pitt 2013). He had been thinking about 49s and wondering why there were only two draws each day, one at lunch time, one at what was still called 'tea time'. Why not have them every half an hour? But first Frater and Grubmuller had to find a way of making sure that their product was, technically, 'betting' and therefore legal in shops. When they got back to the UK they consulted Barry Stapeley of Satellite Information Services (now Sports Information Services), the broadcaster owned by the large bookmakers and responsible for providing content in betting shops, who suggested that they locate an RNG in Bedford in order to produce 'remote events' (Pitt 2013). Frater and Grubmuller were not alone in looking for cheaper, faster products: other bookmakers were experimenting with numbers games based on pseudo-random numbers generated by lava lamps, situated, of course, in secret, off-site locations.

At first the new machines, called the Global Draw, produced a lottery-style draw every half an hour, but once again, the pair realised that this was an arbitrary limitation. After receiving legal advice, they 'came up with the idea of making it every second, as the principle was the same. That's what led to what became known as fixed odds betting terminals' (Pitt 2013). These changes took place extremely quickly. At the 1998 Betting Shop Show the afternoon seminar on the Global Draw attracted a big crowd. At the start of the show the machine drew every five minutes, by the end it drew every ten seconds: Grubmuller couldn't reveal the technology fast enough. The only limitation on the profitability of these machines was the tax on stakes which impeded high-speed gambling, and was very difficult to get around, even with the help of lawyers.

Frater and Grubmuller developed their lottery alternative before the tax change in 2001, using a different business model. At the time, 'tax on turnover ... was 6.75 per cent; our lottery game had a hold of about 10 per cent' (Pitt 2013). They put a dozen of the machines in their betting shop in West Hounslow and at the Betting Shop Show claimed a 50% margin expected to stabilise at around 30% on an average stake per (betting) 'slip' of £3 to £4. It is interesting to note that they were still using betting shop rather than casino terminology. The popularity of the machines and the success of the shops attracted the attention of other bookmakers, as well as arcade, casino and bingo operators. Like virtual racing, they were unloved by traditionalists, but the shops showed that punters would use them and that they could be profitable, despite being shackled by tax. The major piece of the puzzle was yet to fall into place and out of their direct control, as Frater told BOS Magazine:

> 'It was about this time that bookmakers were trying to convince the government to change from a turnover tax to a gross profit tax. I discussed it with Walter and we agreed that if it went to a gross profit tax we could develop roulette and put it on the machines. The gross profit tax was accepted and within a few weeks we'd put roulette on all the machines in our own shops, then we rolled it out to the Coral shops. From the day we put in roulette, it just went like that,' he says, pointing upwards, through the roof and towards the stars. 'When the other bookmakers saw what we and Coral were doing, everybody wanted them.' (Pitt 2013)

According to industry commentators, in 1998 racing accounted for 70% of business in betting shops. By 2007 this was less than half, and by 2014 racing contributed 30%.

Hooked!

In 2007, as the full impact of FOBTs was emerging, both in terms of bookmakers' profits but also in terms of calls to the National Gambling Helpline, I was given permission to conduct fieldwork inside the head office of a bookmaker in the UK. It had taken me more than a year to gain access, but once inside, I was taken under the wing of an efficient and enthusiastic administrator. Lucy asked me what I wanted to know about, and organised my schedule accordingly. I first met Martin in the canteen where we chatted over coffee and muffins. He was bored, had an interest in Anthropology, and was keen to tell his story. He was also self-confident and enjoyed showing off about his job managing the development of what he called 'the machines business'. He told me:

> This is the most important department in the company bar none. You're not from Gamcare[3] are you? They cost £17,000 each and we used to rent them. Now we buy them and they pay for themselves after 50 days then it's just cash. They won't get stroppy or say it doesn't like the way it's being treated or has to look after a sick kid. Imagine the turnover if we make £500 a day profit at 3%! It way outstrips e-gaming [which is] now an entire floor of its own. And OTC [over-the-counter] betting in shops. (Interview 2007)

At first, I assumed that he was bragging. I spotted one of my more dependable sources nibbling a doughnut and asked him, 'What do you think is the most important change in bookmaking?' He didn't even pause to think before saying, 'FOBTs have been the biggest change (after 17 years in betting). Would have said taxation, but FOBTs much bigger.' I moved on and asked someone who had been even longer in the business, who was hiding out from what he calls 'the new breed of shiny suits' in the break room. 'Product development is the biggest change.' He said. 'There was a background of a declining market in the 1980s with only audio, then AWPs then evening opening, tax, FOBTs, online.' Which is the most significant? I asked him. 'Oh, machines, no doubt about that. The only question is how long it takes the government to work out what we're doing and take them away.'

Martin had worked at head office for ten years, throughout the roll-out of FOBTs, and was keen to tell me how he had contributed to their success, so we moved our conversation from the canteen to his office where we sat surrounded by life-size cut-outs of female models who were being used to promote new games and free tournaments in shops. Martin moved a few to one side so that I could take a seat, telling me that he had met 'the blonde' on the King's Road and paid her £200 to pose as a croupier wearing a bow tie, 'these are a few spares – for personal use only' he said with a wink. Martin explained how FOBTs had evolved from poker which paid off at between six and nine months per terminal, which was 'pretty good', to showing roulette, which paid off after eight to ten weeks. He confirmed Steve Frater's story about their instant popularity:

> In Hounslow West they had twelve terminals and queues, waiting boards, but they still had fights. When we saw that, the roll-out was very swift. It was a no brainer. There was no legislation for or against them – it was a loophole. When we had about five hundred of them we went up against the casinos and said that it was still fixed odds betting and the rest is history.

Martin is referring to the case brought by the Gaming Board, the predecessor of the Gambling Commission, in 2003, which was settled out of court. As part of the settlement, the bookies agreed to conduct research into FOBTs and in November 2003 a voluntary Code of Practice was signed between the Department for Media Culture and Sport, the Gaming Board and the Association of British Bookmakers (ABB). The code limited bookmakers to four FOBTs per shop, set the maximum stake at £100 and the maximum prize at £500, set the minimum spin duration at 20 seconds and ruled out the depiction of casino games other than roulette (Woodhouse 2017).

In Las Vegas, casinos are gigantic social experiments and the programming of chance has become an art based on real-life, real-time, data and sophisticated algorithms designed to hook players and encourage them to continue playing (Schüll 2012). In the early days of FOBTs concerns were rather more parochial. According to Martin, the greatest challenge he faced was not designing compelling games, but securing the takings. As he explained, 'I said early on to operations. We're going to need a stronger box. And I was right':

> We were bringing in machines that they [punters] hated at first. We had to make them really strong. AWPs were made of chipboard and crap. You could kick them apart. We soon learned that FOBTS had to be much more robust and withstand much more violence because they

made people really angry! Like in Liverpool, someone lost a couple of grand and wheeled the bloody machine off down to the estate to set fire to it. These are the kind of people you're dealing with. Total animals. And in Brighton. They were trying to burn holes in it!

In Las Vegas slot machines have been developed into a hybrid form of entertainment, combining high-definition graphics, storytelling and celebrity tie-ins. In 2007, ten years after their introduction, FOBTs remained resolutely low tech, but, like the customers in locals' casinos in Las Vegas, who stick with old-fashioned 'steppers'[4] their 'fit' with betting shop customers was unassailable:

> The product on the terminal has been the same for four years. Roulette has not changed, except the payment table, but the same graphics used by about 70% of old-style roulette. Roulette is still 99% of all trans-actions. No other roulette has challenged it. 0.6% of the market is Chinese, we took a red baize and reskinned it, put on Chinese charac-ters and Chinese buttons with Arabic numbers, in Chinatown they do tend to use that version.

During the Gaming Board action against FOBTs, Martin's company had trialled other games, but none of them were as popular as roulette:

> We did have a number of products that had roulette mechanisms but didn't look like roulette. 'Infinity' was a figure of eight, it would stop on a symbol and give you a wild spin. We had five or so products in case roulette was taken away from us. Spoof was quite successful, it was about 2% of turnover at first, but then it dropped off.

Far from halting the rise of the FOBT, the Code of Conduct agreed with the Gaming Board had, according to Martin, been good for business:

> Self-regulation in a way helped us. We had less of a problem with fraud. Someone with a £500 bet on would damage the terminal and say 'give me my money back'. At £100 there was less of an incentive to kick off and it cut a lot of that out. Rolling along with the new constraints we still have a ten to twelve week payout on more than 6500 units.

For Martin the second biggest challenge of 'rolling out FOBTs through-out the estate' was transforming horse race bettors into machine players:

> Our biggest problem wasn't technical, because we already had AWPs. It wasn't software because the games are quite simple. The biggest thing we did was take an old environment, one set up for old farts to bet on horses and dragged it into the twentieth century. Against all the odds. Everyone we spoke to in retail said that punters didn't want machines and gambling in the shops, that they would never take to them but we proved them wrong. Of course they did!

Martin overcame the aversion of punters to machines by creating competi-tions and tournaments, giving away free spins and encouraging managers to 'look after good customers, who could be relied on to spend all their cash':

> Tournaments and free bets were basically how we got machines going and if we have a slow week we still put something on, make people dress up and stand outside with free bets, give some girls a few free bets and ask them to go and flash the punters a few smiles. It works for other things, why not us? First one's free, come and see me when you need some more! Nudge, nudge, wink, wink, job done!

The 'other things' that Martin is alluding to are illegal drugs, which, at least in the popular imagination, are sold by people who offer a first hit for free, in the hope or knowledge that their customers will return either because they want to repeat the experience, or because they have become addicted. Martin added that:

> Once you've got people on these things they will never stop until they run out of money. It's incredible. You see punters literally pouring money into them. When you look at the other sections, talking about margins, how they can make certain bets attractive, how they can cross-sell and get people to buy things they might not want, I feel very lucky. I don't need to do anything. I actually think that it would be much harder to try to stop people using the machines, than to get them to spend more. Honestly, most people, they try them and that's it. Hooked!

A gift from god

By 2007, people working in the bookmaking industry were aware of the distinctive properties of machines, and the fact that they were attracting new customers to shops which had previously been unprofitable. Those who were prepared to speak to me about machines provided a variety of different views. Some, like Martin, were delighted that the machines had managed to reverse the decline in the retail business that betting shops had experienced over the previous decade, 'Machines were a gift from god.' He told me, 'Well, god, and the chancellor. Something that everyone could understand and anyone could play.' Others were more brazen about the extractive properties of FOBTs, including this senior manager:

> FOBTs? Money hoovers. They literally suck up any cash that is lying about the place. I think of us as like a massive cleaner [whistles]. In we go to a neighbourhood. Any spare cash mate? In this slot here! That's it, just shove it all in there. Oh, and enjoy a free cup of coffee while you're at it, you fucking mug.

Or this one:

> They know these FOBTs are on borrowed time. They still can't believe their luck! When they started we were like, 'That won't last'. And here we are, years later, changing our shops into arcades under the noses of the Gambling Commission. We can't believe it. Honest to god.

Some betting shop managers offered very clear ideas about the kinds of people who were feeding the FOBTs, and their motivations:

> These are not punters like you and me, they are not thinking humans, they're life's losers. They are all over the place. Everywhere you go. They can't think for themselves. They've got no common sense – they're greedy. They think they can get something for nothing and they get turned over. They keep doing it, over and over, losing every time, because they don't learn. They are incapable of thinking.

It was very common to hear people in the industry describe machine users in this way – culpable for their own losses, motivated by greed, incapable of exercising self-control, a framing which clears the operator of any responsibility for the hardships caused by FOBTs, and feeds into the responsible gambling narrative which I will describe in the next chapter. However, although this view was common, there were alternatives, markedly among older people who had witnessed changes in the industry, and particularly those who were nearing retirement. FOBTs divided the betting industry as well as the public. Some people worried about customers, and blamed their competitors for a 'race to the bottom' – new entrants to the markets who were focused on machine income and would not have been viable without them. As senior level executive, who had been working for a large bookmaker for 15 years, told me in 2009:

I've spoken to other organisations and everyone is absolutely flabber-gasted. Everyone to a man came up through the shops and in 15 years in shops I've only known one problem gambler. Since I left shops and the rise of FOBTs, every single shop has serious problems with them. The old Act [Gaming Act 1968] wasn't great, but it did hold things in check and at least had that moral position. Now I've got moral issues, and moral issues with the company. It's bothering me to a great extent.

Throughout his career, and until FOBTs were brought into the shops, Charlie understood his company to be providing a legal and trustworthy service for people who wished to bet. He was uncomfortable with the idea of increasing demand, particularly for products which he viewed as not merely inferior to his core product – betting on horse racing – but opposed to that product. Machines were 'gambling' – an activity which was entirely outside his experience and not something he wished to encourage:

I have always been proud to work for the best bookmaker in the UK. I found the work interesting, I liked the people. I could vote Labour, go to church and bring up my kids quite happily. Until FOBTs. You may as well have slipped me into a shiny suit and told me to go and run a casino. I don't know the first thing about it and I don't want to. It's a totally different ballgame.

Among the many dissenters who disapproved of the machines and the direction of travel that they represented was Stan, an independent book-maker from south-east London who had welcomed me into his shops and was proud of his family tradition in bookmaking, 'I'm a bookie through and through', he said 'cut me and I bleed bookmaking'. Stan chose to retire rather than continue to wrestle with his conscience. In 2009 he wrote to me saying, 'I've retired because of the machines. I've sold up. I'm off to Spain. You've got to earn a living but you need to look in the mirror when you shave or else you'll cut your throat.'

The mixed reactions to FOBTs by traditional bookmakers recall the responses that Zuboff (2019) has described by supporters of traditional forms of capitalism to surveillance capitalism, which, to them appears not just creepy but horrifying. Like the bookmakers who responded to the changes put forward by the Gambling Act with a mixture of delight and fear, gambling executives tread a line between methods of extracting money from people that are accommodated within their existing view of the world and those that appear acquisitive or anti-social. In chapters 6 and 7 I discuss the importance of this contrast in more depth, in relation to online gambling, which, like FOBTs, provides corporations with opportunities to make supernormal profits based on repetitive play and highly flexible regulation.

Frater and Grubmuller won the race to create the most lucrative product in betting shops because they had an international approach and – unlike some traditionalists – they were not in the thrall of horse racing; they believed that machines could be profitable in British betting shops. Most importantly, like bookmakers in the 1960s, they saw regulation as a puzzle or challenge to be overcome, rather than a restriction. This approach is far from new. In 1968, Albert Murray, Labour MP for Gravesend, observed in the House of Commons that, 'a coach and horses were driven through the 1960 legislation ... I have no doubt that when the [1968] Bill becomes law Ladbrokes will be quoting odds on the time it will take people to get round it.'[5] The industry continues to evolve in this way, guided by lawyers who come together at annual conferences: 'Changes to regulation are always opportunities to make money. If you can't find the opportunity, you aren't looking hard enough', one senior legal adviser to the UK industry told me in Las Vegas in 2013. Another gambling corporation lawyer explained to me in London in 2016:

I am paid to come up with clever ways of making money lawfully ... just! If the scheme that you have come up with is wholly legal and in the spirit of the regulations, then the chances are that it will not be lucrative. This business is all about spotting an advantage and then pressing it home, getting ahead of everyone else, mainly the competition, but also the regulators. By the time they've caught up you are onto something else.

FOBTs endgame

Theresa May put FOBTs 'on probation' in 2003 (Walsh 2003), although no one was quite sure what the terms of this sentence were, or what punishments would be meted out for perceived transgressions. Despite periodic threats to reduce their numbers or stakes prompted by stories in the media, bookmakers managed to resist any serious changes to their structural characteristics by repeating a very simple message that 'there is no empirical evidence of a causal link between gaming machines and problem gambling' (ABB 2013). This stance was accepted by successive governments, and placed the onus on researchers to produce the kind of incontrovertible proof that rarely exists in public health research, which focuses on combinations of independent and related variables, working in complex systems and causing unanticipated consequences. A task which was already virtually impossible was made even more difficult by the refusal of bookmakers to share their machines or data with independent researchers.

In practice, it is impossible to devise an experiment which proves that FOBTs cause problem gambling for several reasons: gamblers cannot (practically or ethically) be isolated from exposure to other kinds of gambling or other products with addictive properties (leading to questions around causation and comorbidity) while laboratory experiments include less 'noise' but are easily dismissed (particularly by the industry) as poor proxies for natural environments. Demanding evidence of this kind delays the implementation of meaningful reforms, but fits easily into the common-sense narrative of 'evidence-based policy', an idea which has escaped serious critical attention in relation to gambling policy despite its mixed performance in areas ranging from public health (Smith 2013) to school policing (Nolan 2015).

When increasing numbers of those harmed by FOBTs, including the relatives of gamblers who had taken their own lives, gained the courage to speak in public about their experiences, bookmakers and their supporters enforced a commonplace distinction between what was to count as 'empirical evidence' (quantitative, 'hard') and 'anecdotal evidence' (qualitative, 'soft'). They used this distinction to deflect calls for meaningful regulatory changes until 2014 when, under pressure from the government, the

Responsible Gambling Trust (RGT, a charity funded by voluntary contributions from the industry and chaired by Neil Goulden, also the chair of the ABB) commissioned a set of reports into machine gambling in the UK which the government suggested would settle these questions once and for all. The fact that the same person, and particularly an industry veteran, could head both of these organisations at the same time, is extraordinary. The lack of critical attention that the arrangement attracted can only be understood in the wider context, in which gambling was endorsed by the political establishment as a legitimate leisure activity, the harm it causes presented as a function of the weaknesses of particular individuals.

In 2010, those calling for reform, including the newly formed Campaign for Fairer Gambling,[6] were told to wait for the outcome of the research, by, for example, Hugh Robertson (Minister for Sport between 2010 and 2014 and chair, since 2018, of Camelot, the operator of the National Lottery):

> the Government are seriously concerned about problem gambling. This is one of those quite tricky areas where common sense suggests that it is a major problem but there is a lack of evidence to back that up. I very much hope that the major research project that is being undertaken will give us the necessary evidence and, absolutely, once the problem is proved to exist, the Government will act. (*Hansard* 2013)

It wasn't only the Conservatives who used the RGT research on machines to justify their lack of action on FOBTs. At an earlier Westminster event, Clive Efford (Shadow Culture Minister) told the audience, 'If the research that is currently being done for the Responsible Gambling Trust shows that there is a link between the stakes and prizes on FOBTs and problem gambling, then I will call for them to be removed.' I told him that the research would not answer the impossible question, 'Do FOBTs cause problem gambling?', partly because (as one of the researchers had been careful to say throughout) the research was far more limited in scope, and partly because the question, as posed, is a giant, unanswerable, red herring.

The machines research

The much-anticipated RGT-commissioned resesarch on gambling machines was published on 1 December 2014, and launched at an event in London on 10 December. The launch provided an insight into what happens when the collaborative partnership model favoured by industry-supported gambling research charities all over the world is given its fullest expression. It was an absurd parody of an academic conference, with speakers including members of the industry, the UK regulators and researchers. It aped the conventions of an academic conferences, techniques which were deployed most effectively by the commercial interests that were (theoretically) under scrutiny. So, for example, Ladbrokes CEO Richard Glynn impersonated a cross headmaster, repeating the word, 'complex', peering out at the audience over his spectacles and attempting to silence Professor Jim Orford, a retired academic with a distinguished career, by referring to him as a 'provocateur'.

The strange nature of the event was evident even before the speeches began. Outside the entrance to the main hall a stand displaying glossy leaflets was manned by three friendly looking young people. GamCare, or some other treatment provider, I presumed, wrongly. The stand belonged to Featurespace, who had conducted some of the research. Their promotional pamphlets were packed with endorsements: 'Featurespace gives you much more compelling information [than other solutions] at a much lower price point', enthused William Hill. One of the three lively and articulate young people approached me and asked whether I would like to hear how Featurespace can help my business detect fraud. I felt more and more confused. How was it possible, I asked myself, that the company responsible for research that was set to inform UK policy could also be touting for business from bookmakers attending the much-awaited launch?

Featurespace had already launched their report earlier that morning on Twitter by saying: 'World-leading research has shown that the £2 stake limit on #FOBTs is ineffective in reducing gambling harm', a tweet clearly intended to engage directly with the drive, led by the Campaign for Fairer Gambling, to limit stakes on FOBTs to £2. A £2 stake was not the focus of the Featurespace report, nor did the research test this claim. The chief technology officer (CTO) of Featurespace presented his findings during the launch. He had no academic track record that might have qualified him to undertake a project of this kind, nor was it clear how he had secured the commission from the RGT. He had been crunching the numbers of his customers, looking for evidence of harmful play. At the launch, he was presenting those findings to them, in front of policy makers, the press and other researchers. 'How did you manage this conflict of interest?' I asked him during questions from the audience. He looked confused and said, 'What we've presented is what the data says ... It's not us speaking, it's what the data has told us.' The bookmakers in the row in front of me turned around and scowled at me, as did several fellow academics. My question was absolute anathema to the consensual atmosphere cultivated by this event and others like them, run by the RGT (now called GambleAware) and based on partnership, collaboration, mutual learning and co-production. These all sound like positive things, and criticising them appears negative, or even anti-social, until you see at first-hand what it means to have the industry in the room when you are trying to work out how they are making their money, and from whom. The World Health Organization and other public health organisations explicitly exclude industries like alcohol and gambling from discussions between researchers. In the UK, partnership continues to be celebrated, despite calls for 'clean conferences' in this space (Livingstone 2018) and substantial evidence of the deleterious effect of industry participation on the quality of research in many different fields (Lundh et al. 2017).

In 2011 Gary Banks described the double standard employed by the Australian industry in arguments about evidence:

> The industry essentially owes its existence and current size to the lack of an evidence based approach to liberalization ... It subsequently protested only a little at the lack of evidence for most of the (ineffectual) harm minimisation measures introduced over the past decade, despite their compliance costs. But it has been insistent on high standards of proof for measures that promise to be effective. One major industry group even suggested that no measure should be introduced if the possibility of error was more than 1 in a 1000! (Banks 2011)

The situation is the same in every jurisdiction, including the UK.[7] The gambling industry has managed to set the terms on which evidence can be assessed, setting impossibly high standards for effective measures while rolling out low-cost, low-impact measures such as responsible gambling education, often without requiring (or providing) proof of their efficacy.[8] The decision by the government to reduce stakes to £2 was not based on proof that FOBTs cause problem gambling, but on the weight of international evidence which shows that, all things being equal, easily available, high stakes, high frequency gambling is more likely to be harmful than slower, less accessible, lower stakes forms of gambling: something that has been known for many years. In Alberta, Canada in 2011, for example, researchers found that problem gambling rates were three to four times higher for EGM players compared to the general population (Williams et al. 2011: 105), and that 77% of VLT and 72% of slot machine expenditure was accounted for by problem gamblers (Williams et al. 2011: 110). As I argued in chapter 1, the real catalyst for change in the UK was political. People in the UK were simply fed up with the machines and parliamentarians knew that continuing to defend and to profit from them would be unpopular. There are hopeful elements in this story, and certainly lessons to be learned from the activities of both the Campaign for Fairer Gambling and Gambling With Lives, the charity set up by parents bereaved by gambling-related suicides. At times (sitting in the audience of the machines research launch, for example), the gambling industry appeared unassailable; in practice, however, they are vulnerable to the kinds of pressure that can be brought to bear in an open democracy. But, the closer the industry gets to government, and the more dependent the state becomes on income from gambling (as can be seen in Macau, for example, where approximately 80% of government revenue comes from gambling taxes), the more resilient it becomes. In the next chapter I describe how FOBTs affected life in the betting shop, and interrogate another essential element underpinning the expansion of gambling, the idea of 'responsible gambling'.

5
The Responsible Gambling Myth

We take the safety and security of our staff and customers extremely seriously. (Spokesman for a betting company)

I was robbed and stabbed. It's part of the job. (Betting shop manager, central London)

Governments that choose to develop their gambling industries, whether in order to raise income through taxation (for example Massachusetts; see Massachusetts Gaming Commission 2015), because they already have a large illegal market (Vietnam; see Tomiyama 2017), or because they want to attract investment and tourists (Singapore, Japan; see Kyodo 2016) have all embraced the concept of 'responsible gambling'. 'Responsible gambling' has been defined in many different ways, but suggests that gambling can be safe and even 'healthy'[1] for most people if sufficient information is provided to guide their decisions, while acknowledging that it can cause problems for a few people, who should be told how to seek help. The effect of equating gambling regulation with consumer protection is to place responsibility for problems and their solutions with individuals while the structural features of gambling markets, including the supply of opportunities to gamble and the forms taken by these opportunities, are de-emphasised (Livingstone et al. 2014). Despite the growing international consensus that gambling should be treated as a public health issue (*Lancet* 2017), 'responsible gambling' remains the ethical underpinning for gambling regulation all over the world. In 2018, for example, the UK government described itself as determined 'to achieve, in partnership with the industry, a culture of responsible gambling' (DDCMS 2018b). The government in British Columbia in Canada is also 'committed to responsible gambling' (Vockeroth 2014). In Australia, New South Wales has an Office of Responsible Gambling, while Victoria boasts the Victorian Responsible Gambling Foundation.

Responsible gambling programmes and initiatives are also produced and promoted by trade organisations and operators as part of self-regulation. Like invocations to 'drink responsibly' these initiatives are 'strategically ambiguous' (Smith et al. 2006). The compliance officers employed by large companies have a strange job, which one described to me as 'balancing social responsibility with healthy profits'. Another told me that their job was 'surreal': 'on the one hand I'm here to make money for the company like any other employee. On the other I am a threat to good business.' This awkwardness is heightened by the distinctive distribution of profits from gambling. Like many other commodities, but especially those with compulsive or addictive qualities, a disproportionate amount of profits (between 15% and 50%, depending on the jurisdiction and product) come from people who have been categorised as 'problem gamblers' (Williams and Wood 2016). In 2011 problem gamblers accounted for about 50% of gambling expenditure in Alberta, Canada (Humphreys et al. 2011). In Finland more recently researchers found that the overall rate of problem gambling was 3.3% but problem and pathological gamblers accounted for 28.5% of total expenditure among women and 20.8% among men (Castrén et al. 2018). In Australia, the Productivity Commission (2010) estimated that 36% of revenue came from people identified as problem gamblers. In the UK, the amount of revenue estimated to come from problem gamblers ranges from 1% (the National Lottery) to 20% to 30% (for betting on dog racing and fixed odds betting terminals [FOBTs]) (Orford et al. 2013).

Research also suggests that, like alcohol and tobacco, there may be no 'safe' level of gambling. According to an Australian study based on 'large, nationally representative surveys in Australia, Canada, Finland and Norway', 'gambling at any level can be associated with harm. And the more money lost, the greater the risk of harm' (Markham et al. 2016). Because of this profile, compliance officers face a constant conflict of interests: the mechanisms that most effectively prevent people from experiencing gambling harm also have the greatest impact on profits. Their senior managers, tasked with maximising profits for stakeholders, are obliged to engage with 'responsible gambling', at the same time as minimising its impact on income.

Industry-run responsible gambling initiatives are contrary to public health approaches to gambling, and rest on quite different principles. While responsible gambling emphasises individual responsibility, informed choice and treatment, public health emphasises population-level measures designed to reduce harm, or prevent harm from occurring. This contrast has been compared to parking an ambulance at the bottom of a cliff, rather than building a fence at the top. One of the few places in the world that can claim to have attempted to take a public health approach to gambling is New Zealand, where the Gambling Act 2003 required the Ministry of Health to develop 'an integrated problem gambling strategy focused on public health', which must include 'measures to promote public health by preventing and minimising the harm from gambling', 'services to treat and assist problem gamblers and their families/ whānau', 'independent scientific research associated with gambling' and evaluation (New Zealand Ministry of Health 2015). Elsewhere, government and industry acknowledge that gambling is a public health issue, use public health language including referring to the 'harms' caused by gambling, at the same time as promoting responsible gambling measures focused primarily on the treatment of individuals who are already experiencing gambling harm. This is inevitable: gambling cannot be treated as a public health issue while it is framed as a leisure industry and based on policies that are led by the Treasury, as in most Australian states, or by the Department for Digital, Culture, Media and Sport (DDCMS), as in the UK. The priorities of these departments (including the imperative to consider economic growth in their decisions) conflict with the aims of public health. The outcome of these conflicts of interest within companies are responsible gambling programmes like 'When the Fun Stops, Stop' by the Senet Group (a UK industry collective) and 'Nobody Harmed' by William Hill. These initiatives, which focus on individual behaviour and place responsibility for change with consumers, demonstrate that a public health approach to gambling cannot be undertaken by private companies with obligations to shareholders or owners.[2]

In this chapter I use my experiences of working in betting shops to explore how responsible gambling operates in practice. In betting shops in London, codes of practice do not reflect the realities of relationships, processes or everyday life. This contrast, between abstract codes and lived realities, is in no way unique to gambling spaces, and the failures it causes are comparable to other failures of self- and 'light-touch' regulation, including by motor vehicle manufacturers (Copley 2015), social media giants (Rudgard 2019) and banks (Treanor 2013). However, what is distinctive is the way that, in this context, codes operate to deepen structural inequalities between workers and their managers. In this case, the cost of social responsibility, an aspect of public relations implemented in order to legitimise gambling profits, is borne by workers putting their bodies on the line. Betting shops are complex and variable social spaces with their own rules. Abstract codes fail to recognise this complexity; they create contradictions and increase the vulnerability of workers.

Shop life

It's 8 a.m. on a spring Monday morning and I'm working as an unpaid cashier in a busy betting shop on a prestigious street in central London. The shop has recently been completely refurbished – it has 30 flat-screen televisions, polished wooden floors, a glass frontage, chrome furniture and a light and airy feel. Manager Aaliya and I have spent the first hour of the morning preparing the shop for opening at 9. Listening to MTV Base and chatting amiably, we have secured the day's racing newspapers onto the walls using the regulation magnets and restocked pens and betting slips in all of the betting stations. At 8.45 Aaliya changes out of her jeans into a smart pair of trousers and we unlock the door. A man in a suit is waiting. He nods to both of us and assumes his usual position on one of the four FOBTs in the corner of the shop, lighting a cigarette as he sits down. After 20 minutes or so he rushes over to the counter and asks us to change a £20 note. He asks for a Coke and offers payment of 60p, which Aaliya refuses. His drink stashed on the top of the machine, he plays for another five minutes before rushing off to his job as a corporate lawyer. Today he has been unlucky and as he leaves he shouts over his shoulder to us, 'There's plenty of money in there if you need to pay someone out!' Aaliya and I can see from our computer terminals behind the counter that he has spent £600 in 30 minutes. A street cleaner takes his place, picks up £150 immediately and places a £39 bet on the football. During this time Aaliya checks her unsettled bets: 'This is your way to know what is outstanding in your shop then nothing is a surprise to you, no big bet in the system,' she says.

Second into the shop is Mr Narang, a chef who works at a local restaurant and does not speak English. He smiles and salutes me, lifting his woolly hat, and begins chatting to Aaliya in Punjabi. Mr Narang does not appear to know anything about horse racing, and places his bet with Aaliya's help. Aaliya tells me that Mr Narang's colleagues all bet, although they do not share his unconventional system. This morning, Mr Narang hands over his ticket from the day before and it's a winner. He is genuinely amazed. The three of us laugh and Mr Narang receives his £37 winnings. I have a strong feeling that Mr Narang bets in order to spend time with Aaliya, and he is not the only one. In the course of our work we are brought chocolates, cakes, fried chicken and 'proper' frothy coffees. One colleague is given a CD of songs written in her honour with her face printed on the disc by a man whom we refer to as 'The Pest'. She is not pleased. Female staff are encouraged to be friendly to customers, but we are also warned about 'dodgy blokes' to be avoided in what is an over-whelmingly masculine space with very specific rules about how men and women should behave (Cassidy 2014).

The third customer is Steve, a builder in a white hard hat. He begins by collecting his winnings of £600 from the previous day and giving Aaliya £20 'luck money'. He sits down with the racing paper and writes out seven new bets, two win bets and a double on a horse race, a Lucky 31, reverse forecast through the card on traps four and six at Newcastle, and Chelsea to beat Tottenham, Frank Lampard to score first. His stake is £215. He has a brief discussion with Aaliya before leaving the shop with a number of colleagues, also in hard hats, who have congregated in the shop to eat sausage rolls and drink tea. They talk and watch the virtual dog racing, which runs constantly in the background, but none has a bet. While the builder writes his bets several other people enter the shop. Barbara is in her fifties. She came to London to study at the London School of Eco-nomics but in the 1990s she was a victim of a violent attack. She is now homeless and spends much of her day in the shop, making bets of 75p, up to between £2 and £2.50 each day, chatting and bringing us the free papers in the afternoon. Other regulars sometimes share their winnings with her. As Aaliya says, 'Sometimes one of those bets can return £38 and she is somewhere warm and comfortable, betting within her means and sometimes winning, at better odds than the lottery.' While I take Barbara a cup of tea a well-dressed, well-spoken man asks me if we are betting on the Budget speech, and if so what odds can he get on the number of sips of water the Chancellor will take. I call head office to check and they provide me with a 'tissue', a set of odds or 'prices'. An Australian man comes to the counter to ask how he can bet antepost on the Formula One Grand Prix. The well-dressed man decides on six sips at odds of three to one and hands me a tenner.

Lunch is extremely busy, with lots of builders and office workers on their breaks. In the afternoon the rhythm changes as we take bets on UK racing from customers who prefer to lay them at the last possible moment, just before 'the off', mostly as singles or doubles, but also in multiples including Trixies, Yankees, Canadians, Super Yankees, and the ever popular Lucky 15.[3]

We handle large amounts of cash (being careful to place change on the counter rather than in the punters' hands) translate or 'capture' and settle bets using the electronic point of sale (EPOS) system. Mistakes are costly, and can encourage slow counts and other tricks.[4] By two in the afternoon we have completed 485 transactions. We are keeping a particularly close eye on a Chinese man who is very superstitious, and will not place bets with either me or Aaliya because, as he told us, 'You no lucky'. He has been back in the shop for the past three months after spending the previous nine months at a nearby rival. In these three months he has put £215,000 through the till, and taken out £95,817 on horse racing at between £100 and £400 per race. The afternoon passes in a blur and we haven't had time to have lunch or make a run to the bank, the machines and the safe are full and there is money everywhere: as I reach for a mug in a kitchen cupboard great bricks of it fall on my head. Racing finishes at around six and after that people come in to play the FOBTs. By the time we close at 9.30 p.m. we have taken almost 900 slips.[5]

The next shop I work in is near a busy bus station in south-east London. As I walk in I'm struck by the sticky carpet and the stench of cigarettes and alcohol. As I reach the counter it's clear that someone has been urinating in the back corner of the shop. A hand-written sign on the toilet door says 'Closed because you fucking idiots cant [sic] stop dealing drugs. You was warned'. I walk up to the counter and a large man eyes me suspiciously. I open my coat and flash my uniform and he buzzes me in through a rein-forced door. Like liquor stores in New York, betting shop back offices are sealed off from the rest of the shop by 'bandit screens' – once bars, now reinforced glass. A young girl is sitting at the counter doing her nails and says 'hello'. The large man says, 'You must be out of your fucking mind coming here.' There is trouble of some kind every day of the three weeks I'm in this shop, ranging from violence against the machines, punching or smashing the screens, to threats to staff. At the end of our shift we leave the shop together and our manager, 'Big Paul' sees that us two 'girls' get the bus before him. Paul has been robbed at gun-point four times and was robbed at knife-point in the shop while emptying the machines six months ago. During our interview he describes himself as 'a fat, 40-year-old no-hoper with post-traumatic stress disorder'. Our customers are mainly West Indian and Eastern European and we do very little business over the counter. FOBTs account for between 74% and 85% of our income.[6] We spend the day behind the counter, occasionally venturing out in pairs, checking first that particularly troublesome customers are nowhere to be seen, in order to empty the money from the machines.

Live and let live

These two very different experiences reflect the variety that exists among betting shops in London, which provide a very similar range of services but reflect the local area, the competition, the operator, the manager, the staff and the serendipitous conditions under which people choose that particular shop. There are a handful of flagship shops on posh London streets, many more shops opposite pubs (known as 'wet' sites), shops in Harlesden full of West Indian customers, and others in Chinatown where the customers, staff and games are Chinese or British-born Chinese. A few bookies resemble coffee shops where there happens to be provision made for betting and playing machines. A decreasing number are traditional 'over-the-counter' shops, where betting on horses in the afternoons takes precedence and the regular customers are knowledgeable about horse and dog racing. An increasing number are gritty enclaves for machine playing, where over-the-counter business is minimal.

Many shops are notably cosmopolitan. The ruling ethos? 'Live and let live.' Despite deregulation and refurbishments, betting shops remain one of the last resolutely working-class, masculine spaces left on the high street (Cassidy 2014). Etiquette in the betting shop starts with a single, simple rule: people should be allowed to behave in any way that suits them so long as it doesn't interfere with anyone else's ability to do the same. Anyone can go into a betting shop. Unlike pubs, there is no necessity to buy. There are limits to this tolerance. As my manager used to say, 'If you stink, you're out. If you can't leave people alone, you're out. Otherwise, so long as you keep yourself to yourself, you can stay.' In part this is because, 'You can have a punter who looks as though he hasn't got two shillings to rub together and he bets £20 and someone else rich-looking puts on 50p.' Interesting and sometimes unlikely combinations of people form loose associations that coalesce, dissolve and re-form, and may or may not be recognised outside the betting shop.

Bookies are important nodes in the informal economy, where you can recruit labour, fence goods and launder cash. Most activities are more prosaic. I learned to salsa in a betting shop below a community dance hall and pool centre in Lewisham, had my hair cut in a shop in Brockley, and sold a washing machine from the pawn shop next door in a shop in Nunhead. I noted hundreds of small transactions in my diary each week, like Daz, a Rastafarian man, who came in with some LPs and magazines he had found in a skip to see if anyone wanted to buy them in a West Indian shop in New Cross. In the same shop, Willie, one of the customers, provides hot lunches of fried chicken or ackee and salt fish from a polystyrene box he keeps behind the counter, at £5 a pop.[7]

Everyone I met told me not to lend money in the betting shop, but of course money is circulating all the time – as stakes shared, interest, windfalls and debt. Lending and borrowing money was the cause of some of the violence I saw in betting shop, but it was also often done remarkably casually, in the same way as money is distributed between players in casinos in London, Las Vegas and in Macau. Money inside the casino or the betting shops is simply not the same as money outside: transformed into 'winnings' it takes on magical properties, and becomes dispensable and fecund in contrast to the mundane money of everyday life (Zelizer 1994). One of the sets of diaries that punters kept for me in south-east London illustrated this particularly well. A group of nine men redistributed pooled money through betting to the extent that it kept them solvent at times when work was scarce, but it also showed that winnings were shared without any thought of return, and in ways that money earned was not. Two of the nine were brothers, the rest were friends. Their exchanges had no endpoint and there was no equilibrium to be reached. My request to record their transactions temporarily disturbed their system by showing that, for example, the brother who owned the company and provided most of them with work was paying the lion's share. The inequality was explained away: Steve was either 'a lucky bastard' (whether or not this was in general or in relation to betting was left open) or 'a good judge' (of horses).

As well as bewitching money, betting shops also encourage bonds to form between people who might otherwise remain separate. The group of three friends who taught me most about machine gambling in south-east London were Desmond, a Jamaican man in his sixties who ran a barber's shop, Tiger, a Burmese man in his thirties who worked casually in the catering trade, and Chen, a Chinese student. These three spent all their time together, shared tips, winnings and stakes, and consistently looked out for one another. When Chen was forced to pay a debt to the Snakeheads who brought him to London, Tiger and Desmond helped to raise the cash. When this was not enough, Chen hid for months in the back room of Desmond's shop.

On the other hand, when 'strangers' came into 'our' shop, at quiet times, we would inspect them, and pay attention. On one occasion, a white man wearing black clothes came into the shop and as he wrote his bet a radio he was carrying under his jacket crackled, identifying him as a policeman. Everyone in the shop tensed. He turned around to the person nearest to him, who happened to be Jim, a Chinese regular, who was holding a bag of DVDs, and started to speak in an aggressive tone saying, 'What have you got here then? Do you speak English?' He snatched the bag of DVDs out of Jim's hand and yelled, 'This is why we don't want you people in this country!' and stomped out of the door. As he left, the entire betting shop ran after him shouting abuse. He walked a little way before turning back towards the small crowd, who turned themselves and ran for the shop, shouting to the manageress, 'Lock the door Margaret! He's coming back!' We spent the afternoon reliving the event, slapping Jim on the back and agreeing that the policeman was 'out of order'. 'He comes in here', said Reggie, a West Indian, who was the first person to lay a bet in the shop on the day it opened, 'He comes in here throwing his weight around? Insulting Jim? Insulting us? This is my shop!'

Regulars become proprietorial about particular shops and set the tone of the place, as manager Kevin explains: 'If you go to the same betting shop it feels like it's part of you. You get a sense of belonging, It's a habit. People will come in because they feel comfortable coming in.' Regulars have their own routines. Arthur, for example, a regular in an extremely civilised shop in Hatton Garden, who wore a wig and gave his occupation as 'armed robber (retired)' during our discussions, would come into the shop at 10 in the morning, place a chocolate bar on the counter in front of me, nod and say hello and then sit with his legs elegantly crossed, in one of the comfortable chairs to watch the news while reading the paper. At 11 I would take him a cup of coffee. At 12 he would come and stand at the counter watching us take bets and chatting. His favourite topics were: the uselessness of politicians, corruption in the Metropolitan Police, the belligerence of the United States and the breeding of Bengal cats. Between 12.30 and 1.30 he would have lunch (soup and a roll) in the café next door. When he returned he would sit with Berat, a Turkish friend, and bet £5 doubles and singles on his choice of UK racing. He did not bet at Kempton, Brighton or Musselburgh ('bent'). I didn't ever see him play the machines or place a bet on virtual racing which he thought was 'daylight robbery'. Once racing was finished Berat would fetch espressos from the Italian deli and they would chat over the day with us, walking around the shop and leaning on the counter. Arthur would tell tales on other customers, drawing to our attention the myriad ways in which they fell short of the standards required in 'his' shop: 'I saw Steve leave a MacDonald's carton in that corner. That man has no class. Bad enough he eats that shit. Pardon my French Rebecca.' He also knew all of our colleagues, including our bosses, and contributed to discussions about schedules and responsibilities: 'Abby simply cannot be asked to work with Jerome. There's going to be trouble! Move Sarah over to Victoria and be done with it. It's not worth trying to make it work between those two.' My manager would nod and make the change. At the end of the day Arthur would leave the shop with us, sighing and stretching as we locked up, commenting on 'another day, another dollar', 'a good day's work', before wishing us goodbye and saying casually, like any other colleague, 'see you in the morning'.

Regulars like Arthur do not travel far to their favourite shops, and as a result each shop is a reflection of the local area – for better or worse. As Kevin, manager for 15 years, explained: 'In an area like this of 10% scumbags then you'll have 10% of scumbags in the betting shop. In Brixton my old shop I had mad people selling guns and dealing drugs. Here I haven't had a minute's trouble in a month.' In London, this includes the tensions that exist between different groups. In one of the boroughs where I was working I went into a clothes shop and came across a camp Italian tailor who I knew as a fairly macho regular customer in a nearby betting shop. At first, I didn't think that he had recognised me, and as I pondered whether he had a twin, he came over and whispered in my ear, 'They don't let poofs in the bookies.' Although there were shops where multiculturalism ruled, others attracted a homogeneous crowd, and in some urban centres each shop would be reserved for a particular national or ethnic group. I recorded many examples of racist language and actions when these rules were violated, intentionally or otherwise, including countless references to 'Micks', 'Chinks', 'Blacks' and 'Arabs' in my notes, as well as watching Irish punters tell African and West Indian punters they weren't welcome in a particular shop and a Chinese man being robbed of his machine winnings by a group of young Somalian men. Like pachinko parlours in Tokyo, betting shops are intensely localised parts of the global gambling industry.

During the 1980s and 1990s, betting industry professionals debated implementing measures intended to entice more women into betting shops and even designed bets to appeal to them: 'Women make up 50 per cent of the world's population', Anthony O'Hara, nominee for betting shop manager of the year told the *Racing Post* in 1998, 'yet only about one per cent of betting shop populations, so it seems to me the way forward is to encourage this largely untapped market to enter betting offices' (*Racing Post* Staff 1998). However, by the time I began my research, the interest in attracting women had waned. As the retail director of a large firm explained to me:

> if you want to increase the number of women coming into betting shops you've got to try a lot of new things and that is expensive. And you run the risk of doing things that your core customers, men, don't like. If 5% of the population already goes to the betting shop I'd rather try for 6%. Men, yes, but that's a 20% increase. Or I'd rather try to get an extra 20% out of the customers already there. Much easier than persuading women to come into the shops. It wasn't cost–effective.

While direct attempts to lure women into betting shops were unsuccessful, according to a survey by William Hill, changes in regulation (including the smoking ban in 2007) and technology appear to have had the unintended consequence of feminising the environment to some extent (*Gambling Online Magazine* 2008).[8] Before the smoking ban my female manager told me that, 'Women are going to have babies. They don't want to come in here until the new law [smoking ban] comes along. Many people would not want to work in this environment. You could easily be a trolley dolly where it smells of bread!'

Whenever I visited a new shop my presence provoked questions. Did I know that I was in a bookies? Was I lost? Or a sex worker? Someone sent by the council to spy on benefit claimants? Police officer? Spy for a competing bookie? Mentally ill? Looking for my husband? To most punters it was inconceivable that a middle-aged woman would be in a betting shop as a matter of choice. Once I had been around for a while and turned down every offer of sex, I was often treated like an exotic pet. Bets and sports were patiently explained as though I was an alien or a child who had never heard of football or cricket, let alone horse racing. From Aaliya's point of view:

> This is the worst job I could do. When I started twelve years ago there weren't many Asian girls in the shop and I remember I got a job for my friend and her mum made her quit. It's a male-dominated clientele, and the older generation associate gambling with prostitution. I used

to laugh about it. All I need to do now is work in a pub and a strip joint except I can't cos I ain't got the body for it! For an Indian girl to be here is just so terrible. Ultimately a job's a job.

Aaliya enjoyed her job. She put up with sexism, pushing back when she had the energy, but she had been fortunate: despite working in betting shops for three years, she had yet to be involved in a serious incident. Part of the explanation for this is that she was based in a new, flagship shop in the centre of London. Some of her colleagues were not so lucky.

Violence: part of the job

According to the Association of British Bookmakers (ABB): 'The betting industry has a strong safety and security record with the welfare of our staff and customers being our number one priority' (ABB 2013). However, 36 of the 47 experienced, London-based managers I worked alongside and interviewed had been robbed at least once. One man had been robbed eleven times, although he regarded himself as extremely unlucky:

> I was robbed once in a dodgy shop in Brixton before the machines come in. It was one of them things. A desperado and a gun! The shop was known for trouble and you just did your time there and moved on as soon as you could. With the machines things changed. We went from one or two bad scenes a year to three or four a day. Sometimes you couldn't come out from behind the counter to empty the money. I was hit with a baseball bat in 2005. I had a little gap after the baseball bat because I worked in a nice little shop in the suburbs. Then one bloke got a lucky punch and laid me out the first week in my new shop. Since the machines come along it's got worse, so I don't keep tabs any more. It's enough to put you off coming to work.

Female managers had also been robbed, some on several occasions, as Jill explained, 'Worst was when I was stabbed in the neck. I went back to work the next day. Didn't think anything about it at the time. But I've thought about it since and I don't like going to the bank on my own.'[9] Another female manager told me about the first time she had been hurt by a punter, 'When I was at a shop in Bermondsey I paid a man out 2p less than he'd worked it out to. I gave it to him but he threw it back at me. He waited outside the shop and punched me in the face.' For men and women, violence was expected, rather than exceptional: 'I was robbed and stabbed. It's part of the job' (male manager, central London). Although I worked mainly in poor boroughs in London, there is evidence that the issues are more widespread. According to a survey in 2012 by Community, the union representing betting shop workers, 50% of betting shop workers had been threatened with some form of physical violence and 10% had experienced physical assault in the previous twelve months (quoted by Evans 2014). In 2011 a female betting shop worker told the union:

> In my 20 years' service, I have been robbed nine times by gun, knife and axe. One robbery happened when I was pregnant. The robber smashed the bandit screen, pulled a gun on me, cocked the gun to my stomach and pulled the trigger. Thankfully, the gun wasn't loaded but it is an incident that haunts me to this day and I still haven't forgotten the fact that I was asked to work the rest of my shift and face questions and accusations from my bosses. (Percy 2011)

A spokesman from BetFred, responding to allegations of violence in betting shops in 2012, told the *Guardian* that, 'We take the safety and security of our staff and customers extremely seriously' (Murphy 2012). Seven of the 36 people who spoke to me about being robbed had received offers of counselling or support from their companies, including a woman who told me: 'I was robbed late on a Sunday. I had half-hearted offers of counselling. I had four visits to the police. The biggest interest was getting open next day. There's no care, but I guess there never is when you've got shareholders to answer to.' Other male colleagues reported similar experiences, 'My area manager made a joke of it, like. "You won't be asking for counselling will you?" he said. "Tough old bastard like you?" That kind of thing. The time before he just said, "no".' Or, 'My boss just told me, "There's no time for that crap, you've got a shop to run. Shit happens. Move on."' Another said, 'I was told, "You best get back to work. You don't want to dwell on it."'

Experienced managers were afraid of being implicated in crimes that took place in their shop, even when they were victims:

> Every robbery puts a black mark on your name. You're the first one they look at, unless you've got a bloody great knife sticking out of you or something, like Jill got that time. That definitely got her off the hook!

It's like that though. Robberies and other bits and bobs like that can damage your reputation with the bosses.

Robert, the head of security at a small firm where I worked as a cashier confirmed this procedure, explaining that:

First person we look at after a robbery is who was there. If you say you were dismissed for dishonesty then, quite honestly, interview over. If you don't say and you get found out you get sacked. 90% ... no, well let's say 50% of people have been moved on because they think you're up to something. Even me! They might not be able to prove it, but they'll make it difficult enough for you so you have to go. We miss out on some good people because of it.

Individual operators and the ABB are acutely aware of the significance of violence in betting shops, which threatens licences and encourages public opposition to FOBTs. Official figures are difficult to interpret but, according to the BBC, 'Police statistics obtained under Freedom of Information show violent crime in betting shops in Britain rose by 9% between 2008 and 2011' (*BBC News* 2012).[10] At the same time, reports of criminal damage almost halved. The current affairs program *Panorama* has suggested that this was because operators had encouraged staff not to report violence in shops. A memo issued by William Hill, which told staff not to report crimes against the machines unless the perpetrator's name or place of work was known to staff, was used to support this contention. William Hill defended the memo as approved by the Metropolitan Police (Murphy 2012). My research participants had a more nuanced view:

Area managers don't want you to gripe about bust-ups in the shop. It gives us a bad name and the council can come round and take your licence away. Someone smashes up your machine? They bring you a new one the next day. No big deal. It's part of the job now.

Us and them

A spokesman for the ABB responded to *Panorama* by saying that:

Bookmakers offer a modern, mainstream leisure experience to 8 million people each year and the vast majority of our customers bet safely and responsibly. Like any other retailer on the high street we are sometimes faced with anti-social behaviour which is not linked to any particular product. (Quoted in Peev 2012)

However, the people I worked with were unanimous that the change in atmosphere in shops could be attributed to the introduction of machines. All 47 experienced managers I worked with felt that FOBTs had increased the likelihood of violence in shops. All 14 area managers agreed. The only people who rejected the idea that machines have led to an increase in violence against people and property in betting shops were those responsible for maintaining their public image.

Thirty-six of the 47 experienced managers I worked with had been robbed, but they also described a rise in relatively low-level violence that had accompanied the introduction of machine gambling. I asked 57 managers, 'How often do people abuse the machines in your shop?' Twenty responded 'every day', 20 'most days', 15 'once a week' and 2 'once a month'. 'Once a year' and 'never experienced it' were unused options. Working in shops myself, listening to colleagues and conducting unstructured interviews, helped me to better understand the form taken by this violence and how managers accounted for it: 'It started when we got the machines. We used to get grumbling and complaining. Now getting robbed and spat at is part of the job' (Male manager, south-east London). The growth in low-level violence was accompanied by a change in the atmosphere in the shop, and in relationships between staff and customers, which many found quite painful, as two experienced, male managers explained:

I don't actually mind them abusing the machines. What I mind is that we have gone from people who are helping someone have a bet on a horse they fancy to prison guards, stuck behind a reinforced counter, being abused by people who know we are exploiting them, robbing them blind. I can't defend it. I hate the machines. They tell me they've done their money and start spitting at me and punching the bandits and I stand there and think 'Is this what I've sunk to?' Watching the money stack up in a machine I hate in a miserable shithole where poor people come to get ripped off.

I used to love the banter. It was all taken in good heart. That was when we had horses and dogs and people who came in the shop had something in common. Now it's us and them. We are crooks to them now.

We are robbers. Machine fixers! 'You fixed the machine!' That's what we are. No wonder they want to tear our heads off. In their eyes we steal from them.

Low-level violence was virtually continuous in some of the shops where I worked. Machine play produced a staccato soundtrack of punches, slaps, kicks and expletives. In others, including Aaliya's shop, a raised voice or a kicked machine would cause people to stop and pay attention. But the direction of travel, according to betting shop workers, is clear. The increase in tension is made more challenging for staff by the longer opening hours which have accompanied the growth of income from FOBTs, and the rise in what is called 'single manning', the use of one member of staff to man a betting shop. A campaign against single manning is under way in the UK, prompted by the murder of Andrew Iacovou in May 2013 in a Ladbrokes in Morden, south London. Andrew lay undiscovered behind the counter for 90 minutes. Although he had pressed his panic button his body was not visible on the CCTV feed. Despite this campaign and an early day motion in Parliament in 2013, in August 2014 William Hill rolled out single manning in just under 2000 of its 2320 shops, based on 'a risk-based approach' intended to tackle 'rising costs' (quoted in *SBC News* 2014).

The end of the day

It's almost closing time in a quiet shop in London and my manager, Jane, and I want to go home at the end of a long shift. We are both exhausted. But there are two people left in our shop. Richard, and a second customer whom we don't know, who has been playing a FOBT for four hours. Richard is homeless and leaves his belongings in the shop for days on end, with Jane's tacit agreement. I sometimes find a shoe on the shop floor, or a rucksack stuffed in a cupboard out back, 'It's Richard's' says Jane, when I ask her about these things. Richard enjoys certain perks, and although he asks people for money as they play on machines, we tolerate and even indulge him. He is 'harmless', a category which is meaningful in this context. We can see from our terminal behind the counter that his new companion has spent over £300.

We have a chat about how to handle the situation. Do we (a) go over and ask him nicely to leave as we are now closed? (b) Let him know we are closing from behind the counter and if he doesn't leave, switch the machine off? We agree that it's likely that he is waiting for the machine to pay out, and will not want to stop playing. We decide that one of us will stay behind the counter while the other goes over and has 'a word'. I draw the short straw (literally – we pull rolled up betting slips from Jane's hand) and set off. My heart is beating fast, and I go through everything that I have been taught by colleagues: 'Be feminine!' 'Be friendly!' 'Don't nag!' '99.9% of men won't hit a woman!' As I get nearer, the stranger gets up from his stool and says, without looking away from the screen, 'Come any closer and I will fucking stab you, I swear.' The hair on the back of my neck stands up. Richard looks slightly surprised. 'Out you go!' I say breezily. 'Time we closed up. We told you half an hour ago.' I look back at Jane who nods encouragingly.

We stand for what seems a long time but is probably only a minute or two, before the man yells suddenly, 'Fuck off! I am warning you!' I haven't moved and I try again but this time more firmly. 'I'm afraid we need to close. Security will be here in a moment to check the premises' (a lie). Another moment or so is spent frozen in silence, except for the 'click, click, click' of chips. The next spin seems to take forever, but as the ball finally drops into a slot the stranger suddenly explodes. He jumps up, and wrenches the machine towards himself. Richard and I run for the counter door. The machine rights itself and the stranger stands, pounding and kicking it, swearing and shouting. As quickly as his outburst began, he stops and I notice that he is crying. He leaves the shop, heaving the door open with such force that the lower pane of glass shatters. 'What a nutter!' says Richard, now safely behind the counter with Jane and me.

Jane calls our area manager to let him know about the damage to the door. The first question he asks is, 'Is the machine broken?' To which Jane replies, quick as a flash, 'We're fine, thanks for asking!' While Jane gives the manager a piece of her mind, I venture out into the shop to lock the door and eject Richard into the well-lit street where shoppers are passing by, oblivious. We are safe, but we are together, 'What if I'd been here on my own?' asks Jane. What if you were working in Lewisham or Green Lanes, I think. The Safebet Alliance's voluntary code of conduct suggests that people working together should leave in pairs, keeping a look out and avoiding dark alleys and unlit exits. It doesn't provide any advice for people working on their own, but Big Paul's seems about the best I found, 'Keep your head down and run like hell.'

In 2013 the ABB published its *Code for Responsible Gambling and Player Protection in Licensed Betting Offices in Great Britain* at a time when pressure was being placed on the government by the media to reduce stakes on

FOBTs (ABB 2013b). It suggested that, in order to encourage responsible gambling, staff will be 'actively encouraged to walk the shop floor, in order to allow them to initiate customer interaction in response to specific customer behaviour' (ABB 2013b). In this chapter I have described everyday life in betting shops in London to show how this approach to reducing harmful gambling is not just impractical, but dangerous. It places betting shop workers, already occupying complex positions in the nexus of punters, machines and colleagues including senior managers, under additional pressure. Poorly paid, they are incentivised (both positively and negatively) to maximise profits on machines as well as (theoretically) hold the line on responsible gambling when their marketing efforts prove too successful. Like compliance managers and gambling bosses, they are utterly compromised. It is no surprise that the Facebook group set up by betting shop managers to share information and offer support to one another is called, 'I No Longer Fear Hell, I've Worked in a Betting Shop', a group which, in July 2019, had 18,046 members.

6

The Bookmakers' Lament

At the same time as fixed odds betting terminals (FOBTs) were transforming betting shops, the internet changed 'remote' gambling, from a low-frequency credit facility provided over the telephone, to a high-frequency trading proposition which enabled punters to arbitrage using exchanges or to bet continuously on the infinite instant markets provided by betting during an event, known as 'in-play'. On the production side, operators became increasingly like banks, handling millions of transactions each day, and using algorithms and platforms borrowed from financial services in order to produce tradable risks and profitable systems. As online products recolonised the space between finance and gambling they generated discussions about the 'proper' ways to profit from risk: examples of the boundary-making activity that Zelizer (1979) also observed in the legitimation of the market for insurance in the United States.

This chapter focuses on the action that took place on the trading floor of a UK bookmaker, which I will refer to as Warringtons,[1] as they switched between two ways of making prices for betting markets, attending to expert knowledge and exploring how profitable risks are created and legitimated. The purpose of the chapter is to show how different ideas of risk, competition, fairness, trust and freedom are cultivated under changing conditions. Members of the gambling industry invested their practices with social meaning and value until the internet arrived and revealed their contingency. At this point, work began to bring in new people, and to create a new system, starting from a different set of assumptions. I describe the outcomes of this process in the next chapter. But first, I describe how betting markets were made at head office, when horse racing was still the most important source of income, before the online revolution.

In 1998 anthropologist Caitlin Zaloom worked at the Chicago Board of Trade as open-cry trading was replaced by online systems, a very similar shift to the one that I witnessed at Warringtons. Zaloom's ethnography shows that traders did not view the change as a simple transition from one system to another, and indeed that they endowed each system with distinct moral and social values (Zaloom 2006). Defenders of the older system of open-cry trading argued that it was a more stable, more efficient, more liquid and more transparent way of working than the online system that was to replace it. In 2007, while working at Warringtons I observed a similar crisis unfold as one method of producing betting: a high-margin, qualitative approach, based on superior knowledge and market dominance, was defended, but ultimately replaced by a computerised, low-margin alternative. This change provoked a commentary on the morality of lucrative risk taking and also on the more general movement towards abstraction of which it was deemed to be a part. It was marked by a change in emphasis from one sport: horse racing, to another: football, and a related changing of the guard, from odds compilers to traders. The purpose of this chapter is to show that traditional bookmakers were not online natives, and that the internet did not sweep through the industry, cleansing it of socially embedded processes and replacing them with numbers and robots. The takeover was more difficult, faltering and partial than conventional descriptions imply.

Disruption

The first online bet was made in 1996 by Finn Jukka Honkavaara, who won a measly $2 from a $50 bet on the outcome of a football match between Tottenham Hotspur and Hereford United. Establishing the template for online gambling as a quintessentially border-crossing activity, the bet was placed with Intertops, an Austrian service licensed in Antigua and created by Detlef Train, a German-born bookmaker with a British licence (*iGaming Business* 2008).[2] As in many other areas of e-commerce, where the early entrepreneurs went, the established industry (with far more to lose) followed cautiously. William Hill launched their online service, 'Sportsbook' in 1998 but it was deemed unreliable and could not offer betting in-play. Their own software was eventually written off at a cost of £26 million in 2008 when they signed a not unproblematic deal with software provider Playtech (Bowers 2008). They have since flourished. Ladbrokes launched its online service in 2000 and also developed in-house technology, spending £50 million. In 2012, when online betting was growing fast, Ladbrokes' digital profits halved (Ebrahimi 2012). They made a belated deal with Playtech but had already fallen way behind William Hill and online specialists including bet365.

I started fieldwork at Warringtons in 2007 in order to gauge the impact of the Gambling Act, which was due to come into force in September that year. However, the Act turned out to be a historical footnote to the shift from tax on stakes to tax on profits. Much more pressing was the revolution taking place in front of me: from 'retail' (betting on horses and dogs in shops) to online (called 'e-gaming' at the time). An embodied practice based on specialised knowledge and exclusive relationships was being replaced by abstract systems which used algorithms and data to create profitable uncertainty. Traditional ways of making a book were fading, but not going down without a struggle. Older systems and workers were clinging on, surviving serial restructures and redeployments because, it seemed, no one knew whether it was really possible to make 'prices' (the odds that are offered to a backer or punter by a bookmaker) without people. Old timers, those with knowledge of how the tried and trusted systems worked, were retained, just in case, only to plough up and down the corridors telling anyone who would listen that we were all going to hell in a hand cart. On the trading floor, human and mechanical calculations, inside knowledge, 'mental filters', 'gut feelings' and algorithms combined in jarring ad hoc combinations.

It was clear from the very first day of fieldwork that the company was in turmoil. I was greeted by a gloomy odds compiler whom I had met during my time spent as an intern on the *Racing Post*, the daily racing newspaper in the UK. 'Welcome!' He said. 'You are witnessing the end of bookmaking. If these people get their way, in the future I will be replaced by a very fetching robot who can't tell one end of a horse from another.' This was the first of many narratives that I collected which focused on the expansion in volumes of betting and the related shift from the traditional markets of horse and dog racing, to sports of all kinds. People who did not know how to use email, including my former colleague, were making prices for online competitions about which they knew nothing. Offices were filling with computers, only to empty again the next week – they were 'lemons' bought by someone who knew nothing about technology. Board rooms where people could have discussions were first replaced by individual offices and then individual offices were knocked through to provide more space for open-plan desks. Job titles changed constantly. It was chaos – people couldn't find each other, and were often late for meetings because they didn't know where they were going or who else would be there. Once they arrived they often couldn't see the point of the meeting or of being there. And in the coffee shops and common areas it became clear that the upheaval was also affecting people's sense of themselves and of their work. According to the bosses, they were no longer working for a bookmaker: from now on this was to be a technology business – an odd suggestion to someone like my former colleague who did not own a mobile phone.

Numbers

Warringtons' headquarters is a large, ugly building on the outskirts of a big city. My guides were Bill and Jeff, both veterans with over twenty years' experience, a qualification which earned them the description of 'total dinosaurs' from their smart phone early adopter rivals in the Sales and Marketing department. Bill and Jeff told me proudly that their respective domains, the Bet Acceptance Centre and Trading, were 'the hub of the estate'. When Bill described the 'vast changes' that had taken place over the past two or three years, he emphasised the decline of traditional over-the-counter (OTC) betting and the growing importance of FOBTs, telephone betting and the internet, 'Three or four years ago e-gaming was not there,' he spluttered, 'now it has an entire floor.' Business was also shifting, he said, from horses, to sports:

> In bet acceptance we've had 71,000 calls in seven months. Ten years ago it was all horses. No night racing, we used to have two afternoon meetings. Cheltenham used to be exciting. Now we get 600 sports calls a week and 400 horses. From markets for just horses and dogs we've gone to vast numbers.

'It's unbelievable,' he continued, 'the expansion. Incredible to think we now have up to 2500 matches available to bet on at the weekend, with seven markets on each match.' Bill was incredulous, but just five years later each match provided over 120 markets, a figure which continues to rise. As well as the increase in numbers of events, there was also a diversification: HQ was no longer home to horse racing experts, along with football experts who dabbled in cricket or rugby. Now there were all sorts. He took me upstairs to show me the rows of people sitting with miniature national flags in front of them and explained:

> Sports odds compilers used to be three people doing everything. Now it's like a bus station. All different specialist areas, all capable of making odds and taking decisions but responsible for certain areas like cricket

or American football, volleyball, Bundi, cycling, speedway, handball, all the Scandy sports. It's like the United Nations up here.

The department was already creaking under the weight of additional work and changing practices, which Bill continued to imagine as extensions of the existing systems. The sense that a paradigm shift had taken place was not yet fully apparent. For example, some of the systems for calculating liabilities in 2007 were not yet computerised. Remarkably, the Betting Acceptance Centre still kept physical 'books' of outstanding bets: 'We have one red file of everything that's live. One book for golf and cricket. One for rugby union and league, one for normal sport any other and a black book for anything else, the Mercury music prize, *Big Brother*. Oh, and one for American sports,' explained Bill.

In this fluid space where old and new systems were colliding, the method for setting prices was a delicate hybrid. Horse racing maintained a thin patina of glamour and exceptionalism: odds compiling in this section was still presented as a lucrative intellectual endeavour connected to a long and distinguished history. Odds compilers were highly knowledgeable individuals, some of them well known and coveted. They were depicted as sartorially challenged introverts who had renounced human interaction. Within earshot, Bill described them as 'strange fruit'. 'The building could be burning down and they wouldn't notice,' he added. The horse desk was a throwback, with telephones but no computers, and strewn with remnants of the bookmaking past: *Timeform*, the *Racing Post* and other form books, apple cores, chocolate wrappers and dirty tea cups. Bill described the desk as 'the engine room':

> where everything begins. Day to day. Early prices are available 9 or 10 or 11.30. We get prices for every race from the Antepost desk over there. They spend their lives in form books. Prices are just people's opinions on a horse's chances. They'll pick a race. Three will get together and then 'call over'. They'll read out the prices for each horse.

The horse desk is the source of the market, creating 'tissues' – initial or 'early' prices for every horse and every race. 'Tissues' are 'the first word', the foundation of a market. Getting a price for a horse wrong would result in an influx of money, creating huge liabilities. At the same time, the tissue must be competitive in order to attract business, as Bill said, 'The most volatile moments are in the early minutes of a market being formed for a race – that's why the horse desk is paid the big bucks.'

The tissue is a message which carries weight and significance. When Warringtons had the shortest prices on a winning horse the abrasive Channel Four Television pundit John McCririck used to shout at viewers, 'They knew!' On the other hand, the tissue gives good judges, or those with inside knowledge, an opportunity to get good value before the market starts to 'talk'. The tissue is an informed reading of the race, based on variables including the type of race, the ground, the weather, the trainer, the jockey, the form and the breeding of the horse. The construction of tissues implies that judgements of these kinds (a) can be made and (b) can be profitable. As Bill said to me when we were inspecting the odds compilers like so many prize bulls, 'Other companies would kill to have my staff. They make me 3 or 4 million [pounds] a year easy.' Discerning customers, including users of early prices, include individuals described by Bill and Jeff as 'shadies' and 'shrewdies'. Shrewdies are 'on the level', 'good judges', 'pros'. Shadies may either know (or think that they know) something about the race and are 'dodgy customers', 'bad karma' or plain 'villains', more of whom later.

The sociology of knowledge behind odds compiling is conventional: it is the idea that a judgement made by someone knowledgeable about horses and racing may be valuable, in the same way as stock market value was once based on the properties of the commodities traded. As the race approaches, a different process takes over, with a different logic. Prices are changed to reflect the bets which have been filtered through the shops, telephone and internet, and in order to attract or repel 'business', or what sociologist Erving Goffman (1967) called 'action'. Unlike odds compilation, this process de-emphasises the properties of the event itself and focuses on the collective 'weight of money', the internal logic of the market that now assumes a life of its own. The market maintains a relationship with the tissue – the tissue is one of the most important pieces of information for those seeking to profit from the race. But the market itself may now move away from the tissue, overlaying it with knowledge and strategies from other sources, including shadies and shrewdies. Management of this knowledge and its impact on prices takes place at the Bet Acceptance Centre.

Permission to lay?

At the Bet Acceptance Centre (a large table seating six male staff), a stream of telephone calls alerts us to bets being placed in Warringtons' shops. The calls are from managers who control the flow of bets using 'permission to lay' (PTL). PTL is an essential part of staff training and drummed into all cashiers. Notes taken during my training session repeatedly make this point: 'We do not accept all bets.' 'You cannot accept a large bet at long odds from any Tom, Dick or Harry, who walks in off the street.' Bill settled this question by adding, 'We aren't a charity.' Bets above a certain stake require managers to call the Bet Acceptance Centre to ask for 'permission to lay' – permission to accept the bet. A full table of limits is prominently displayed behind the counter of each shop, as well as on electronic point of sale (EPOS), the system used to accept bets in shops. The decision of whether or not to take the bet will be based on the event, the bet, the market, and the record of the punter.

To get an idea of the market for a race Bill uses a 'fieldbook': 'a snapshot of about 500 shops', 'I take what they're doing, multiply it up to see what's going on. We also have a shop ticker, the stream of actual bets in ticker form, you see patterns developing, you can marry the two.' Calls are varied and come in constantly. A request for a bet on a Scandinavian football match, one for the Tour de France, a market which has been suspended due to rumours of drug taking yet again, a request for the time of the kick-off of a match between Portsmouth and Fulham, a request for an accumulator on league winner and relegation which Bill takes 'at small money' because the two markets are connected, 'we don't want to get too heavily involved in that ...'

The majority of these bets are accepted in less than 30 seconds, by Bill in person, who is almost always first to the phone (he suggests the phone should be answered before 6 seconds, but I rarely hear it ring for more than 2), even though there are five other men sitting around the table. Occasionally a bet comes in which warrants more attention, including one for £1000 at 25/1. 'A thousand on Royal Academy,' says Nick across the table. 'We're longest for a reason, so take it', says Bill. 'I've got a thousand too', says Arthur. Bill pauses. 'Same horse? Which shop? If it's London let's have a look at the handwriting.' Bill can see the slip as it was entered into EPOS by the cashier in the betting shop. To my continual amazement, he is able to recognise the handwriting of hundreds of customers, even, apparently, when they try to disguise it. The punters piling in on Royal Academy might be new customers, he explains, but you ask all the usual things, 'Have you seen her before? Does she look like she knows what she's doing?' 'Let's give her £500 at 25 and the balance at 16 or 20s', he says.

As well as PTL, Bill uses a number of other techniques to manage the price of betting. He wants to attract 'good' customers (losers), while at the same time managing his liabilities and limiting business with 'bad' customers (winners). This is the traditional business model of high-margin bookmaking where companies use two systems to manage their liabilities: PTL and 'monitoring'. Bill explains this process as follows:

> We've got 18,000 monitored customers, as well as credit customers who are monitored. When you get a new customer you take the bet, scan it and put down 'blue eyes' 'n', new and still evaluating. If it's a 'u' it's unprofitable. They may be using us because they are getting a better price. Like an unfaithful husband. If they are unprofitable they are selective in what they do. They are welcome and we are happy to have them, but we may not give them £3000 at the early price of 7/2 because maybe it's 3/1 with [our competitors]. It's like the customer who comes into Tescos and only buys peas. It's not good for business. We'd only give them £2000 at EP [early price] and the rest at SP [starting price]. Also 'p' for profitable. And 'e' for elite customer, high stakes, high loser. Give them anything they want, tickets to Ascot, anything, and send them to the hospitality department.

These front-end policies limit exposure to risk by managing the acceptance of particular types of large bets (the 'each way' market is particularly carefully policed as in small races it may be a way for punters to 'buy' value) and also bets from individuals known to be 'unprofitable' (regular winners).

The same systems were also used to manage liabilities online, as Bill explains:

> On the internet events are set up with limits depending on the nature of the event and the market. You will be given a maximum on that event as an internet customer. So today a Catterick race might be £1000. After a while you get to know your customer. Everyone starts at 1.0. If they're profitable you raise them to a 2.0 so they can have a maximum of £2000 or 5.0 or so on. On the other side of the coin if you're shady you get 0.5 or 0.01. If we really don't want the business, then we make them a 0 and they get called through to this desk.

The formation of a market for a race in 2007 was a constant weighing up of different kinds of information, as recorded in my field notes:

> We are sitting talking about *Big Brother* when a call comes in to Bill. Horse was 7/1 first thing. Now at 4/1 he has an enquiry for £7000. He gives him £1000 at 4/1 and £6000 at 3/1. He was trying to put him off but he took it. Leaves us with an £18,000 liability. The history shows the punter isn't all that successful. We go back to chatting. Then Mr A calls. He's a 0.1 and he wants £6000 on the horse. We look up his profile. Before today he's had £500 total and now he's £7000 today. What's that about! And he's 87 years old! We look at the bets in time order on the ticker. There are lots of reds ([£]50s and [£]100s) at 7/1. Then £250 each way for a 1.1. He's 1.1 because I want to see his bets for information, explains Bill. Then a 0.05 has £1000 each way and Bill offers him a lesser deal thinking he won't take sixes, but he does. He's becoming increasingly uncomfortable so he changes the price to 5/1 at 10.15. It's still being taken by shadies at 5/1. Then we go 4/1 at 10.27 and then after the 87-year-old at 10.42 we go to 3/1. Then a bunch of customers get into it at small stakes. And the 0.1 after sixes. At 11.30 it's 3/1 then 5/2.

The betting market is not a free-for-all. You can't simply walk in off the street, slap down a wad of cash and demand a large bet on the favourite at Haydock, particularly if you, like the horse you fancy, have 'form'. The business model is based on attracting and retaining losing punters and turning down business from winners.

Pulling the plug

PTL and monitoring are not the only ways in which bookmakers manage their liabilities. Punters who continue to be 'unprofitable' may have their accounts shut down completely, a constant source of frustration to professionals and successful punters alike. However, to Bill this is simply good management, 'We are not obliged to keep on taking a battering. It makes no sense to keep on taking business that you know is going to cost you. We don't turn down business very often. Only when we know that someone's got an edge. Then you pull the plug.' Bill showed me letters sent out to punters and I have since started my own collection, given to me by punters who have had their accounts summarily closed, usually after a big win, or a run of small ones. The highest balance on the account that I saw was £38,848.60. 'Fair enough!' I said to its recipient, but he was outraged, 'Bollocks!' he replied, 'I won that fair and square, and it's a travesty that they can shut me down for winning!' Most were for far smaller amounts, including £7867, £345, £144. Different bookmakers are known to have different tolerance levels for winners. However, decisions that I was aware of on the horse desk seemed fairly unsystematic – after all no explanation was necessary. As the letters indicated, 'This decision is final. Please see our terms and conditions for more information.' 'Didn't feel right,' said Bill, after closing down someone who was in profit by £6.

Some determined punters find ways around this controversial feature of the betting market. Barney Curley, the legendary Irish punter, trainer and owner of racehorses, used to employ people to place small bets in shops on his behalf. I laid a few bets on behalf of a professional punter in the summer of 1999. I wasn't paid, but I was able to add a few quid to my boss's lump, enabling me to double my student loan and live like a queen on overpriced racecourse pizza and champagne for a few months. However, I had to return to more conventional sources of income once it became evident to racecourse bookmakers that the young woman with the camera bag full of cash was not so clueless after all.

Hedging

Unlike Bill, who was primarily focused on individual bets, the traders at Warringtons viewed the entire market: all liabilities on an event across the shops, phones and online. As head of trading Jeff, who had been with Warringtons for 27 years, explained that, 'From a company perspective, we have tools to protect profits. That's our job as traders. Although, contrary to popular belief, we can lose':

> Personally, I work from the phones and the internet. The fieldbook includes all bets on the telephone and internet. The one for the shops is just a sample. During the morning the phone traders will decide liabilities. As we get closer to the race retail takes over – [...] shops is a much larger volume of betting. Their liability might be £150,000 to £200,000 compared to £34,500 on the phones and internet.

At the time, liabilities in the shops still exceeded those on the telephone and internet by a factor of five or six, and determined the market that Jeff wanted to create. As the race approached he assessed a number of factors:

We might do nothing. But depending on the quality of the race, the type of track, the weather – it's better if it's raining than if it's sunny, and depending if we are having a good day – if we're having an okay day so far we will take a bigger liability.

As far as the quality of the race goes, there's the analysis of trends in different races. Broadly speaking we divide them into handicaps and non-handicaps. Handicaps should be harder to predict the winner because the weight they are carrying is supposed to even up their chances. We'd be more comfortable having a liability on a handicap than a non-handicap. So we know that a selling race at Catterick will make a certain percentage, for example, a handicap at Ascot a different percentage.

In 2007 roughly 80% of Warringtons' business was done 'at SP' or 'starting price'. That is, bookmakers paid winning customers at odds which were determined by a 'show' of prices taken from the course just before 'the off' (the start of the race). The starting price system was created in 1874 to allow betting to take place off-course, at a time when the betting ring was the best indication of the weight of support for each horse in a race, and it has endured, despite the reversal in the relationship between on track and off-track betting. Starting prices are still defined as, 'the odds generally available to good money' with a sample of bookmakers in the racecourse betting ring, with 'good money' defined as a bet to win £500. The system is not entirely foolproof (Wood 2013). As Jeff explained:

> About 15 minutes before the race we get a racecourse 'show' – people on course look at all the boards and send back an average of them. It used to be the gentlemen of the press, but now it's SIS.[3] We return the starting price once the race finishes. The whole industry works from that.

If Jeff was not comfortable with his liabilities, then he had only one option: 'the only way to affect SP is by hedge betting on course'. As he explained, 'If Rio Tafetta is 6/4 and a big liability we give x amount to a man at the track and he will go around and put bets on and hopefully get the 6/4 down and reduce the liability for less money than you spend.' This didn't always work: particularly when the market on course is strong, 'At big meetings it's difficult. At Royal Ascot we might have a 6/4 we want to shorten and the person on course will say how much to make it shorter and we can't do it.' It also requires careful management to ensure that on-course bookmakers don't just 'trouser the bet without changing the price', as Jeff explains: 'We don't just put losers into the market. We do put live money in. Because otherwise they might always know it's hedging and may not even change the price. We don't want them always to assume that.'

In the summer of 2007 bookmakers were still acting as traditional brokers, controlling their liabilities by limiting their exposure to poor risks. They were also market makers, intervening in the market on course in order to limit their liabilities in betting shops:

> The on-course market is a lot smaller than the off-course. So if a horse will cost £3 million if it wins and it's 4/1 and just gone out to 9/2, each time it moves out it costs you £200,000, [then] we will send money to the racecourse through reps. It's not the money won by backing it, it's that backing £10,000 or £20,000 will bring the price in, saving us off-course by bringing the price in. From £4 million to £3 million just by shaving a point off the price. People say it's unfair but bear in mind the different sizes of the market. And it pushes out the other horses, if one of those wins you get better odds. We have to protect our 3 to 3.5%. We've been computerised for seven years and it's made it much easier to protect.

The high margins of their products, the 'overround' (the sum of the quoted probabilities across all horses in a race, often presented as the profitability of a race for the bookmaker) charged on the majority of races, was the price that punters paid in order to bet legally with a supplier whom they could trust. This model was based on the economics of running betting shops:

> for every £1 taken we make gross of 16–18%, take out the overhead shop running costs and you get 3p. That's our bottom line, sometimes 2.75 up to 4.15. We must manage that 3p very carefully which is why it's all computerised. Liabilities used to be a straw poll. Now we have total precision we can see what liabilities are. Which means we can hedge by sending to the racecourse or with competitors.

The computerisation referred to is EPOS, rolled out in shops in 2000, which recorded every bet passing through each shop for the first time. While this phase of computerisation allowed Bill and Jeff to better manage their liabilities and in doing so made the existing system more profitable, the next phase, of betting exchanges and bet in-play, increased choice available to punters, and in doing so revolutionised the way that bookmakers manage risk.

Before online betting was made accessible by changes to technology and particularly the rolling out of broadband and smart phones, the majority of punters in the UK faced a stark choice between bookmakers offering similar products at similar prices, all with policies of turning down 'unprofitable' business, a practice that continues. As head of trading at Warringtons explained at a conference in Dublin in 2012:

> If you are a regular player beating the bookies you are going to be restricted and you are going to have to be clever as to how and where you play. I use them as information. But shareholders want to see profit. The bet acceptance team at Warringtons sees every bet. They will know your handwriting; they will know how you write your 'j's.

In 2007, 'getting on', whether online, via the telephone or in a shop, was subject to PTL and monitoring, starting prices were influenced by off-course business and the odds were stacked against punters. And then along came Betfair, which blew away the advantages of the established bookmakers and completely changed the ways in which prices were formed: shifting the power from bookmakers to punters.

The Betfair betrayal

In 2000 former traders Andrew Black and Ed Wray launched Betfair by parading a coffin through London and proclaiming the 'Death of the Bookmaker':

> Person-to-person betting to me was a very obvious application of the internet. In fact, there are other people who had tried it before Betfair. I think the aspect of our model that was truly original was the realisation that you could have odds on the screen exactly like the stock market – the mechanics of the stock exchange can really work with odds. Everything else really followed from there. (Andrew Black, quoted in Bowers 2003)

Betfair allowed people to bet directly with one another, without a bookmaker acting as an intermediary. At first, the established bookmakers were unruffled. Many agreed with *Racing Post* journalist Jim Cremin's view that, 'The only place Betfair will ever rival Ladbrokes is in newspaper coverage. Out in the real world of the betting shop, ordinary punters are, and always will be, cash players' (Cremin 2003). However, when Betfair began to enjoy some success, the bookmakers turned on them, presenting a rare united front. By September 2003 Betfair's volume of matched bets had reached £50 million and was growing fast. A vicious public fight ensued (Davies 2013). Racing journalist Richard Evans reported that, 'any pretence that this relatively new form of betting is not hurting the High Street chains has been unceremoniously binned' (Evans 2002).[4] Bookies were fighting wars on several fronts: online-only bookmakers like bet365 were flourishing, unencumbered by shareholders and with low operating costs and large marketing budgets. At the same time, odds comparison sites like Oddschecker, EasyOdds and BetBrain made it possible for punters to 'shop around' to find the best prices, increasing downward pressure on margins. However, Betfair was the primary focus of the most hostile attention (partly due to their provocation of the traditional bookmakers whom they delighted in annoying) and was accused of depressing the margins of bookmaking to the detriment of the horse racing levy. In 2010 Ralph Topping, CEO of William Hill, told *Betview Magazine*, 'I call Betfair the choirboys of the industry – "look at us we're so innocent" – actually the exchanges are the biggest Masonic lodge there is. They're a massive secret society where illegal gambling is taking place' (quoted in Davies 2010). The challenge posed by Betfair to traditional bookmaking invoked ideas of 'fairness' and good behaviour: not just competition between two rival business models, this was a clash of cultures, bookmakers in one corner, City traders the other.

Betfair changed the distribution of risk. Unlike traditional bookmakers, who were themselves acceptors of bets, Betfair facilitated bets between account holders. Their profit was not a margin built into prices they set themselves, but a commission of between 2% and 5% charged to winning customers. In both cases profits came from punters, but the way that profit is arrived at, the function of the bookmaker, the place of knowledge and skill, the significance of (inside) knowledge, is very different. Betfair's tagline drew attention to the impact of this change by declaring, 'Winners welcome', drawing an implicit contrast with traditional bookmakers who limited or closed down unprofitable business. Betfair also enabled punters to lay bets – to bet *against* something happening. Most importantly, punters could back and lay in running, that is, during an event, a feature which became increasingly important as the main focus of betting shifted from horse racing to football.[5]

While some punters used Betfair to bet traditionally, finding better prices and with the added flexibility of being able to lay, from the outset others saw the potential of the platform for trading and arbitrage whether manually or using automated programs. It was this activity which particularly offended traditional bookmakers, who claimed that in order to be respectable, a bet must place something at risk. As Bill said, 'Proper punters bet with bookmakers. If you are deviant, you can trade on Betfair.' At first, 'arbers' using Betfair profited from differences in prices that existed throughout the betting ecosphere. However, as on-course bookmakers began to use Betfair themselves, arbing was replaced by betting in running, creating the arresting sight of men on ladders dotted around the racecourse, trying to be first to see if a horse fell, in order to accept risk-free bets.

At head office, PTL and monitoring were presented as legitimate approaches to risk management in contrast to the 'tricks' of trading on Betfair. As Bill exclaimed:

> They make money from some poor bastard with a slower internet connection or picture feed. They see a horse has fallen and they hoover up any bets on the horse before the other poor bastard has got the feed. How's that a fair bet? That's wrong, isn't it! To take a bet you can't lose.

For odds compilers and traders at Warringtons, Betfair traders personified 'the City', viewed as an asocial realm of automated profiteers:

> These guys are all City guys. They've learned their trade at Morgan Stanley or whatever. They see spreadsheets and pick up on a trend or make one up and profit from it. When they get caught they pay the fine and move on. Do the same thing again. They are exploiting the little players, the punters that we represent. They get involved in this business and they think they can plug in their Amstrad and start setting the world alight. They don't realise they're up against sharks.

Traders were stereotyped as either geeks or greedy megalomaniacs:

> Betfair traders? They're your Gordon Gekkos. 'Greed is good.' That sums them up. They are a different breed. They do all this market manipula-

tion, the Gambling Commission hasn't got a clue about it, and it's going on right under their noses. Bastards sitting at home with their feet up, press one button, 50 grand, press another button, another 50 grand. What kind of life is that? All that money, without graft? Makes you sick.

Where traditional bookmaking was presented as accountable and transparent, Betfair was anonymous and threatening:

> Our name's above the door. You know who we are and we've been taking bets for a hundred years. What do we know about these cunts? These Johnny come latelys? Who is taking your bet? You just don't know. It could be the brother of the goalkeeper for all you know. It could be the wife of a tennis player. It could be Al Capone. You haven't got a clue who they are or what they know.

But most of all, traditional bookmaking was presented as fair:

> We give punters a fair crack of the whip. Our worry is that Betfair, with all its technology and big players, will wipe that out. We make a market that's fair, we give everyone a piece. Betfair takes a little bit of money from a lot of people and gives it to a very few with the best technology. It's a con and it will run its course. If you aren't risking anything then you aren't betting, you're stealing. You should be ashamed of yourself.

On the trading floor, in a reproduction of the tensions felt between traditional open-cry traders and the new breed of online financial traders described by Zaloom (2006), the old guard clashed with the new. The horse desk viewed the incomers brought in to respond to this new trade – mostly football traders – as 'utter yobs', 'always shouting', 'brash' and yet naïve or somehow unworldly: 'nerds'. They were both too moved by money and not sufficiently grounded in the real world. Like traders on Betfair, their computers had unfettered them from the social relations that constituted betting markets. They had become anonymous and automated. The impact of this separation was predicted to be a crash of sorts – a trader naïvely following his computers would be duped and the company would be compromised. It seemed incredible, and dangerous, to the traditional bookmakers, that a computer program could possess the necessary sensitivity, honed over many years, to detect a 'shady' 'pulling a fast one'. They just didn't have either the nose or the stomach for it. Despite the increasing use of algorithms and trading systems, many bookmakers continue to believe in the importance of intuition: 'Ultimately', a senior executive told me in 2018 'Warringtons will always be human.'

Betting, trading, gambling

I've been in head office for several weeks now and I'm starting to recognise at least three different registers. The first is BETTING, strongly positively valued as a measured risk based on experience, knowledge and undertaken with sober reflection but with openness and hope, generosity and acceptance that losing is possible and to be faced with Corinthian good humour. Bets are made by sportsmen through traditional bookmakers. The next is TRADING which relies on locked-in profits emerging from mismatches in information expressed as millions of datapoints that are not discernible to humans but susceptible to algorithmic exploitation. Trading is BAD/not really in the spirit of things. Trading takes place on Betfair. GAMBLING is taking risks which depend on dumb luck and the logic of the lottery in which 'it could be you'. But it's highly unlikely. Viewed as shameful for punters but potentially highly lucrative for the industry. Gambling takes place on FOBTs/virtual racing/in-play. (Field notes, head office, 2007)

Traditional bookmaking enjoyed 40 years of comfortable growth, unchallenged and relatively unchanged. Three huge companies emerged from the thousands of independent bookies who had taken licences in 1960, protected by the licensing regime, buoyed by economies of scale and brand recognition, they became complacent and innovation waned. A business model evolved which allowed operators to charge a relatively high price for a service the supply of which was strictly limited. By the time the internet provided a new channel for betting a bottleneck had developed in traditional bookmaking, building up pressure for change, which was resisted by regulation and the slow embrace of technology by firms which were relatively homogeneous and successful.

By 2007 traditional bookmaking was clinging on in the face of the increased choice presented by new entrants online. Using a language that they had developed over a period of 40 years, market makers were accustomed to presenting their work as creating value as well as profit, and were eager to convince me of its rectitude and morality, despite the many ways in which it preserved their advantages over punters: they were protecting legitimate business from 'shadies' and 'unfaithful husbands' trying to 'buy value'. Their own position as gatekeepers was not open to critique. Their use of inside information was structurally justified. Monitoring customers, shutting down accounts, hedging on the racecourse were not only 'perfectly legal' but necessary. They created equilibrium and made the socially productive process of creating betting markets sustainable and 'available to everyone', a singularly resilient variety of risk fetishism complete with supporting metaphors and exclusions.

At times, the most institutionalised workers at head office depicted themselves as offering a benign public service, in contrast to the dangerous business of trading on Betfair. A few had already realised that the future of bookmaking lay online, with sports and at low margins. However, in 2007, the trading floor was still dominated by graduates from betting shops who had been rewarded for using recognised, incremental methods to grow business in shops, by creating even more expensive, higher-margin products and increasing the numbers of events, or by reducing liabilities on the phones, online or on the racecourse. Simply put, they were looking down the wrong end of the telescope. Had I arrived a few months later, by which time both Bill and Jeff had (reluctantly) 'moved on to pursue new opportunities', I would have been introduced to the brave new world of algorithms and Big Data by Mike, who came from a telecommunications background and summed up what he knew about horses by saying, 'One end bites, the other end kicks!' Instead, I witnessed bookmaking's last stand.

Betting, traditionally understood, was in terminal decline, trading and gambling – both better suited to the high-frequency media that created more opportunities to generate profit, were on the rise. Horse racing – the traditional medium of the British betting public, was diminishing in importance – by 2011 the respected analyst Paul Leyland went so far as to describe it as 'irrelevant' – at least in relation to betting (GamblingData 2011: 7). The demise of betting on horse racing was mirrored by a rise in the importance of high-frequency gambling on slots, football and bingo: this brave new world is the focus of the next chapter.

7
Online in Gibraltar

We say we don't want problem gamblers, but what's the difference between a problem gambler and a really good, loyal customer? (Senior executive, 17 years in the betting industry)

The changes I experienced in betting shops and at Warringtons' head office were part of a revolution, the repercussions of which are being felt all over the world. Even as machines halted the decline of the traditional bookies, the centre of the industry shifted, from dismal office buildings in London suburbs, to shiny tower blocks in semi-exotic offshore locations with favourable tax regimes, high speed internet and unlimited secure server capacity. Markets were no longer localised, or limited to working class men with a proclivity for horse racing. The production of gambling, and of gamblers, was changing.

In this chapter I draw on fieldwork in Gibraltar to describe how workers in the new gambling industries understand products and customers, and how the idea of 'responsible gambling' takes shape when its subjects are account numbers, data points and disembodied voices. I start by exploring the origins of online gambling, background that has been effectively written out of the history books, before describing the repercussions of the decision by the UK government to create the only open market for online gambling in the world.

The Wild West

Online gambling was pioneered by software developers and entrepreneurs prepared to operate in offshore locations, illegally targeting American customers. Several sites claim to have been the first online casino, including the imaginatively named Internet Casinos Inc., which went live from the Turks and Caicos Islands in August 1995 offering 18 casino games and access to the National Indian Lottery (Janower 1996). At first, online gambling was an appendage to pornography. In fact, one of the people responsible for its creation, speaking in Berlin in 2012, told me that, 'Early days it was porn and casinos one and two. I seriously remember thinking that the internet would only ever be used for porn and gambling, and in my mind they were one industry.' He cited the example of Starnet in Canada as 'the most obvious case, packaging together porn and casinos until they got raided and had to pay back $4 million. It was pretty wild back then.' He described the racy cast of characters that made up the nascent industry, including British bookmakers, Israeli entrepreneurs and Canadian ex-cons. Some, like an American entrepreneur who spoke to me in Macau in 2014, greatly enjoyed their notoriety and reputation for law-lessness and risk taking, presenting it as a necessary part of their success in this unruly, masculine space. His description of this period reinforces Peter Adams' (2007) suggestion that the gambling industry might produc-tively be thought of as an extractive industry, its participants as pioneers:

> Shit, yeah, I was a pioneer. You had to be ruthless. And lucky. The greatest feeling was when you take a virgin territory, somewhere people are wealthy but not too educated. You could literally dig for gold! What was life like? Taking risks. Bad guys who didn't play (by) the rules. There were gunfights, actual shoot outs in some of these places. I was a young man! I fucking loved it! The days on these sites with my buddies and the nights creeping around with women. I had everything.[1]

Even people who did not contribute to the development of online gambling were well versed in these kinds of stories, which have spawned numerous books, and films like *Runner Runner*. The only dissenting voice came from one of the few women I managed to find who had played a key role in the creation of the offshore industry, who described life in Costa Rica as 'quite boring and very lonely'. A highly respected London-based analyst offered a more mundane explanation for the industry's early lack of structure, telling me that, 'Everyone says that online gambling was the Wild West, but it was less Wild West and more a loose collection of utter morons without any proper idea of how to make money.' He described how this gradually changed when:

> you got more business people coming in, the established bookmakers eventually woke up and capitalised on their brand and the regula-tors emerged from the dung heap. Now online gambling is more like

banking – compliance, regulation, managing millions of transactions, Big Data, whatever you want to call it, reducing costs, mergers and acquisitions and share prices.

As the internet developed and the scale of the opportunity became clearer, the industry began to evolve, separate itself from porn, and develop a more acceptable public face, fostering this image through trade organisations like the Remote Gambling Association, led by wily former civil servant Clive Hawkswood, in new publications and at hastily arranged conferences, primarily in London, where the long established 'bricks and mortar' market attracted interest from people who could see the potential of regulation for protecting and growing profits. This progress was described by a middle-aged London-based entrepreneur when I spoke with him in Las Vegas in 2014:

> I started seeing more casino sites online in about '97. I went to a symposium in London in 1999 and I think it was their second or third, so you had enough business to warrant an industry meeting by that time. The symposium set the tone of all of the gambling industry conferences I've been to since – high on sleaze and hype, low on data of any value. Everything was exaggerated, exactly as you would expect and can see today with mobile and social [gaming]. There were differences too. The link with porn has more or less disappeared.

In 1994 Antigua and Barbuda (which, alongside Costa Rica, had become the base for many of the illegal companies serving the US market) had passed the Free Trade and Processing Act, enabling them to grant the first licences for online gambling. However, these licences were not recognised by the US government and a row erupted between the two, which rumbles on, despite the intervention of the World Trade Organisation (Miles 2018). By 1999, the industry was maturing, and cleaving, into websites dealing in illegal markets and, on the other hand, in the UK in particular, companies that sought regulation, respectability, stock market investment and, gradually, political influence. In order to achieve stability, they needed 'light-touch' regulation and a cheap, well-connected base from which to access large, profitable markets. New Labour, with cross-bench support from the Conservatives, provided the first piece of the puzzle, in the shape of the Gambling Act 2005.

The Gambling Act 2005 created the first regulatory framework for so-called 'remote' gambling.[2] Specifically, it created an open market for online gambling at a time when many jurisdictions, including Australia and the US, were implementing full or partial bans. In 2001 Australia passed the Interactive Gambling Act, which made it an offence to offer gambling services other than wagering and lotteries to Australians, and limited the provision of these services to operators licensed in an Australian jurisdiction. As well as prohibiting games of chance, including slots, roulette, blackjack and poker, the Act also banned 'in-play' betting and instant-win scratch cards (Australian Government Department of Communications and the Arts 2019). In 2006 the US passed the Unlawful Internet Gambling Enforcement Act (known as UIGEA) which 'prohibits gambling businesses from knowingly accepting payments in connection with the participation of another person in a bet or wager that involves the use of the Internet and that is unlawful under any federal or state law' (United States Treasury Department 2006). In Europe, despite the fact that online gambling and sports betting were legal in many jurisdictions and far more accepted than in the US (where sports betting is still considered 'mob dirty' by many), no one imitated the UK. Sweden, Finland, Norway, Belgium, Hungary, Austria and Greece maintained full or partial state gambling monopolies, despite the efforts of bookmakers (described in more detail in the next chapter) to draw the attention of the European Commission to their anti-competitive behaviour.[3]

As well as creating extraordinary conditions for growth, Tessa Jowell, Secretary of State for Culture, Media and Sport, announced that she wanted the UK to become a 'world leader' in online gambling, offering a 'hallmark of quality' to players all over the world (*BBC News* 2006). However, when Gordon Brown took over as Prime Minister in June 2007 he appeared, once again, not to have read the New Labour memo, and imposed a tax of 15% on remote gambling. Companies based in the UK moved offshore, able to provide services to UK customers as long as they were licensed in 'White Listed' countries, which included all those in the European Economic Area, as well as Gibraltar.[4] In 2013 the Gambling Commission estimated that the UK remote industry was worth £2 billion (HM Treasury 2013), most of it based in the Isle of Man, Guernsey or Gibraltar, where companies advertising and doing business in the UK, including William Hill, Ladbrokes and Coral, paid a 1% tax on turnover, which was capped at £425,000 (Stradbrooke 2013).

Gibraltar: gambling and banking, pirates and lawyers

> Gib is tightening up. They used to be pirates, but they want to be seen
> to be running a tight ship to attract the big companies and protect the
> reputation of the jurisdiction. Alderney is a weird little place. I quite
> expected people to come out and start eating my head. (Male CEO,
> London, 2012)

Low-tax betting by telephone had reached Gibraltar by 1989. Early online
specialists like 888 and PartyGaming arrived in the 2000s, bringing
welcome investment and helping to establish Gib's reputation as a regulator 'in the UK mould' (described by my participants as, 'light-touch',
'sensible', 'realistic') (Atkinson 2006). Although several operators returned
to the UK when gross profits tax was introduced in 2001, by 2010/11 they
had all returned to Gib. By the time of my first visit in 2012, Gibraltar
hosted most of Europe's leading online gambling providers, including
Ladbrokes, William Hill, Betfair, bet365, 888, Victor Chandler and Gala-
Coral, all of them attracted by low tax and the chance to be regulated in
a European jurisdiction that was trusted by punters and shareholders.
Along with financial services, gambling is a key part of the diversification of Gibraltar, away from its dependency on income from the UK and
towards a kind of independence. According to GibraltarOffshore.com 'its
unique status within the EU [European Union] makes it the jurisdiction of
choice for certain types of investors or traders'. The site goes on to claim
that there are over 60,000 companies registered in Gibraltar, 'more than
two per inhabitant!' Gibraltar itself denies being a 'tax haven' preferring to
describe itself as a 'low-tax regime' (Badcock 2017), however some writers
have criticised its links with companies involved in international scandals
(Bullough 2017). Gibraltarians enjoyed emphasising their traditional role
as middle men and facilitators in international trade: 'We were pirates!
And we still are, really', muttered one lawyer, active in both gambling and
banking, in the margins of a conference in London.

  During fieldwork, my research participants estimated that between 40%
and 60% of online gambling in the UK took place in Gibraltar. Spending
time there allowed me to see how the various businesses worked, how
people came to embody and reproduce the roles of entrepreneur, customer
service provider or VIP manager, how they understood and related to their
colleagues and customers, and, more generally, what life in Gib is like for
people who sell gambling. I interviewed 116 people and spoke at length

and less formally with many others, recording our conversations in note-books or on a handheld device. I went to training sessions, call centres, observed VIP and customer services desks, shadowed managers, sat in on meetings between companies and the Gibraltar Gambling Commission, and with lawyers and accountants. I followed up invitations from people I had met at gambling conferences as well as making new contacts. Some people didn't want to talk to me and told me to 'get lost', but many were surprisingly forthcoming in the warm sunshine of Gibraltar. Some of them were disenchanted with their work: 'I hate my job and so do 99% of the people who work here', said one, while others enjoyed the opportunity to set me straight on a few things, 'Academics haven't got the first fucking clue about gambling', said another, cheerfully.

Learning the ropes

I'm sitting on a bench in La Linea in Spain watching a man on a moped. He looks about 40, and is thin as a rake. He is pulling packets of ciga-rettes out of his jacket, which bulges uncomfortably on this hot day, and throwing them into the trunk of an old car parked on the street. He seems unperturbed by my presence and gives me a wonky smile before slamming the trunk shut and puttering off, back to the border with Gibraltar, a few hundred yards away. I've come to Gibraltar to experience a different kind of cross-border activity: online gambling, which generates as much as 25% of GDP in this, one of 14 remaining British Territories Overseas. I'm waiting near the border for my guide to all things gambling in Gibraltar: Dan, a seasoned professional who has worked for several different com-panies for over a decade. He turns up in ripped jeans, T-shirt, flip flops and Raybans and says that we had better get going because he plans to be in a hot tub 'with four babes and a bottle of Jack (Daniels)' by lunchtime at the latest. I sigh, accustomed to Dan's bullshit, and we set off, passing through the border together and across the airstrip where I landed the night before.

Dan is a 45-year-old entrepreneur whom I scraped up off the pavement and decanted into a taxi when he had got drunk and been mugged after an industry party in London in 2010. He describes himself as 'a typical gambling industry arsehole' before asking me rather doubtfully, 'You do realise that we are all cunts, don't you? I sometimes think you still don't get it!' Dan left school at 18 and started working at a betting shop before moving into low-level IT in search of better pay. After four years of data entry he was 'bored out of my head' and decided to return to gambling in a newly established online division of a leading bookmaker. According to Dan his colleagues had little or no idea of what they were doing, 'If you could log on without shitting yourself they thought you were a fucking genius', he said. I am in Gibraltar to learn about betting in-play, the phenomenon that is driving expansion in the UK industry, and to understand how it has changed relationships between punters and operators.

Dan's first trick is to take me to coffee by the marina and point out how many people he knows, and which companies they work for. Without a trace of humour, he informs me that he can tell just by looking at someone's haircut whether or not they work in the industry. He does a pretty convincing job of demonstrating this skill, and insists on introducing me to people when I doubt him. Between 6000 and 9000 people cross the border that connects, or divides, Spain from the isthmus every day, including 2600 of the 3000 who work in online gambling (Grocott, quoted in Select Committee on the European Union 2017). Parking is a nightmare, and there is almost always a long tailback from the border – the line grows even longer when the Spanish authorities decide to slow things down in order to make a political point. As a result, a lot of people park just outside the border and, like Dan and I, walk across the border, security badges flapping in the breeze.

When low-tax remote gambling first came to Gibraltar in the 1990s companies like Stan James employed hundreds of people in purpose-built call centres. However, as gambling has shifted from fixed-line phones to desktops, then smart phones, less labour is required. Recent initiatives to reduce costs even further focus on Artificial Intelligence and automation, and the remaining human resources are concentrated in marketing, security and managing customers, including so-called VIPs, a euphemism for super-profitable customers, more of which later. Some of the companies I visit are exceptionally open and welcoming. Two of the largest are nervous and elect to give me guided tours, limiting my access to people who are well briefed and inscrutable. In one case, I am assigned a minder who accompanies me wherever I go. She is marginally less happy than I am about this arrangement. When I meet Dan for lunch he is appalled and calls in a few favours, introducing me to people who are more open, some of whom seem desperate to talk.

The central business district where I'm working is a medium-rise, joyless collection of nondescript office buildings where established brands jostle with newcomers keen to: 'either find a new product, or new customers, or both, make money, sell up, move onto the next project or, if you're really lucky, retire'. In the online space, established brands like bet365 and William Hill enjoy all kinds of advantages – scale, first mover, huge brand recognition, heavy presence on television through both commercials and sponsorship (my participants refer to a survey in 2012 which found that 61% of men claimed to have seen the bet365 advert featuring Ray Winstone's head urging them to 'Bet in-Play Now'). Their vast budgets underwrite sign-up bonuses and offers including free bets. Equally importantly, they generate huge amounts of data which they use to learn about customers, allowing them to generate personalised marketing which increases profitability, a process that is constantly developing (Busby 2018; William Hill 2019). The companies I worked with were all set up and run by men. I encountered female senior executives only rarely and, in the four years that I attended online gambling conferences, I calculated that 4% of speakers were women (often the same woman). Denise Coates, the UK's highest paid executive, co-founder and CEO of bet365, is a notable exception to this rule (Chapman 2018).

Hanging around with Dan and his colleagues I learn that the gambling community in Gib is a small, relatively tight-knit world. In the words of a male executive who had relocated from the UK, 'The gambling community in Gibraltar is insular – people go to the same bars and restaurants, know the same people, and behave in quite similar ways, like lads in the 1980s, only older.' Earnings are above average, and the way to increase them is to move, often sideways, between companies, as was common: 'this is not a loyal industry', he added. Employees are paid a 'finder's fee' if they can bring in new colleagues (Atkinson 2006). On the other hand, it was difficult to leave the industry entirely as salaries in similar fields were not comparable. Some people loved the drinking culture:

> I'm so much happier at [Rocket] than I was at [Twister]. The line between work and play has been more and more morphed. I really like that. Our CEO is great. Out getting monstered every night and still in there at 9 doing deals. Great when you respect your CEO and when you can socialise together and share things and don't need to be different.

Others recognised that 'This industry sucks you in, and it's hard to get out of it, whether you like it or not.' Although jobs are advertised to Gibraltarians first, some specialised workers from the UK are paid to relocate to Gibraltar, and many arrive without connections. Whether by choice or for lack of an alternative, they often build their social lives around work. They described being absorbed into a relatively homogeneous way of life that was initially exciting but ultimately less than fulfilling:

> New people arrive and you meet them and you think, 'They remind me of myself when I arrived' and a few months later they are exactly like you. It's hard to get out of the way of life here because we all do the same thing and we all come from a similar place. The work is not that exciting, but it's well paid. The weather is better than the UK and you can still go to Marks and Spencer's and get your pants so you don't miss home. It's boring, basically.

One analyst described it particularly thoroughly and suggested that 'gambling industry culture' was a fitting subject for an anthropologist because, 'Different sectors within the industry have their own tribes', of which, 'the internet sector is certainly a young person's industry ... you'd see very few ties or suits. That changed a bit as the industry has matured and they've gone for funding from investment banks.' He suggested that both in Gibraltar and the other offshore hubs, there was a distinctive approach to life, 'It's a cliché but I'd say it's a work hard play hard atmosphere.' Asked to describe his colleagues he spoke without hesitation, saying, 'I think they quite revel in being a bit on the edge, based in offshore jurisdictions. Some of them push the law in terms of regulation and I think some of them enjoy being in a grey area ... the more corporate elements would try to distance themselves from that.'

Not everyone fits in of course, or chooses to adapt, and some people told me that they actively avoided the rest of the crowd. A night out with Scott, for example, a senior executive in a new company, is spent hiding from colleagues: 'I come from communications!' he says, looking at me as though the difficulty was self-evident, 'The majority of people here in gambling are complete arseholes. I don't fit in with them at all.' I asked another relative newcomer to tell me how he got into the industry and he replied:

> You mean how did I fall into the seventh circle of hell? You know that Dante put the bankers in the seventh circle of hell. Along with the rapists. But I don't think he put gambling operators in there ... luckily Gibraltar had stacks of room.

'Bet in-Play Now'

The 2014 World Cup was a milestone for people working in online gambling in Gibraltar. The sheer volume of betting – more than £1 billion, twice as much as in 2010 – was unprecedented, the rhythm and frequency of betting had also changed: no longer limited to the outcomes of matches, instead there were infinite opportunities to bet 'in -play' on hundreds of micromarkets (the number of corners or yellow cards, for example) within each game. For the first time, the majority (60%) of these bets were placed using mobile devices (*Sky News* 2014). The tournament was also remarkable for the prominence and volume of gambling advertising, which increased by 600% in the first six years after the Gambling Act (Sweney 2013), and exploded again during the World Cup.[5] Companies, including bet365, William Hill and Ladbrokes, spent fortunes on marketing, scrambling to recruit customers ahead of the imposition of the new point of consumption tax which came into effect later in the year.[6] In 2012 more than half of the money bet on an event with Ladbrokes came from live betting. By 2015, 80% of bet365's sports betting revenue came from betting in-play (Jackson 2015). In Gibraltar, the 7–1 thrashing of Brazil by Germany was quickly forgotten: the 2014 World Cup was remembered as the clearest indication yet that the future of gambling lay in heavily advertised, live betting on televised football, accessed online via smart phones.

Live betting works by chopping sporting events like football or tennis matches into smaller and smaller pieces, making it possible to bet continuously, on individual points, fouls or other markets. As a senior executive from a large UK bookmakers told me at a conference in Dublin in 2012, 'Bet in-play is simply sports book roulette. It's addictive, it's a 24-hour clock. It's completely oriented to keeping people on the website; you've got enough content not to navigate away'. The analogy between live betting and casino gaming was commonplace among experts. Dan, for example, used language familiar from Natasha Schüll's (2012) description of electronic gaming in Las Vegas to explain that, 'Betting in-play is about turning a sporting event into a slot machine. Get someone hooked on that constant flow of events and they will play to exhaustion.' Recruiting people to this new form of betting was also relatively easy, at least initially. As Dan explained:

> The Premier League was our biggest recruiter here and overseas. People love to bet on the Premier League. Something about how Sky has put

that together is just perfect for betting. It's clean, for one thing, you've got glamour, transfers, money, lifestyle. People just love it. The big difference … Fans don't just bet on their own team any more. They will bet on any given match. That's the main difference from traditional betting.

The exhaustive coverage provided by satellite broadcaster Sky, including heavy promotion backed by sales of rights and subscriptions as well as advertising (including from gambling companies), has changed the way in which people watch and bet on football – no longer focusing solely on their own team (putting 'skin in the game' as American sports bettors would say) but seeing football per se as a betting medium. The biggest challenge faced by Dan's company was recruiting punters ahead of the competition:

There are two models: strip them quick and move on, or do it slowly and try to retain them for longer. The economics have changed. When we started up you could just rape people. Nowadays it costs too much to find new mugs. You're better off taking them out for dinner first. Amazing what people will do for a £10 bonus.

Dan's company learned that in order to make money you had to present an appearance of giving money away. Bonus culture spawned increasingly restrictive terms and conditions which required players to 'play through' any winnings a certain number of times before they could be cashed out. Marketing departments also work constantly to reduce risk and increase house edge by, for example, promoting bets which encourage the illusion of control, such as combination bets at long odds, or encouraging people to bet more frequently (Newall 2015), or simply by closing 'unprofitable' accounts. Punters, on the other hand, are explicitly forbidden from using what are referred to as 'minimal risk wagering patterns' . As one leading company explains on its website:

We offer bonuses and promotions to enhance your enjoyment of our games and wagering. We expect you to participate in all bonuses and promotions fairly. We consider certain types of play to be unfair and in breach of these Promotion Terms. These include: a) using minimal risk wagering patterns (e.g. low risk wagering, zero risk wagering or equal betting patterns).

As the rush to secure new customers at the lowest possible CPA (cost per acquisition) continued via affiliate and company websites, so-called, 'bonus abuse' or 'bonus whoring' – individuals using borrowed identities to open up multiple accounts in order to benefit from deals designed to attract new customers – became the primary concern of large and growing security sections.

Pivotal in the new business model, supercharged marketing departments were the focus of huge amounts of energy. One expert explained how he sold behavioural marketing to initially sceptical bookmakers:

> We started out selling online analytics for fraud detection. But we could see that 'loyal' customers – actually just people who stick with you for a long time – have increased lifetime values [LTV]. Well bookmakers love LTV as you know. We knew that casinos use loyalty data to tailor marketing. But marketing is expensive and you can't always predict how effective it'll be or if it'll reach the right people, so we started to look at individuals rather than segments. We found some research which showed that most people found generic messages really irritating and counterproductive, and promoted the idea that we could tailor messages but without any additional cost. The bookmakers lapped it up because they are so tight.

Behavioural marketing yielded instant results that bookmakers loved, 'Getting smart on marketing and bonuses was a turning point. It made what we were doing beforehand look primitive and really helped us to retain punters when the market became much more competitive,' a senior executive explained to me, showing me figures demonstrating that, in his company, tailored messages had resulted in improvements in key metrics, specifically: increases in reactivation and numbers of active customers, higher gross revenues and increases in frequency of interaction. 'This is where you defend your business,' he explained, 'finding cheap ways to reduce churn by making sure good customers stick with you and nudging them to bet more than they really want to'.

Marketing activities based on these insights are constantly developing. For example, GVC's presentation to investors in 2019 described how: 'Analytics and insight are the most influential enablers of sustained player engagement and growth', showing how they capture 'customer DNA' by using a combination of 'optimised acquisition' through 'data driven targeted advertising', that is (a) personalisation: presenting 'the most relevant content at the right time'; (b) 'next best action': sending 'the right message, bonus, contact or strategy for each individual customer at any stage of lifetime' and (c) 'real-time targeting': increasing 'customer engagement through real-time communication and offers pre-match and in-play' (GVC 2019). They illustrate these processes in relation to UK online customer relationship management (CRM), showing how a customer who bets £100 per week is targeted by adverts based on his past behaviour on a Friday ('activation') and Saturday ('cross-sell and up-sell') through a combination of ten adverts, email / SMS, offers and push notifications. GVC's aim, from 2020 onwards is to 'cultivate loyalty, not just satisfaction', particularly through partnerships with football, and by using a 'single voice' that is 'persistent and consistent' (GVC 2019).

According to live betting experts, breakthroughs in marketing turned out to be far more influential than the algorithms that data analysts had been hired to create, much to their disappointment. As Josh, a 30-year-old programmer at Warringtons explained:

> To be honest there was much less skill involved in working for Warringtons than I expected. It was really just a massive marketing machine by the end – whatever new product the marketing team put together we just pushed it out. There was a lot of automation, virtually no skilled odds compilation. We just followed the Asian markets and chased soft retail money all day.

'Chasing soft money' involves customer profiling and 'factoring', as Dan explained simply, 'Basic economics: we close out or restrict smart players and focus on selling high margin products to losers'. According to Dan and Josh, the limits set for losing players can be between 10 and 1000 times those of selective punters. John, another senior executive and bet-in-play expert, also confirmed that the way in which odds are set has changed profoundly since I worked with traders at head office in 2007, now taking a lead from the vast Asian markets. According to John, 'The market in Asia tells you so much. The market in Asia will tell you Wayne Rooney has a sore toe before his wife knows.' Expanding on this theme, he explained that, 'Odds used to be compiled in-house by specialists. Now they are driven by Asia and by the demand to bet on anything in any country.'

In a change since I worked on the trading floor in 2007, marketing is now controlling the business, even on traditional products. Senior executives, once responsible for creating new products and trading prices, are now subservient to marketing, as one explained:

> [The] Marketing [department] now tell[s] trading the price they want and traders have to accept that ... we used the Champion Stakes by going 2/1 [on the favourite]. I did scan the figures and it was 14.9% on retail on turnover – huge on the day. You can't price that as a marketing event.

While some companies in Gib make a fortune by turning sport into roulette, others focus on transforming gambling from a bad habit into a harmless bit of fun, particularly for women.

Lucky Day

By 2012 mobile phone gambling had been a topic of discussion at conferences for several years, but its potential was always seen as limited by tiny screens and minuscule buttons. Some of the fat-fingered senior executives with backgrounds in 'retail' (betting shops) were still shouting into early-model Nokias, and would scrunch up their noses in annoyance when younger colleagues evangelised about frictionless payments while waving the latest BlackBerry. It was only after the launch and rapid uptake of smart phones, and the spread of mobile broadband, that it became interesting, making so-called 'mobile-first' investors look like savants. When I visited their London offices in 2012, new company Lucky Day was growing fast and George, its creator, was suitably enthused:

> It's brilliant. I love it. Because you are living through a revolution where everything changes but it just does it every couple of years. It's great. It changes faster than It ever has done. A year ago only about 20% of our customers were using mobile phones or android. Now it's about 60%.

Lucky Day provides a service direct to customers (B2C) and also a white label service to other businesses (B2B). Like many people I interviewed, George argued strongly that traditional bookmakers had been slow to see the opportunities in online gambling. Cash-rich, accustomed to regulation, technophobic and notably risk averse, traditional bookmakers were 'doubtful' about online gambling until as recently as ten years ago. Looking back, bookmakers describe the hesitant early days with bravado – having prospered, they can afford to:

> [Ralph] Topping was first tasked with setting up an online division in 1999. Why? Incredibly, this was because after having sent an email to his sister in Canada, he was the only senior member of staff at William Hill to have used the internet ... (*EGR Magazine* 2012: 69–70)

To put this in context, undergraduates have been using email since 1993, Amazon and eBay were launched in 1995. According to Topping, who went on to become CEO of William Hill in 2008, William Hill Online 'began with this team of three in a cupboard in Leeds' (*EGR Magazine* 2012: 70). The subsequent success of William Hill's online business means that this story can be told with the swagger that is typical of the industry, but this conservative outlook drove technology-savvy newcomers crazy. As one of the pioneers of online gambling told me after giving a talk in Barcelona in 2012, 'This industry is killing innovation with the wrong people, poorly planned incentives, internal politics, non-agile cultures, big teams and the "not invented here" syndrome. I could never give this presentation at Facebook – they would laugh at me. Here they are just so behind.' When I told him that I was interested in innovation he said, 'In that case you are looking in the wrong place. They are not innovating here. They are copycats.'

With limited backgrounds in technology, but in possession of recognisable and trusted brands, traditional bookmakers had to rely on outsiders. Unable to catch up with online-only firms like bet365, which had created their own in-house technology and software, established bookmakers became publishers, subcontracting the creative and technical work to four or five third-party (business to business, B2B) suppliers and creating a market in which customers would find the same products on all of the major websites. Newcomers, often with backgrounds in communications or finance, were amazed, as Ryan, a company director with a background in media who was trying to sell a new product to established companies in Gib, explained:

> When we entered the market, we expected it to be risk taking, fast, hungry for differentiation, and they are none of that. It took us a while to work out why. They are preserving their advantage. They don't need

to innovate or differentiate themselves from their competitors and in fact to do so is a risk.

George's 'right-hand man' is Mike – managing director, Commercial. When I ask him what that means he says, 'I keep the money rolling in.' Like Ryan, Mike comes from a media background and, once again using the language of both colonialism and the extractive industries that often accompany them, describes the B2C mobile sector as 'a land grab': 'All of these companies are trying to harvest new customers from a limited pool and you have to use every means you can think of to make sure they come to you rather than your competitor.' The way to do this, according to Mike, is to promote the brand, preferably on terrestrial television:

It's all about building trust. You have to convince people that you are reliable, that it's safe to gamble on their phone, to spend money. We've found TV is the best way to do that. Ads on TV made a huge difference. We had a huge bump after that. TV still has that old-fashioned cachet for people, or at least it does for our customers. It's really comforting and reassuring. It tells them that they can trust us. It made a massive, massive difference.

The success of Lucky Day showed traditional bookmakers and mobile-first companies that the two businesses could coexist: playing slots on smart phones turned out to be something that appealed to women, and to people who had not gambled before. For Mike, this meant that he could sell Lucky Day products to traditional bookmakers. As he explained:

89% of our customers haven't gambled online before, don't have any other accounts and don't think of themselves as gamblers. This is our market, and they are all new to gambling, which is great, because book-makers can use our product and know that we aren't hurting their existing business.

For George, the idea that 'our customers are not gamblers in the traditional sense, they are phone game players' was highly significant. He was happy to present Lucky Day as offering a form of entertainment, but less eager to associate himself with what he saw as 'harder' forms of gambling, like sports betting: 'Most of our customers play for a few minutes, on the sofa, or the train and that's enough for them. They aren't looking for the next race or the next bet, and they aren't under pressure to play when they don't want to.' This implicit contrast with the traditional industry was referred to throughout the company. As managing director Scott explained:

> It's karma isn't it. You don't want people getting into problems. We've had some really sad stories here that George has been involved in and I've been involved in. And we have paid money back. Not many times, but we have done it. Maybe not commercially ideal but it's karma isn't it. If you hear that someone's partner is out of control, they have a real problem and they might lose their house, you have a choice. I may be too much that way inclined but I think it's one of the things I like to maintain in the company. There are other companies where that wouldn't be possible.

Customer service

The customer services team at Lucky Day occupies a small set of rooms on the fifth floor of a nondescript building filled with other gambling companies in the business district of Gibraltar. Monday morning is surprisingly busy with a constant stream of calls. 'They are mostly technical or financial', team leader Adam explains. 'They want to know how to deposit, when their winnings will arrive, when their bonus will come through. That kind of thing.' Adam is always first to the phone, answering quickly and efficiently, his English has just a hint of a Spanish accent. Two colleagues, Trev and Nicole, follow in his wake, equally professional, but not quite so driven. At the same time as answering queries, Adam is receiving new accounts from Michelle, who takes care of verification and VIPs. Frank and Bob head up the fraud section.

Trev is dealing with Michael, a customer who would like a refund: an account has been opened on his phone without his permission, and £480 deposited. Trev asks for his mobile phone number and date of birth, finds his account and confirms the amount spent, 'If the account has been set up fraudulently, Michael, then you need to inform the police,' he says. As Michael replies, Trev mutes the phone and says to me, 'It's him. He's done it. They call and say it wasn't them but they won't report it because it was him.' 'Okay Michael,' he says, ending the call, 'Thank you for calling.' Adam and I look at Michael's account and we can see exactly how much he has deposited, and when, which games he has played and his personal details. Adam thinks that, 'He gambled the whole lot, got to the end of the month when he had to pay the bill and said it's not him':

> We know it's him 'cos it's done through his mobile and all his details. The thing is we can't tell him we know it was you, you've got to just … if it wasn't him he will go to the police, report it and get a fraud reference number which is what I would do if that happened to me. But he's not gonna do it. For one thing, he's gonna go to the police and they are going to say to him you've got nothing to prove it you haven't got a leg to stand on. Your mobile is your responsibility. If I've got a gaming account and I leave it unlocked and I leave it there and you play it, it's my fault. I'm sure he played it because it was over a month and a bunch of deposits was made.

Meanwhile Nicole is on the phone to a customer, Annie, who does not want to send in copies of her identification documents in order to set up her account, and has become very anxious. Nicole reassures her and explains that they are obliged to ask for them, but that if she doesn't want to, she doesn't have to send them. Annie finds it hard to hear and understand what she is saying and Nicole has to repeat the same information several times, 'I'm going to end the call now Annie', she says gently, 'Because we are just going around in circles'. Adam is dealing with a customer who is returning to gambling having self-excluded. He asks to have a limit of £30 per day. Adam agrees to set that up and asks whether or not he spoke to GamCare or any other organisation – he didn't – Adam makes a note of the conversation on the man's account.

According to Adam, 'the typical customer is like, working-class to be honest. We don't get high-end customers; to be honest, other than the VIPs, they don't spend that much':

> When you check an account it tells you the address and we've got people that live in the best places in London and you know from the way they speak they are posh, then at the same time you get the other side of the spectrum you get someone who is a single parent and on the other side. It's a bit of everything.

The name of the company, the website and many of their products (including slot machine tie-ins with popular TV programmes) are designed to appeal to women. There is a widespread assumption in the traditional gambling industry (supported by statistics which show that the majority of sports betting account holders are men) that women prefer slots and bingo, while men prefer betting. At Lucky Day, unlike sports betting companies, women are well represented. The team speaks with 'as many men as women, bang in the middle'. Where there is greater differentiation is in the games played, 'When it comes to games, you check a man's history of games and it's different. Women like bingo, slots, that kind of thing.' Roulette, 'more of a man's game', is the most profitable game at Lucky Days.

Scott estimates that about '15 to 30 people a month out of thousands playing' might have a problem with gambling, 'We're all mindful of problem gambling. We're not in the business of taking people's money if they can't afford it':

> We have a responsibility to protect those who have a problem from themselves. But some of them are just gambler's remorse or a pisstake – after their credit card bill arrives they say, 'that wasn't me' 'someone took my card'. We have a 0.3% chargeback rate.[7]

Frank, account manager, looks up from his book (*Currency Trading for Dummies*) in order to disagree:

> Our problem is that we have to be 'it's all about responsible gambling'. It's not. And I don't agree with it completely because I think people should be responsible for their own actions. The way it's written in the regulation says we have to make sure that people aren't doing their brains. I just think people are weak. If you get addicted it's because you are weak, you have no will power. Maybe I'm harsh. I see everything in black and white. I am addicted to cars because I want to be.

Bob chips in, supporting Frank and adding that, 'most people play the games without any problems except running out of money. So it can't be the game, it must be the person playing. End of.'

VIPs

> VIP line Michelle speaking, how can I help you? Hiya Jill, how are you? How are the boys doing? Where are you on holiday? Anywhere nice? Oh. Lovely. Ooooh lovely. Oh I bet it's nice. I hope the weather's nice. What else can you ask for? I can actually hear them in the background.

How's everything been? Apart from Mark … is he okay? You just sit back for a bit and enjoy the scenery Jill. Oh excellent, oh that's lovely. I'm a bit behind, I'm just going through it all now. I'm just coming back from holiday myself! I'm just going through all that now. Have a nice little sherry while you're sitting there and I'll send you a little text message when it's done. Give me about 20 minutes and I'll let you know what's going on. Alright Jill my love. (Puts down phone and says to room, 'I love Jill' to which Adam replies, 'Yeah. She's sound.')

Michelle 'takes care of' 18 superVIPs and 256 regular VIPs, all of whom get regular bonuses. VIPs are selected from a list of 'good depositors' which is automatically generated each week from Lucky Day's approximately 1 million customers and sent to Michelle, who looks over them and decides who she will invite into the VIP club. 'I have to speak to them first', she explains, and then, if all goes well:

They get a £50 bonus as a welcome gift if they accept our invitation. They get 100% cashback on their first deposit every Sunday and they also get 10% cashback on the rest of their deposits every month up to £200.

Michelle is also responsible for downgrading customers who no longer fit the category of 'good spender'. Although she explains that 'everyone gets the same treatment', Michelle exercises a certain amount of discretion in her dealings with VIPs:

If they phone up and say, 'Look, can I have a little bonus, I ain't got nothing to put on today' and they've obviously spent quite a lot in the past few days then I'll give them a £10, £15 bonus. Someone that's spent, say, a couple of thousand, I'll give them £20, £30 bonus, you know.

Equally, Michelle admits that, 'I'm not going to lie, there is the odd one that's more annoying than the others': 'If they're not spending nothing and they're calling up every day asking for a bonus, they're not gonna get one. Because you can't be giving bonuses out to everybody.' Michelle describes herself as 'chatty' and prides herself on the relationships she has with customers, which she creates and nurtures almost exclusively over the telephone, 'A lot of my customers I get on very well with. I get to know them, I know their family's names and they know my children's names. Jill, I spoke to her yesterday, she's had certain problems, she speaks to me about. It's nice to have that relationship.' A small number of VIPs, mainly women, phone Michelle every day, 'they tend to be the ones that are either living on their own or maybe a single person and it tends to be more women than men':

> I don't know if it's 'cos I'm a woman and we can talk. Having a woman's voice over the phone might seem a bit more comforting than having a man's voice. If I was a man and mostly talking to men they might enjoy it and they could talk about manly things, maybe when it's women they like talking to another woman, having a little joke with her, and with another woman I can just speak to them as a normal person. I don't speak to them as a customer. I speak to them like someone I know. Because I basically do know them. Yes, over the phone, but there is a little relationship that has been built up there throughout the year.

The majority of calls to the VIP line are to ask for bonuses, but sometimes people also phone up when they have had a substantial win, these are Michelle's favourite calls and she lights up as she describes some recent examples:

> People ring me when they win – oh it's brilliant. I love those calls. We all love those calls ... That's another rewarding bit of the job I think. When you hear people say I've never been on holiday before, I'm gonna take my family and they've never been abroad or, one his girlfriend was pregnant and he was gonna be able to buy everything for the baby, just little things like that, it's really, really sweet.

As well as answering calls and checking IDs for new accounts, Michelle is in the midst of planning a trip for some of the superVIPs, 'It'll be great fun,' she says, 'They're all great people and we have a laugh together.' Earlier in the year she took a small group to a comedy club in London, 'I basically went for the top depositors. And because it was my first time I went local so I looked for all my customers that lived in London. And then thought "Right, who's been with me the longest?" I was trying to keep the cost down.' Although 'it was a bit weird at first, a bit nerve wracking' eventually everyone seemed to enjoy themselves:

Mona, one of the VIPs I invited, she was one of the first to arrive at the hotel and she settled in and we went and got a drink and we hit it off really great. She even invited me round to her house the next day for her son's birthday party bless her. I'm like, I've gotta go, I'm leaving tomorrow. And she was teaching me about certain tips on cooking, stuff like that.

Some of the superVIPs have said that they would like their next trip to be to a casino, but she is not sure:

I'd prefer to keep away from gambling. I don't want to see my customers … I know they gamble, I know how much they gamble, I know when, but I don't think I'd want to sit with them in a casino and watch them do it. I might have banned them all the next day and said, 'God, you've all got problems!'

She laughs half-heartedly. Michelle is aware of the dangers of gambling, fond of her customers and eager to do a good job for her employer. Her ability to balance these demands is limited. In particular, she does not want to see her customers gambling. She shudders as she explains that:

I go to the [local] casino sometimes, pop to the loo, or get a drink and you do see the same people sitting there every day, you know, and it looks like if you were to talk to them they would rip your head off, you know, for disturbing them. So to take someone out and see how focused they are on one thing. I don't want to see that.

Michelle is well trained, well supported and aware of the problems that gambling can cause. She describes upsetting cases, but at the same time she hopes that the relationships she nurtures so carefully with customers will prevent them from coming to too much harm:

There has been the odd reality where, this woman spent thousands, absolutely thousands, and didn't realise until she called up and she'd done it in the space of two days. And we closed it and she went ballistic at me for closing her account. She called up wanting a bonus 'cos she'd spent so much money and I saw how much she spent and she was a good spender anyway, so I thought okay, and gave her a bonus, she called back asking for another one and then in the conversation she said she'd maxed out her cards and she was trying to win her money back. You don't try to win your money back. That's a no no. She was getting really upset. I said, 'I'm closing your account.' 'You can't do that!' 'You should be doing what I tell you to do!' I said 'you're doing something really silly. You're gonna lose more money trying to win it back.' It was a quite upsetting phone call actually because she was then getting really hysterical and really upset and I think it started to dawn on her what she herself had done. So obviously hearing someone, knowing that, you know, it's gonna take them a long time to get back on their feet after that and there's nothing I can do about it. I mean I work for a gaming company but I don't want to see people on the floor neither.

Michelle frames her understanding of problems in terms of responsible gambling and the formal steps that she must go through if she suspects that someone is being harmed by gambling:

Usually if I see something bad they come to me. Now I can't make them say they have a problem. If they're adamant they haven't then I can't make them turn round and say 'yes'. I will offer them a limit. Nine out of ten times they'll say, yeah, okay, so there's a little indication, but sometimes they'll call and say, yeah I need to stop and we offer six months, a year or permanently.

On the other hand, Michelle clearly wants her care to prevent people from suffering. She does not describe addiction as an illness, and regrets that some people *choose* to gamble more than they can afford. In Michelle's experience, gambling harm is something that people do to themselves, *despite* her hard work:

I don't gamble and I think I could not hurt myself like that and spend my money that I've worked for, yeah I play the lottery, couple of tickets, couple of pounds, if I win, [I win,] if I don't, I don't. At the end of the day they are customers but they are still people.

A bit of fun

In 2017 an estimated $107 billion was spent on gambling globally, more than on film and music combined, much of it online: casino players alone now account for 11% of total internet traffic (Jones 2018). Mobile gambling makes up an increasing portion of this spend: at the end of 2016 the market was estimated to be worth $41.78 billion and by the end of 2020 it is predicted to reach $80 billion (Stocks 2015). The UK was at the forefront of this growth and is now the largest regulated market in the world. Smart phones and mobile broadband catalysed this growth, enabling companies to create responsive, personalised gambling, available all the time, everywhere. Where it was once illegal, heavily stigmatised or niche, gambling has been diversified and promoted to a wider range of users, through new products and advertising designed to reassure customers old and new that gambling is socially acceptable as well as always available. Football coverage is peppered with advertisements for gambling on everything from dynamic billboards and players' shirts to the tracksuit bottoms worn by the goalkeeping coach. In the UK in the 2018–19 season, for example, 9 out of 20 teams in the Premier League and 17 out of 24 teams in the Championship (which is also sponsored by Skybet) had gambling companies as their main sponsor (Djohari et al. 2019). So-called 'pink gambling', such as 888Ladies and Pink Casino, has joined bingo in attracting female players to sites which provide stereotypical experiences designed for women, including opportunities to 'chit chat', catch up on celebrity gossip and indulge their love of kittens. The established, respectable feel of the industry is reinforced by cuddly 'brand ambassadors' like national treasure Barbara Windsor and professional 'geezer' Ray Winstone.

Gibraltar is a key site in the transformation of the public image of online gambling, from an illegal trade based in places selected for their lack of extradition treaties to a business like any other, run by respectable people. The industry finds physical expression on the Rock, notably when a sizeable chunk of the 3000 workers descend on the Quay on a Friday night to drink and socialise, see and be seen, comparing fortunes in their companies and contributing to the maintenance of particular understandings of products and people. People who work in 'gaming', as they often call it, correcting me when I speak about 'gambling', are either part of, or acutely aware of, a way of life that is quickly normalised among newcomers and can be summed up by the tired cliché: 'work hard, play hard'.

Driving this business are new products including betting in-play, which is modelled on electronic gaming and shares many of its structural characteristics (fast and immersive) but with the important difference that the interface is mobile and personalised, and casino games designed to be played on smart phones. No more inconvenient trips to the casino. Betting in-play has grown symbiotically with football, particularly the relentlessly promoted English Premier League, not just in the UK, where remote gambling expanded by 300% between 2014 and 2017 (Jones 2018), but all over the world. The growth appears to be unassailable: in 2018, the amount bet on the World Cup doubled once more, as it had during the previous competition, to £2.5 billion (Ellson 2018). Because the most expensive part of this expansion is recruitment and retention, it requires huge investments in marketing (almost a third of online gambling operators' cost base in 2014; see Stocks 2015), including sign-up bonuses ('free bets') for new players and cashback schemes for 'profitable players' (losers) (Payne 2019). Risk management is one of the remnants from the traditional trading floor: start winning on 'selective bets' and your stakes will be limited, automatically and almost immediately (MF 2017). Carry on losing on long odds accumulators or random guesses, on the other hand, and you will be welcomed and rewarded, in cash, to keep playing (Witherow 2018; Ford 2019). In this way, bookmakers have downloaded the risks generated by their products onto their customers.

Technology has domesticated gambling, moving it from casinos and betting shops into homes and, most recently, pockets. Mobile casino gambling is expected to continue to grow, boosted by new markets, including in the US, which is set to be serviced by companies that cut their teeth in the UK and Gibraltar. This new image of gambling: regulated, safe, unthreatening, uncomplicated, accessible and personalised, has proved popular with women who would not dream of visiting a betting shop and may not have time to go to bingo in person. They can grab their phone and spin a few reels from the sofa, safe in the knowledge that their bank details will not be sold (as they might be on an illegal site) and any winnings will be paid into their account within five working days, just like any other online transaction. If they do have problems with a deposit or a game they can phone customer services and chat to someone friendly. And if they are good depositors they may be invited to join the VIP club.

'Mobile-first' companies were created by outsiders with experience in communications technology or the media, and have carved out new spaces in Gibraltar. They are hyper-compliant, embracing and sometimes seeking regulation. They talk openly about problem gambling and think that responsible gambling is 'very, very important'. They explicitly distinguish themselves from traditional companies by taking 'an ethical approach to gambling', a possibility that rests on the core idea that informed customers cannot be harmed by gambling, unless they choose to be. This creates a strange situation in which traditional bookmakers recognise 'responsible gambling' as a social construction and treat it as such – a necessity which makes it possible to trade in the current milieu – while newcomers appear to regard 'responsible gambling' as something objective and tangible. In the next chapter I show how these flawed ideas develop and are reinforced through interactions between regulators, academics, executives and politicians at conferences and other industry-sponsored events.

8

The Regulation Game

If we can't convince people with the carrot or the nice lunch we pick up the stick. (UK gambling executive)

As someone brought up in England, where the majority of newsagents sell lottery tickets and betting shops, bingo halls and casinos are a common sight, it's sometimes difficult to imagine that in many parts of the world, getting caught gambling or enabling other people to gamble can get you fined, arrested or worse. Until very recently, the United States limited gambling to either state-run lotteries or specialised locations like Las Vegas or Atlantic City. Sports betting is still illegal in most of the US and bookmakers are regularly imprisoned (Amsel 2018). China also bans most forms of gambling and arrests and imprisons people who break the law. Last year officials warned that they would 'seriously investigate and severely punish those companies and individuals involved in enticing and organising Chinese tourists to gamble in overseas casinos' – widely interpreted as a reference to the 18 executives from an Australian company who were arrested in 2016 for allegedly promoting casino gambling to Chinese VIPs (Stradbrooke 2016).

Most Islamic countries also ban gambling in principle and many, including the United Arab Emirates and Brunei, rigorously enforce those bans. In Indonesia people convicted of gambling can choose between corporal punishment or imprisonment and are flogged in front of crowds of locals and 'tourists from Malaysia' – one lash for every month of their sentence (Hariyadi 2018). Pakistan bans all forms of gambling except betting on horse racing, although Ghas Mandi in Karachi has been described as 'the largest gambling den in Asia' (Habib 2012). Sports betting is also both incredibly popular and illegal in India, where match fixing has dismayed the cricket community. Lotteries are legal, as well as casinos in Goa and Sikkim, which can also provide sports betting for tourists, but the big money goes on cricket. The recent arrest of Sonu Jalan, supplier of betting software to illegal bookies, revealed a large-scale operation mostly focused on the Indian Premier League (Singh 2018). Until recently, only foreigners were permitted to use casinos in Vietnam (Stradbrooke 2018b). In Singapore, online betting is banned, sports betting is permitted in shops run by the Singapore Pools, and locals must pay an entry fee or 'levy' of S$100 to use the casinos, while tourists can go in for free – but don't expect a Las Vegas style welcome from the security guards.

Members of the European Union (EU) take a range of different approaches to gambling. As described in previous chapters, the UK has encouraged a commercial industry to develop and thrive. Sweden maintained a state monopoly until 2018, Norway and Finland continue to do so, despite legal challenges from companies licensed in other member states (Lund 2018). The variety of approaches reflects different relationships between church and state, and different approaches to government. It also reveals something about gambling, which continues to provoke strong reactions and, despite work by the industries and several governments in Europe, remains essentially feral – wild but temporarily tamed – rather than fully domesticated.

In this chapter I use data gathered at conferences and during interviews with regulators, politicians and operators to see how the scripts which constitute gambling's facts are produced and maintained. Conferences like the grandly named annual 'World Regulatory Briefing' (WRB) claim to inform and educate – bringing the latest changes to regulation to the attention of industry and regulator alike. WRB London 2018 discussed 'How has regulation changed and what have been the impacts? What tools are available to help operators reach and exceed its compliance targets?' and, strikingly, 'Utilising Responsible Gambling as a driver for growth within the industry'. These events are also opportunities for the gambling community to network and to establish shared understandings of political shifts and their impact on markets. In this chapter I describe these collective activities and how they shaped changes to the regulation of online gambling in the aftermath of the financial crisis in 2008.

I started work on online gambling at a time when the UK was held up by operators and trade organisations as providing exemplary, 'light-touch' regulation, offering an open market, while the rest of the world was a mixture of state monopolies, limited licences or outright bans. During my fieldwork this picture changed, and a number of different governments regulated online gambling, either in order to profit from an internal market which was being serviced by offshore operators (Italy, Norway,

Greece, the US), or by acting as a base for offshore operators (Jersey), while the UK rowed back somewhat on its liberal approach by imposing a point of consumption tax set at 15% of gross profit. Regulation was often presented as a response to borderless, frictionless trade, at the same time as it re-inscribed boundaries according to the logic of economic patriotism, and presented restrictions on supply as customer protection. Discussions at industry conferences and meetings show how national interests were represented, and how very different systems and approaches were accommodated within, for example, the singularity of the EU. This struggle for respectability mobilised lawyers, operators and regulators, all battling to convince politicians of the rectitude or inevitability of their positions. Like the regulation of financial services, this process is not one of passive description of objective facts (though it is often presented that way) but an active process of market creation (Mackenzie 2008). Although the industry often rails against regulators, denigrating them for their lack of knowledge and/or market instincts, regulation creates opportunities, niches to be explored by companies eager to profit when proven products are introduced to customers unburdened by experience.

A smorgasbord

> Each Member State of today's European Union has an approach of its own to the regulation of gambling and for the foreseeable future this is likely to remain so. (Littler 2007: 357)

About fifty people, the majority of them men dressed in dark suits, circle one another watchfully ahead of a long session at (yet another) gambling regulation conference. Most of us already know one another from similar meetings, and are reluctant to commit to a seat next to a colleague who doesn't fit with our mood. A few of us need to speak to someone in particular and scan the room, seeking them out: some of us use this ploy in order to escape boring neighbours. The chair of the session encourages us to take our seats and settle down before the first of many speeches, generally regarded as the least interesting part of the event. I look around my table and it is hard to resist the feeling that I am part of a natural experiment. 'This Anthropology is a doddle, is it not?' says Anthony, the Irishman sitting next to me, reading my mind. 'Sure, you have everything you need right here laid out in front of you!' I look around again: the Swedish pair are blond and blue-eyed, the Frenchman is stylish, slightly aloof and coolly sipping an espresso, while the Spaniard and Italian are engaged in a heated exchange involving wild hand gestures and raised voices. 'It's just as I told you,' chuckles Anthony. 'It's the Eurovision song contest without the spandex.'

The diversity to which Anthony has drawn my attention is reflected in the swiftly changing map of gambling regulation that each of us keeps on our laptop: black for an outright ban, yellow for a state monopoly, green for a free market (hello UK) and orange for anything in between. We keep the maps on our screens as we listen to the speakers, ready to update them the moment we hear that Russia has decided to ban casinos (again), or Hungary has decided to offer licences for online poker. I soon realise that this is a pointless exercise – it is impossible to keep up. Unlike telecommunications, energy, transport and postal services, gambling monopolies have survived the attention of the EU, each state able to set its own rules, within certain limits. The result is described by one lawyer from Gibraltar as a 'smorgasbord of dysfunction, a most eccentric mash up. But very good for business.'

Gambling law in Europe has historically been a patchwork, reflecting a range of attitudes towards both gambling and governance. In the UK, as mentioned, there is a relatively long tradition of legal gambling supplied by commercial operators. Despite recent changes to policy, it remains the most open and diverse market for gambling in the world. Most of the other large markets, including France, Germany and Spain, have been much more restrictive, to the huge frustration of the industry. In several Scandinavian countries the state is the sole supplier of legal gambling. Controlling the supply of gambling was of course far easier before the advent of online gambling, which is an intrinsically border-crossing service and very difficult, both technically and politically, to contain or eradicate within national borders.

Online gambling came to the attention of the EU in the early 1990s and in 1992 the European Council decided that, 'on the basis of the principle of subsidiarity', plans to harmonise gambling law would not be implemented (Littler 2007: 358). This decision was the basis for the local licensing approach, which has survived despite the efforts of trade organisations such as the Remote Gambling Association in the UK, which has called for a single law to govern the supply of online gambling across Europe. In the absence of harmonisation, case law has been very active: in 1994 the first of more than forty challenges to national law was brought by Gerhart and Jörg Schindler, representatives of the German lottery who were attempting to import marketing material into the UK. The European Court of Justice (ECJ) upheld the principle that the UK could restrict or prohibit lotteries from other states, on the basis of the 'peculiar nature' of gambling, saying that: 'It is not possible to disregard the moral, religious or cultural aspects of lotteries, like other types of gambling, in all the Member States' (ECJ 1994). This judgment had a profound and lasting impact on the way in which the European market for gambling evolved. It is notable that the ECJ recognised the peculiarity of gambling at the same time as the UK government was preparing to argue that it was nothing special and should be subject to the same laws as other kinds of goods and services.

The Schindler challenge was followed by Gambelli's in 2003, which established the limits of the ECJ's tolerance. Gambelli was an agent collecting bets on behalf of Stanley Bet, a UK-licensed company, in Italy. In this case, the ECJ found that the justification given by the Italian government for the prosecution: crime prevention, the protection of players and the reallocation of profits, were not sufficient to justify protectionist measures (ECJ 2003). The Gambelli case established that economic justifications, in this case the protection of tax revenue, were not an acceptable basis for restrictions on gambling and that public order justifications also needed to pass what became known by lawyers as 'the hypocrisy test', as this lawyer explains:

In the past, state monopolies were justified on the basis of player protection, and that also led to a lot of hypocrisy and double talk. It's a very difficult position to maintain, pushing products at the same time as saying that you are the last line of defences against the rapacious commercial gambling industry. The industry points out the obvious poor value that most monopoly operators provide and sits back waiting for customers to vote with their feet. Virtually, of course. (London-based lawyer, 2013)

Public order justifications could not be invoked in this case as Italy was itself pursuing an aggressive policy of gambling expansion, through its monopoly.[1]

Other cases followed, each closely watched by operators eager to gain entry to valuable new markets. At the same time, national legislators have become more adept at honing regulation so that it fits with the existing case law while also protecting their interests. A kind of dance has emerged. At times, the threat of involvement by the European Commission (EC) has been sufficient to prompt action, though mostly in slow motion. In 2005, the EC started infringement proceedings against France, prompting them to open their market, although they did so in a way that bookmakers found deeply disappointing (expensive licences, high taxes), one telling me, 'France has the worst system in the world and has learned nothing from the rest of Europe.' Similar proceedings were closed against Italy in 2010 after they also agreed to amend their legislation. By 2010 the EC had asked Denmark, Finland, Greece, Hungary, the Netherlands and Sweden to amend their laws in order to make gambling more open to competition from other member states. According to an experienced lawyer based in London:

> There are different motivations and ways of measuring success for regulating gambling: getting the EU off your back if you have a state monopoly; keeping the market small; protecting incumbents; protecting monopolies, but in line with the EU laws. Many different priorities … success is to not have a furore: if you don't get headlines in newspapers, you're winning.

Despite workshops and speeches about best practice, latest evidence and shared approaches, gambling regulation is, as one regulator put it, 'a political journey':

> The biggest driver of reform in gambling is a change in government. See the Netherlands. Especially when combined with an economic crisis. See Greece. So take Belgium, gambling is a very sensitive area, it gets too much negative attention and so you get a particular balance between player protection and creating an attractive market. In Italy they need to generate revenue so it's more encouraging and so on. You can go around Europe and pick out the particular circumstances that constrain or enable gambling. And it is constantly changing, it's very difficult to keep up with.

In 2012, as we limped through the aftermath of the Eurozone debt crisis, political upheaval was rife and creating an especially fluid picture. At conferences, investors were full of excitement: the crisis had produced an unprecedented opportunity. 'Out of desperation, comes hope', I'm told by one excited venture capitalist. 'Chaos', I say. 'Opportunity for whom?'

I ask. His response is contained in a breathless, rousing speech to the conference:

> I think these are new times. It's a new era. It feels like 2000 again. We've had the Wild West, the car crash that was PayPal and Visa, then 2005 and poker, and now this is a third epoch. This time we've got the opportunity to really grow this market. The game is very much on again.[2]

The 'game', as this investor puts it, was regulatory arbitrage and was being played in Greece, Germany, Ireland and Italy: some of the largest markets for gambling in Europe.

The year 2011 had been a pivotal one for online gambling. The EC launched a Green Paper, suggesting that they would play a more proactive role, but 'fell at the first hurdle' (a euphemism loved by all bookmakers) when it proved impossible to agree on a definition of 'online gambling'. 'European harmonisation?' One consultant looked at me with mad eyes when I raised it, 'The Green Paper was like rounding up cats. Regulators wouldn't sign up: can we even define what gambling is? Backgammon is gambling in the UK, not in Germany. There's morals and ethics and history and all sorts of things national licensing reflects these things.' 'The EU did it solely to be seen to be doing something,' I was told in 2014, by a regulator who had been an integral part of the process, 'None of it was serious.' Into this vacuum stepped national regulators of all stripes, motivated by a range of issues, but all eager and willing to provide an unpredictable variety of 'local licensing'.

Who's in charge?

> I have a feeling I shouldn't be here. (Regulator wearing a shiny red-sequined hat and holding a large cocktail, sitting in a hot tub accompanied by young women employed by a gambling company).

> This is very tastefully done isn't it? I should think it's quite interesting to you, from a professional perspective. As an anthropologist, that is. (Regulator watching a burlesque strip tease in a bar in a European capital city, during a conference).

Regulators are surprisingly lively company. Some are burly former policemen or upright military men who like to boast about their inside knowledge, telling me that they know 'where all the bodies are buried' from the unregulated era when 'any fool with a laptop and a ticket to Antigua' could set up a gambling site. These men proffer a robust, 'common sense' approach to regulation, including over plate smashing and dancing at a conference in Greece in 2012:

> The more you restrict gambling the less able you are to control it (smashes plate). You get value and security from good-quality operators. Look at France! (Twirls around and grabs another plate.) You've got people playing in unlicensed casinos, plus the government got the tax totally wrong which created enormous leakage, only 25% of players are captured. (Smash!)

The 'common-sense' approach of ex-security men holds sway in offshore jurisdictions which are competing to host large companies in what some self-styled 'respectable' regulators with large internal markets called a 'race to the bottom'. They are eager to stress the similarities between gambling and other service industries, and to emphasise the changes that have occurred, including regulation, which have brought respectability, 'It's a different marketplace to 15 years ago and all the laws of big business are now in place,' a prominent regulator told me in 2012, '95% of what we do is the same as any other industry; 5% is the same as any other financial services industry, and needs light regulation. Mind you, light regulation did get us into trouble that one time ...'[3] Another explained that the problem lay not with gambling, but with a lack of understanding on the part of policy makers and the general public:

> You see most people are terribly ignorant of everything around gambling, the technology, the standards, the customer services, the new products and so on. These are listed companies, entirely respectable, selling a first-class product to increasingly discerning customers. Flying the flag. We should be shouting their praises, but you see people are very small minded and they hark back to a time when gambling was stigmatised, something to be ashamed of. It's very unfortunate.

Unsurprisingly, this is a position which enjoys wide support among operators. One CEO of a gambling and media company told an audience in Dublin, rather colourfully, that: 'The idea that gambling should be treated differently than any other kind of commerce is an abomination and something they came up with when they thought witches should be burned.'

Regulators of jurisdictions with large domestic markets have different priorities. In contrast to the jolly ex-policemen, they include self-confessed geeks:

I came from local government and I am one of those rare people who actually enjoys ploughing through paperwork. I take pleasure in precision. I think of myself as a sort of reverse Walter Mitty. I work on gambling which sounds glamorous. Occasionally I get to meet beautiful women at events like this. But most of my life is spent in an office with my nose in my computer.

This man was described as 'Clark Kent, but without the alter ego', by a droll female Scandinavian regulator. 'Where you have a large domestic market you need a bureaucrat,' explained one UK lawyer in Barcelona in 2014, 'The more boring the better, to avoid the *Daily Mail* effect and help the politicians sleep safe at night.'

By responding to the urgings of industry trade bodies and issuing infringement proceedings, the ECJ curtailed the range of options available to governments seeking to respond to the growth of online gambling in their countries. Laws which were primarily prohibitive were replaced by those which aimed to permit gambling of particular kinds and under specified circumstances. As one regulator of a small offshore jurisdiction explained:

Until the 1960s we didn't acknowledge that gambling existed. Then there was a pragmatic recognition that a number of individuals were offering bookmaking illegally and so, as there were a certain number of bookies operating, we made a law that allowed that number of bookies to operate legally. The first line of that law is 'all gambling is illegal'. You can't do anything except x. But since the 1990s-ish this way of framing laws has changed, European legislation says you must now provide a basic framework of what you CAN do and regulations that say HOW you can do it.

This regulator was sanguine about the changes that were subsequently made to legislation in his jurisdiction, but explicit about the impact of the ECJ:

This isn't unique to this jurisdiction, but it changes everything. We have an erosion of sovereignty due to the development of the ECJ and so on. We have a move to a generally permissive law which then means if it is not captured by regulation then it is allowed. The default position under the old law was that it wasn't allowed.

Under these conditions, and the many differences in their circumstances and priorities, regulators who control access to lucrative markets present a liberal front, relating regulation to the safe and efficient operation of markets, mindful of the role that the ECJ has played in forming the ecology of online gambling. Denmark's regulator, for example, introduced changes to legislation by explaining to a rapt industry audience that:

> In 2004 our monopoly systems began to crack under aggressive competition from foreign operators who started to offer customer support in Danish, as well as higher payouts made possible by being unregulated. Turnover on the lottery dropped. In response, we made a liberal, viable, responsible market where the state does not lose out.

This is an explicit, if rhetorical attempt to hold in tension the expectations of domestic constituencies and those of the EC, to legislate in ways which reflect the place of gambling in Danish society while speaking to the market-based logic of the EC. Denmark's approach, which was to create a relatively open market in the mould of the UK, can be contrasted with that of Norway, which has continued to restrict access to gambling. The origins of this difference in two jurisdictions which otherwise have a great deal in common (similar political and social systems and the same approach to gambling regulation pre-financial crisis) have been traced to a decision by Norway, made in the early 1990s, that the state would not benefit from gambling revenue (Jensen 2017). Based on the striking subsequent divergence of policies, Jensen argues that, 'deviation from this path towards further liberalisation only occurs if the state cedes having a financial gain from gambling' (2017: 120). Not surprisingly, once the state becomes a recipient of funding from gambling these relationships become virtually impossible to disrupt (Steketee 2015).

The light touch

As in financial services, many European regulators, operators and governments endorse 'light-touch' regulation, although their understanding of this phrase can vary. One UK-based operator summarised the idea as, 'free markets and the idea that gambling is a leisure industry with certain risks'. Another provided a lengthier description, starting by identifying, 'Minimal interference in what is a highly efficient market.' And going on to set out a rough theory of market economics and its application to gambling:

> Badly run operators will go bust. Government should recognise that some people will harm themselves gambling, but that's not something the operator can stop happening. Those people are damaged goods and the only way you can stop them doing it is to totally restrict gambling which would prevent the normal man from enjoying himself and also mean you end up with an illegal market that doesn't protect people and can offer the same products cheaper, driving out your legitimate companies.

In the UK, this approach has led regulators, politicians and operators to express the shared opinion that commercial and social goals are not merely compatible but synergetic. This position underpins the Gambling Act 2005, and has been naturalised: rendered a part of 'common sense', despite its distinctiveness in global historical terms. It was neatly summed up by a senior director of the Gambling Commission speaking at a conference about problem gambling in Westminster in 2014:

> Let's start with a quick recap of where gambling fits into the current public policy framework ... Since the late 1990s gambling has been positioned by successive governments as a mainstream, mainly adult leisure activity. Second, while most people who gamble do so safely, most of the time, gambling causes harm and sometimes serious harm, and you don't have to be a gambling addict to experience harm. And the third concept – and I think this is a point that is often lost in discussions like this – gambling is also fun. People who gamble do so generally because they enjoy it, they make an adult choice to gamble because they want to, and in an open and free society like ours, that's a decision they are perfectly entitled to make, provided they are not harming themselves or others.

These assumptions, and in particular their presentation as a non-position, is very popular with operators and their representatives: 'We like the Gambling Commission, we are beholden to them. Even though they're expensive and arrogant. They have done what we needed them to do. They make us sound kosher' (Lawyer acting for a bookmaker). It is also in striking contrast to the approach in New Zealand, for example, where the Ministry of Health 'focuses on public health and on preventing and minimising harm caused by gambling' (Ministry of Health 2014).

The idea that legislation should produce a 'healthy gambling industry', as Tracey Crouch, Parliamentary Under Secretary of State for Sport and Civil Society, put it shortly before she resigned (Crouch 2018a), plays well at conferences; however, a few non-conformists continue to cultivate contrary positions, denying the advantages of competition and maintaining that outright bans and state monopolies are, in the immortal words of one maverick regulator speaking at a conference in Greece, 'the healthy option for our people'. 'Communist!' shouted a gambling industry veteran from the audience, making me jump. 'Get lost!' yelled another, provoking the crowd to raise the volume of their tutting and grumbling. The regulator was not accustomed to such rough treatment and became very angry, shouting, jumping up and down, sweating into his smart suit, and staring menacingly at the elderly ringleader. 'If you are operating illegally and you come to my country,' he said, 'I will arrest you!', adding an unmistakably hostile hand gesture before sitting down and handing over to the next speaker, who stood, a little shocked, and reiterated the usual banalities. This was a memorable moment precisely because, like policy makers, most regulators and operators do not wish to draw attention to the trade-off between commercial and social goals that gambling represents. They would far rather equate the one (commercial efficiency) with the other (social justice), arguing that a profitable, responsible gambling industry is the best way to protect consumers from exploitation by illegal operators, as reiterated by this US casino operator speaking in Tokyo:

> We all want the same: scholars, operators, governments, users of our products and even, God bless them, people providing much needed support for poor people who are suffering from various kinds of addictions. We want a safe, healthy industry, where people can enjoy our products and have fun in our wonderful facilities.

Writing regulation

Where does regulation come from? Even some people who were closely involved in its production were not too sure: 'So much regulation is based on received wisdom and mythology and I don't think anybody really knows where half of this stuff comes from,' explained one consultant. Of course, some regulators liked to give the impression that devising the rules that govern gambling in their jurisdiction was a highly professional and coherent process: 'We spent a year looking at examples of best practice throughout the world,' explained one in Barcelona, 'meeting with experts, discussing the pros and cons of different approaches and consulting with a wide range of stakeholders about what would work best in this context.' Others were more candid: 'It was the first time that any of us had done it, so we just copied and pasted a lot from Singapore and a bit from Nevada,' I was told in Tokyo. A trawl through the paperwork shows that there is a lot of recycling of established ideas and practices, described by one regulator as 'the pick and mix approach'. In the Commonwealth I was told, 'We used UK laws as templates for our own laws and regulations on licensing.' Some governments brought in outsiders to help them: 'We were the first African jurisdiction to use modern standards. We brought in people from the UK to help. We met them at conferences in London.' 'Consultants' with backgrounds in regulation and / or the industry provide some of the routes through which 'best practice' is shared, and suggested that this process was 'quite flexible, more of an art than a science', undertaken with 'connections, people you know well and trust not to put you under a bus', and, most importantly, dependent upon, 'the political mood of your current overlords'. As a consultant with influence throughout Europe, South America and Africa explained to me:

> The regulators set technical standards which they borrow from somewhere else. Then they set up a meeting and people known for their expertise in this field all get to put in their tuppence – the consultants looking for work and the academics polishing their profiles – and that lot all get paid and at the same time provide arse coverage from politicians for the regulator, who in turn provides arse coverage from the press for the politicians.

Meetings with operators and their lawyers are part of this process. In the UK, close consultation with the gambling industry is a given, as in other fields of public health including alcohol. In some Scandinavian jurisdictions such invitations would be counter-intuitive. Operators insist on being heard, maintaining that they are not operating illegally if the law in a particular jurisdiction contradicts that of the EC, in their view, or the views of their lawyers. Operators described how they pushed particular arguments during meetings with officials from countries in so-called 'grey' markets, where online gambling was unregulated:

> We have a clearly laid out argument which doesn't alter much because it's based on common sense: regulated gambling is safer than using illegal sites and will create tax revenue. Which part of that argument we stress depends on the jurisdiction. How hard we go, our approach, even how we dress, to an extent ... you know the unconscious things you do in meetings to reassure the other party that you have shared interests, that you are human even. If we can't convince people with the carrot or the nice lunch, we pick up the stick: 'Your monopoly is a violation of European law.' The consequences of that should be obvious.

An example of this approach can be seen in the actions of Betfair, which, in 2011, filed a complaint against Germany with the EC, arguing that planned regulation was 'protectionist' and would 'solidify the existing monopoly'. 'If Germany failed to carry out the necessary amendment', the complaint continued, then 'Betfair would like to invite the commission [EC] to consider the initiation of infringement proceedings against Germany for breach of EU law' (Wiesmann 2011). 'Uncertainty in Germany is playing havoc with our share price,' an executive at Betfair told me over coffee when the complaint went public: their share price had halved since listing in 2010.

The co-production of regulation means that different interests are variously promoted and suppressed. The interests of some participants lie not in the outcome, but in being part of the process, and of similar processes in future. Consultants, for example, described the practical considerations which shaped their contributions:

> I don't want to offend the government who've employed a couple of 20-year-olds to write gambling regulations and the whole thing in my view is likely to go quite wrong. I don't challenge it because I'm mindful that I need to earn the next crust to pay the bills.

Consultants and lawyers also described the conflicts of interest which arose from working both for governments and also for companies:

I know the other guys in the room very well, I've worked for over half of them. They are sharp guys, and I know exactly what they are doing when they push for a certain thing; and I can also see that the civil servant, whoever he or she is, Mr Bean for all I know, has not a clue about the issue, knows nothing in fact, and is no match for them. I have to plot a course through that.

The conflicts of interest that characterise these processes generate lacuna and silences which can easily be mistaken for approval and encourage conservative outcomes which strengthen the networks that produced them. Academic researchers are part of this mix, invited to offer expert opinions under circumstances that do not always promote the free flow of ideas, as one senior academic, who is approaching retirement, told me:

I am there to provide cachet and I do so by nodding and appearing to approve when they say, 'responsible gambling'. Many years ago I thought that I would make a difference – better me doing it than someone who is corrupt. Now that seems entirely naïve. We are all as bad as each other.

Those who relied on government departments felt under particular pressure:

One of the fundamental flaws of the proposal is that they are predicating an awful lot on a very small survey of gamblers that was done about three years ago … Now I haven't had the temerity to say anything about that yet, and of course not because I want to win a contract from the Ministry of Justice and Finance.

Relationships between regulators and academics are highly variable, and suffer from some of the same structural problems as relationships between academics and the industry. A few academics have called for 'clean' conferences, and will not accept money from industry, or attend meetings that the industry has sponsored or been invited to attend (Livingstone 2018; Adams 2016). Others are more tolerant of such conflicts of interest and become known for their 'collaborative' approach and, as a result, get to spend more time with both regulators and industry. The trust that they build up as a result of these activities can be converted into funding, access to 'natural' data and opportunities to participate in legislative and regulatory processes, particularly when industry has a seat at the table.

Some regulators also cultivate close relationships with the industry, believing that this is the best way to understand their needs and to find ways to enforce regulation. As one explained: 'I consider myself in partnership with the industry. It's my job to ensure that I am clear about what I need to happen, and to listen to the practicalities of what's possible. The more open we are to each other, the better. This is a partnership.' On the other hand, there are some who deliberately adopt a more pronounced distance: 'I wouldn't go for a drink with anyone from the industry on my own. I pay for lunch. It's a basic integrity thing. I'm bound by certain codes of conduct.' In some jurisdictions in the US, regulators may not be recruited directly from industry and must undergo a two- or three-year period of so-called 'gardening leave', much to the annoyance of one industry-connected regulator, 'This is total bullshit ... Regulators should know the industry inside out. It's absolutely essential that they do.'

Spreading the word

As well as contributing to the terms of engagement, lawyers, operators, consultants and paid researchers are responsible for communicating the fruits of their labour to people outside the group, a process that was described as 'changing hearts and minds'. When I entered the conference scene in 2010, asking naïve questions, I was subjected to a lot of this education. Very typical was one US operator who patiently explained to me that: 'A lot of ideas about gambling are based on total ignorance. Old-fashioned ideas that come from a religious background, moral arguments that are totally ignorant of modern gambling and what it's about. We have to educate those people, open their eyes to the truth.' Or, in the UK, a lawyer explained that, 'A lot of people think gambling is dirty or dangerous, they have this old-fashioned idea of what it's like. My job is to show them it's clean and modern, a big part of the leisure and entertainment industry.'

At a recent conference in Prague, a 'cadre of former regulators and legal experts' urged the gambling industry to 'keep regulation away from "emotional" politicians' (Ewens 2018). The idea that politicians (like independent academics and women) are emotional, volatile or self-interested was often expressed by lawyers acting for the industry, some of whom also play an important role in lobbying:

The difficulty of pitching to politicians about gambling is that they are such a diverse group. I see my role as education. To open up their minds to the idea that gambling policy has consequences, that it has wider implications for jobs, and that it can be part of a diverse and safe leisure offering. It's not at all easy, because you have a lot of polarisation. Either they are already on your side or they are never going to be, or opinion shifts and you are more likely to lose people than gain them. From a lawyer's perspective, this is why evidence-based policy is a bit of a red herring. It draws a veil over a lot of more complicated economic and political issues. (Lawyer working in Europe)

Gambling companies retain specialist lawyers, some of whom have come up with lucrative arguments which create or protect sources of revenue or delay changes to legislation which might reduce profitability. Although many of them acknowledged that being a lawyer is intrinsically boring, they also suggested that gambling was among the most exciting of fields because 'we can make stuff up and try it out':

We are paid the big bucks to work out strategies that are to the advantage of our clients. In gambling it's good fun because there is no precedent. We make it up as we go along and this means that lawyers working in gambling are often quite individualist, mavericks who see a challenge there and like to make something new, or find ways to get around new problems.

Many of them also enjoy working for the gambling industry:

The gambling industry is really diverse. Mostly they are very demanding to work for, they have high expectations, they don't suffer fools gladly, they are aggressive. But there is also a lot of variety. So Betfair is more willing to litigate. There are some sensible people and some nuts and cowboys. More so than in other industries, definitely. Never a dull moment! (Lawyer in London)

Part of their role is to win support for the industry among politicians. They are mindful that this task is complicated by the peculiarity of gambling, but they are accustomed to using language that politicians can reproduce which speaks to a particular kind of 'modern' which is 'market-led', understood as efficient and safe:

My role is to educate. To win hearts and minds. Gambling is a complicated subject and politicians don't have time to understand it. It's all about politics, just look at the US. It's like herding cats and most of what happens is entirely unpredictable. You have so many different interests to try to anticipate. Politicians, regulators, law enforcement. You have to see where the power lies and that's not always obvious and can change fast. Then you have to understand that there is nothing inherent that gambling shares all over the world. Sports betting in the US is mob dirty. It cannot be a part of the campaign to make online legal. Now where in Europe could you imagine a similar situation? These things are very distinctive. Everything about them, the way that power works in the system, and the way that people gamble. (Lawyer for the gambling industry)

Some of the lawyers I worked with were unconcerned about the impact of gambling on people, but this was not just (or always) cynicism, but a particular way of imagining personal responsibility that fits well with the variety of market-driven and -moderated gambling that they were responsible for promoting. The lawyers I came to know well were not all cynical but they shared a particular worldview, something that we discussed regularly, although this discussion was inevitably focused on my left-wing bias and their objectivity:

In general, I think that as lawyers we are in favour of an idea of human nature that sees people as free and intelligent. Able to make choices and to compete with one another so that someone who achieves more is better rewarded than someone who sits on their backside all day. We are competitive, we play a lot of golf and tennis. We have more of an affinity with free market thinkers than academics who are all closet or open lefties. And our understanding of gambling is that way too. Is it lawful? Can it be presented as such under the current regulations? These are our questions. Not 'Is it harmful?' Everything is potentially harmful, whether that's food, alcohol, driving or whatever. We advocate light-touch regulation that nurtures commercial activity, creates jobs and provides a top-level service. (Lawyer acting for the gambling industry)

This lawyer was indulgent of my interest in his work and the world it created. Like many others in the field of gambling, he regarded himself as representing a legitimate, if misunderstood industry which 'did more good than harm', and was the victim of an undeserved reputation which was based on bigotry and ignorance. This view is so dominant within gambling that some people have forgotten the role they played in creating it. However, some people also change their minds, as one executive wrote to me 18 months after his retirement, having taken time to speak with people harmed by gambling. He wrote:

> It was an echo chamber. I can see that now I'm retired. I'm talking to different people ... My life is completely different. I'm not trying to justify my behaviour. You've known me a long time now. I've always been genuine about what I'm doing. I'm trying to get at what was going on. It wasn't cynicism or greed. I went to work every day very happy and sincerely believing that I was doing a good job. What I realise now is that the job I was doing, the products I made were harming people. I honestly just didn't see it like that at the time. I was totally genuine and completely wrong at the same time.

A political game

Gambling regulation is a 'political journey', a process that both reflects long-term and established approaches to governance and is also affected by sudden, unpredictable events. In 2004, for example, all of the bingo halls in Brazil were closed down after a video was shared which appeared to show a senior lottery official taking a bribe from a mafia boss. The film caused chaos in the Brazilian stock market and briefly threatened Lula's government (BBC News 2004). In Europe, gambling companies that consider themselves at the mercy of politicians have started to enter into political disputes. In June 2018, Niklas Lindahl, managing director of the Italian division of online gambling operator LeoVegas, engaged in a public spat on Facebook with Italy's new Minister of Labour and Economic Development Luigi Di Maio. Di Maio defended the proposed total ban on gambling advertising which was due to be introduced in 2019 by comparing the promotion of gambling to that of smoking, referring to the movie *Thank You for Smoking*. He acknowledged that gambling generated 'several billions' in tax for the government, but added that 'the social costs generated by pathological gambling are at the same level' (Stradbrooke 2018a). Lindahl countered by saying that, 'It's an insane law that goes against [...] the law in the European Union, the law that guarantees liberty of competition, free trade and competition. Other countries are looking at Italy as a bad example right now.' He added that:

> As for our secondary objective, we do think that sooner or later, a new government will come. We spoke with the opposition and they also think that this new law is completely out of line, so we do hope that when a new government comes, that they will calibrate this law into a more sensible law. (Quoted in Patel 2018)

The idea that a gambling company should have a shift in the Italian government as a commercial objective illustrates the extent of the dependency of gambling industry on politics, as well as their ambition. In the UK, this dependency has already been exploited by a relatively small group, the Campaign for Fairer Gambling, which succeeded (eventually) in forcing politicians to reduce the maximum stake on Fixed Odds Betting Terminals (FOBTs) from £100 to £2. Their campaign undermined the position shared by both industry and government (that there was no evidence to suggest that FOBTs caused problem gambling) by focusing instead on the wealth of circumstantial evidence which showed that FOBTs, like other forms of high-frequency electronic gambling, were associated with greater harm than other less addictive products. They helped to make the already disliked products even more unpopular by building powerful alliances with a range of groups, including people harmed by FOBTs, sympathetic politicians, journalists and organisations like the Local Government Authority. After a lengthy consultation in 2017, and despite the Gambling Commission's recommendation of a reduction in maximum stake to between £2 and £30 (Cox 2018), it was obvious to politicians that anything other than a £2 stake would have been incredibly unpopular among voters.

Unpacking these processes, and showing the effort that they require, indicates that regulation is a range of possibilities, and that the status quo is one among many, rather than inevitable and therefore beyond criticism (Lazzarato 2009). In this and other ways, the current expansion of gambling has much in common with other financial projects which emerged during the 1980s, including the deregulation of financial services (Burton et al. 2004; Knights 1997). Gambling is also an example of 'risk-based regulation', which redistributes potentially negative outcomes from the state to the citizen. This process and its outcomes can be seen in the work of regulators, the development of policies and in the games that we play. As in other fields, regulation attempts to shape particular kinds of subjects to fit into wider historical processes. Gambling continues to divide opinion: the ways in which it is formally managed and legitimated can help us to understand how those in power think about luck, reward, thrift, class and progress. More hopefully, it also shows that while it is often depicted as a triumph of common sense, the inevitable result of changes in technology, or a response to processes described as 'market realities', gambling regulation is actually a political compromise and therefore a reasonable focus for collective action.

Conclusions

A huge social experiment has taken place in the UK since the 1980s. Risks which were previously managed by the state have been privatised and loaded onto the citizen, including via the stock market and the housing market (but also in social care, education and health): a process presented as a democratisation of speculation. These compulsory encounters with risk have been punctuated by booms and busts, including the financial crisis of 2008, and encompassed the subsidiary idea (not one of Margaret Thatcher's, but embraced by her successors) that gambling should be treated like any other commodity and supplied in quantities limited only by the extent of demand, boosted by marketing and promotions. The deregulation of gambling epitomises the process of 'rolling back the state' which was central to the political philosophies of both Margaret Thatcher and Ronald Reagan, and the arguments and principles on which it is based exhibit many of the same features, and the same logic. The outcome of this logic has been referred to by Horowitz (2013) as 'anti-statist statism' – in which strong central support for particular industries (financial services and 'defence', for example) is combined with a philosophy of market freedom. To understand gambling deregulation, including the ways in which certain arguments, activities and ways of behaving are deemed legitimate and encouraged, while others are ignored or devalued, is to understand how society is produced under neoliberalism.

This book focused on the production of gambling, the ways in which policy makers and corporations work together to align policies, regulation, products and desires in profitable combinations. It undermines the idea that the gambling industry comprises a homogeneous group of greedy sociopaths whom we cannot hope to understand, let alone influence, because they are so different from ordinary people. On the contrary, like all communities, the gambling industry includes people with a range of views, some of whom have been highly critical of the direction taken by their industry (Grierson 2016). More significantly, the ideas which enable members of the gambling industries to sell products which are known to be harmful are entirely mainstream and unremarkable, and feature in the kind of soft neoliberalism that is in evidence on British television each morning courtesy of Piers Morgan, or in the right-wing media including the *Daily Mail* (except, interestingly, when they are writing about gambling). An expanding gambling industry does not require extreme views in order to prosper, it thrives on low-level libertarianism and, particularly, an irresistible idea that is virtually unopposable: that people should be free to behave as they please.

Equally importantly, government and the gambling industry are not pitted against one another, the latter ruthlessly exploiting the naïveté of the former. On the contrary, they have shared interests, including through taxation and employment, but also, less obviously, as fellow bearers of a shared 'episteme', an understanding of what exists in the world and how it fits together, which is propitious for both groups (Foucault 1970). Commercial gambling and late capitalism are not merely compatible, they are mutually beneficial and rely on the same narratives, including those that insist that neoliberalism is a description of the world, rather than a political philosophy, and that collective responsibilities are unacceptable restrictions of individual freedom (Sahlins 2008). The gambling industry is part of society, and it is our episteme – the ideas which we take for granted – which permits gambling expansion and the exploitation of the poor and vulnerable that it entails. To critique the gambling industry for its greed or inhumanity is a misdirection. The real struggle is to create more equitable forms of social life.

Informed choice and responsible gambling

The concept of 'responsible gambling' is a central plank of self-regulation and one of the key ideas underpinning the growth of gambling which has taken place over the past four decades. As Ladbrokes stated in their *Responsible Business Performance Report* in 2006, and repeated in *Fair Play. Performance Update. Corporate Responsibility Report* in 2016: 'Responsible behaviour is not only central to our licence to operate, it also fully supports our strategy for growth' (Ladbrokes 2006: 3, 2016: 6). Politicians eager to accept revenue from gambling but cautious about being perceived as promoting harmful products use this idea as a fig leaf. As one UK politician told me in 2012, 'gambling companies can expand in this market as long as the industry is seen to have invested in comprehensive programmes of responsible gambling. It's the spoonful of sugar that makes growth easier to swallow.' This MP uses the economics jargon that has become standard among his colleagues to describe the actions of the industry: responsible gambling programmes are things in which to 'invest' and which must be 'comprehensive'. At the same time, there is also the admission that these measures are superficial: they are introduced to make expansion more palatable, literally to make it taste nicer. Self-governing, informed consumers are the basis for neoliberal expansion. According to this logic, as long as people understand what they are getting themselves into, they should be free to buy guns, drink alcohol or smoke cigarettes. The problem is that gambling, like alcohol, is 'no ordinary commodity' (Babor et al. 2010) and has the potential to alter the biology of the brain (Worhunsky et al. 2017).

Like neoliberalism itself, or the notion of 'informed choice', 'responsible gambling' is not a natural fact. It was not discovered under a rock or distilled in a test tube, but created and nurtured by groups of policy makers, members of the industry and academics. It obliges gamblers to behave properly – that is, in accordance with the rules and ideas that enable orderly expansion. In the UK, the rules state that gambling must be fair, free from crime, and the preserve of adults. But there are also more subtle but equally powerful ideas embedded in documents like the Gambling Act 2005 or in Ladbrokes *Responsible Business Performance Report*, for example, including the idea that:

> For most people, gambling is an enjoyable and harmless activity. However, for very few others, gambling can become a serious behavioural problem. As a company that earns its living through betting and gaming, Ladbrokes has a responsibility to help tackle problem gambling, understand its causes and promote its treatment. (Ladbrokes 2006: 4)

This framing of gambling, as a source of pleasure to 'most people' and a potential source of problems for 'very few others', has a powerfully normalising effect, creating two groups of people. The 'normal' people who gamble without ill effects, and the others, whose response requires an explanation, often relating to exceptional individual psychology. It is constantly reiterated by ministers, operators, policy makers, regulators and journalists, and renders gambling control an exercise in tyranny. As one MP explained at an event in Westminster:

> The question is, do you ban everybody from doing something because a small proportion of people have a problem? ... All forms of gambling will lead to some people having an addiction, and problem gambling,

that's just a fact, and nobody should deny that; we should all accept that and that is one of the things. The issues are, how do we help to minimise that, and what do we do to help those people who have a problem? The solution shouldn't be to say, well, because some people have a problem let's ban everybody from taking part in that particular activity, that's a crazy ... it's a crazy system.

The proper response, according to this argument, is to inform consumers about the risks and let them make their own choices, or literally 'take their chances'.

Responsible gambling discourses have a huge impact on gamblers, including those who are battling serious addictions. The people who spoke to me about suicide related to gambling had little else in common: not all were poor or in debt, or appeared depressed, for example. Despite their different circumstances, they described gambling problems in similar ways. They did not expect to receive any sympathy from family, friends or health care professionals, and indeed they felt that anger would be a wholly justifiable response. For some of them, this was based on bitter experience.[1] The majority of them had not sought help for their gambling from their family doctor, or from services like GamCare or Gamblers Anonymous, because they were too embarrassed, didn't think they could be helped or because they didn't feel as if they deserved help. They are not unusual in this regard: international research suggests that fewer than one in ten gamblers with problems seek treatment (Hodgins et al. 2011). In short, they were ashamed, and blamed themselves, or, to be more precise, they thought that they had caused the problems that they were experiencing by being physically predisposed to addiction, or because they lacked self-discipline: the ability that others had to 'take it or leave it'. They based this self-assessment on the easy availability of gambling, as Jenny, a married, middle-class woman who had considered suicide after a bout of online bingo during which she lost £27,000 told me: 'It's all over the telly. They wouldn't allow that if it was dangerous.' Shortly before he killed himself, Jason, a young man I got to know while working in a betting shop in south-east London, told me: 'I don't know what makes me do it. I can't stop myself. I must not be made the same as them others who can take it or leave it. It's like a drug and I can't get myself off it.'

'Responsible gambling' encourages people who are suffering to distinguish themselves from 'ordinary people', increasing their sense of isolation. As Jason said, 'If everyone is doing it, having fun, why am I so fucked up?

I can't get my head around it.' During these periods of introspection Jason puzzled about his own situation using the resources available to him in the media, the betting shop and at home. He had not sought help for his problems with gambling, nor did he see himself as someone who would ever do so: 'They'll just tell me I'm a loser and I've got a problem, so why bother?' Like Jenny, Jason blamed his predicament on his own flawed psychology: 'The government wouldn't allow it if it wasn't safe: there must be something wrong with me,' he said.

The Reno model

The blueprint for responsible gambling, referred to by the majority of its supporters, is 'the Reno model', written in 2004 by three of the most influential scholars in the small, dysfunctional field of gambling studies. The Reno model frames gambling as 'a choice' while 'responsible gambling' depends on 'informed choice'. As the authors put it:

> Unjustified intrusion is likely not the way to promote responsible gambling … Responsible gambling is best achieved at the direction of the player by using all of the information available. The guiding principle of responsible gambling practices is that people have freedom of choice regarding their decision to gamble. (Blaszczynski et al. 2004: 312)

Like other market-based solutions to social issues, the Reno model is emphatically and explicitly presented as 'science' outside of, or free from, 'politics': the full title of the paper is in fact, 'A science-based framework for responsible gambling'. The authors stress the need to develop what they describe as 'socially responsible policies that are founded on sound empirical evidence', which they contrast with policies 'that emerge solely in response to anecdotally-based socio-political influences' (Blaszczynski et al. 2004: 302). This opposition: between 'science' and 'politics' and 'myth' or 'anecdote', has travelled very widely in gambling circles. In Tokyo I listened carefully as a representative of a large American casino corporation addressed an audience of nervous local politicians as they contemplated legalising casino gambling, saying:

> if you look at jurisdictions where large-scale integrated resorts or regional resorts operate, in cities across America, the *science* will show

you that you do generally not find any increase in problem gambling and in many cases you find significant increases in quality of life.

Similarly, in the UK, a publication entitled 'The truth about betting shops and gaming machines' produced in 2013 by the Association of British Bookmakers (ABB), 'welcomes the Government's pledge to ensure that any policy changes it considers are based not on concern and anecdote alone, but are supported by firm evidence and factual foundation' and seeks to 'dispel seven myths commonly pedalled by anti-betting shop campaigners' (ABB 2013a: 20).

Trade organisations all over the world have embraced the opportunity to promote 'responsible gambling', eager to show that their 'scientific' measures will enable people to use their products safely. In the UK, the ABB is 'firmly committed to the concept of responsible gambling, where customers are given the self-help tools to avoid excessive or irresponsible gambling and thus avoid gambling-related harm to themselves or others' (ABB 2013a: 4). According to Clubs Australia (2015), the trade association for the institutions where most of Australia's poker machines are located, 'the majority of Australians enjoy gambling in a responsible way', while 'problem gambling is a serious issue for a small number of people. We are committed to making sure that clubs provide a responsible and safe environment for community members that choose to participate in gambling.' In the US, the American Gaming Association (AGA 2017) 'and its members pledge to our employees, our patrons, and the community to make responsible gaming an integral part of our daily operations across the United States'. In Asia, 'responsible gambling' has been emphasised in the Macau Chief Executive's annual policy address each year since 2007 (Ho 2013).

The idea of responsible gambling is also used to open up new markets. In Tokyo in 2014, for example, a vice-president of a large US casino corporation was asked 'What is problem gaming and responsible gaming?' And 'What kind of measure is usually used in overseas operations and how effective is it?' He responded by referring to gambling addiction as a brain disorder, saying, 'we need to acknowledge the fact that there are people who are addicted to gambling, but their addiction is a brain issue, a brain disorder that is going to exist whether or not there is legalised gambling in the environment.' He went on to describe responsible gambling as the solution to problems which may be associated with, but not 'caused' by, legal gambling, saying that, 'the notion of responsible gaming is very real, it's very identifiable, it's very consistent country to country in various parts of the world and it is something that is readily applicable here in Japan.' The idea of 'off-the-peg' measures that can make gambling safe was very comforting to Japanese legislators hopeful that casinos could bring new income into their regions: 'In Japan there is a lot of disagreement about gambling,' one senior regional politician told me. 'I am concerned too. I don't want to see my son gambling. But today we have learned that gambling can be safe. It can be good for most people.'

As well as being used to reassure jittery politicians in new markets, responsible gambling programmes are developed in an attempt to delay or halt anticipated changes to regulation. In the UK, for example, public concern about fixed odds betting terminals (FOBTs) led to the creation of a Code of Practice which held off regulatory intervention and left FOBTs 'on probation' for more than a decade. More recently, the UK government has said publicly that the online gambling industry 'must do more to develop and implement more effective approaches to customer interaction and harm minimisation', explicitly threatening to introduce regulation should these measures not be forthcoming / effective: 'If operators fail to demonstrate sufficient progress then the Government and the Commission has powers to introduce additional controls or restrictions on the online sector.' However, no time frame or conditions are specified (DDCMS 2018b). The industry's response, which was warmly welcomed by government, was Bet Regret, a 'major multi-million-pound advertising campaign led by GambleAware, around responsible gambling' (DDCMS 2018c).

In Macau, despite the references to 'responsible gambling' by the CEO of the Macau Gaming Inspection and Co-ordination Bureau in his annual policy address, gamblers themselves were sceptical about the impact of measures like pamphlets about counselling and help kiosks in casinos. They reacted with hilarity and disbelief to my suggestion that someone might go publicly to a booth in a casino to discuss their gambling habits, telling me, 'You joking? No one go there. To bring shame on you. Your family. Like that. I don't know anyone who go there.' In 2015 Davis Fong, Director of the Institute for the Study of Commercial Gaming (ISCG) at the University of Macau, told *World Gaming Magazine* that 50 people (of the 5000 estimated to have problems with gambling in Macau) had sought treatment (Scott 2015). Even operators acknowledged the limitations. Melina Leong Sio-mok, vice-president of public relations and community affairs at the Venetian Macao, captures the absurdity of her position (and that of all compliance officers) by saying that:

> the company was dedicated to fulfilling its corporate social responsibility, but it was not logical to ask people to stay away as gambling was its core business. 'As a gaming operator, I think it is very conflicting and unconvincing if I ask people not to come to gamble,' she said, adding that the business could not over-disguise its true nature. (Quoted in Ho 2013)

Asking gambling corporations to self-regulate in order to make gambling less harmful is like demanding privacy from a surveillance capitalist, something that Zuboff (2019: 192) has compared to 'asking old Henry Ford to make each Model T by hand. It's like asking a giraffe to shorten its neck, or a cow to give up chewing. These demands are existential threats that violate the basic mechanisms of the entity's survival.' In Gibraltar I worked with a company which was determined to behave differently from those around them: partly because they were outsiders, new to gambling and didn't really know the business. Their general manager, Scott, told me that when 'responsible gambling' appeared on the agenda of an industry meeting he thought, mistakenly, that the purpose was to have ideas about how to keep people safe. In preparation, he had sketched out a scheme for sharing information about customers who were causing concern. 'For most companies here,' he told me, referring to Gibraltar, 'social responsibility starts and ends with the poster they put up in their call centre which has the number for GamCare … I wanted to see if we could do something different together.' When he presented his scheme to his fellow operators they laughed in his face, 'Why the fuck would we share our best customers with you?' they said. 'Even the regulator looked embarrassed for me', he said. In subsequent meetings Scott kept his head down and listened to briefings from the regulator, like the other attendees. He didn't ever regain the trust of his competitors and was viewed with suspicion:

> Either they thought I was scamming them, looking for VIPs, or they thought I was a wet liberal. It was like school. I was the kid with a snotty nose and glasses who did his best to rescue the injured animal while the big boys tried to stamp on its head.

Even UK industry consultant Steve Donoughue, staunch defender of light-touch regulation and fierce critic of 'militant academics' (2019: 46), agrees that 'making operators responsible for preventing problem gambling and money laundering will always be problematic, due to their primary objective of making money from gamblers. To get them to stop doing this goes against the reason they get out of bed in the morning' (2019: 47).

From 'responsible gambling' to 'harm prevention and minimisation'

The Reno model of 'responsible gambling' is currently under attack from a small but dedicated group of researchers (Hancock and Smith 2017; Young and Markham 2017) against a backdrop of widespread evidence that similar approaches have failed in fields ranging from alcohol in the UK (Hastings et al. 2010) to junk food in Australia (King 2011). The language and focus of gambling research is gradually shifting, particularly in New Zealand and Australia, away from education and the treatment of problem gamblers, and towards preventing and minimising the harm caused by gambling at a population level (Baxter et al. 2019). The relevant image, familiar from other areas of public health, is of a stronger fence built at the top of the cliff, rather than an ambulance at the bottom. Rather than attempting to estimate the number of people who have developed problems with gambling, and how this number might be stabilised or reduced, this approach aims to quantify *all* of the harm that gambling causes individuals, families and communities. It suggests that you don't need to be a gambler to be harmed by gambling, for example, if your relationship breaks down due to your partner's gambling, or your business suffers because an employee is struggling with a gambling problem (Langham et al. 2016). When measured in this way, the total volume of harm caused by gambling in Victoria, Australia, for example, was found to be comparable to major depressive disorder or alcohol misuse and dependency (Browne et al. 2016).

As well as suggesting that gambling creates a larger volume of harm than had previously been thought, public health approaches have also produced a shift in the understanding of how that harm is distributed. In Victoria, Australia, only 15% of the total harm caused by gambling was attributable to problem gamblers (Browne et al. 2016, 2017). The vast majority of harm occurs among low- and moderate-risk gamblers, a pattern consistent with those seen in alcohol use and which can be explained by the larger number of cases that fall into these categories. This way of framing gambling implies a change in policy, from 'downstream' interventions, which encourage individuals to 'gamble responsibly' and advocate the provision of treatment for people who have already been substantially harmed by gambling, to structural interventions which target the whole population and are aimed at preventing harm from occurring in the first place.

The idea that harm can be quantified, captured and compared in this way is, of course, part of audit culture and financialisation, essential elements of the broader neoliberal project (Shore and Wright 2015; Strathern 2000). While the outcomes of this reframing may appear progressive compared to those of self-regulation, they are integral parts of the process that led to deregulation and their consequences are, as yet, unexplored. The idea, for example, that the harm caused by the suicide of a young man as a result of gambling could eventually be placed on a scale along with the pleasure generated by a game of roulette reproduces the same logic as that which spawned 'responsible gambling' in the first place, and reduces existential questions to cost–benefit analysis. An alternative can be seen in the approach of, for example, road safety campaigns in Melbourne, which use this logic to jar, rather than reassure. In one road safety advert, people on the street are asked 'How many deaths on the road each year are tolerable?' When they come up with a number they are then invited to pick out that many people from a group, a deontological grenade tossed casually into a utilitarian exercise.[2]

Rebound

As the gambling industry has grown, touched more people, and impacted cherished areas of UK life, notably football, attitudes have changed dramatically. When I began my fieldwork, the majority of people were uninterested in gambling. Gradually, as the volume and visibility of advertising grew and coverage in the press intensified, this changed. In the past five years, tolerance of gambling expansion has evaporated, replaced by anger at the behaviour of the industry, particularly in relation to FOBTs and the impact of advertising on children. Recent front-page headlines both reflect and encourage this change and include 'Epidemic of child gamblers' (*Daily Mail*, 21 November 2017), 'Gambling sites forced to stop luring children' (*Sunday Times*, 22 October 2017), 'Crackdown on rip off gambling companies' (*Times*, 29 October 2016) and most distressing of all, 'Online gambling drove my son to suicide' (*London Evening Standard*, 27 April 2016). The day after politicians voted to delay the reduction of the maximum stakes on FOBTs the front page of the *Daily Mail* screamed, 'Blood on their hands' (1 November 2018), part of a broader campaign to 'Stop the Gambling Predators'.

Hostility towards the industry has been fed by their internal bickering, antagonistic briefing and by intense competition within the online betting sector, which led to vast sums being spent on intrusive advertising, promotion and sponsorship, particularly around live sport, especially football. The British love of football, carefully nurtured and exploited by the broadcaster Sky, was a huge factor in the massive growth in betting in-play. The gambling industry literally capitalised this passion, but by doing so without measure, they are, in the words of one executive, 'killing the goose that lays the golden eggs'. Some football fans are beginning to complain that betting companies are ruining, rather than contributing to, their enjoyment of the game. They are also angry about the impact that this exposure to advertising could have on their children (Collins 2013; Freedland 2019).

A change in personnel at the Gambling Commission has also been significant. When Sarah Harrison took over as CEO in 2015, she took a tougher approach to rule breaking, an approach that has been maintained by Neil McArthur, who was appointed in 2018. In 2016 Betfred paid £800,000 in 'compensation and in contribution towards socially responsible causes' after failing to prevent one of their customers from gambling with stolen money (Davies 2016a), while Paddy Power made a voluntary payment of £280,000 (the equivalent of three hours trading, according to the *Guardian*) to a 'socially responsible' cause for the same offence (Davies 2016b). Bookmakers either failed to heed the threat, or calculated that continuing to push the boundaries was worth the risk. Like bankers, executives describe fines as 'part of the business model', or 'a cost of doing business – you just swallow hard, pay up, and carry on. At the end of the day shareholders would rather see a fine and a profit than see your bottom line suffer because you're not pushing hard enough.'

The policy of fining rule breakers continued and includes a record £7.8 million for online company 888 for failures in their self-exclusion systems (Davies 2017a); £1 million from Skybet for continuing to allow hundreds of people who had self-excluded to bet and sending promotional material to 50,000 more (Davies 2018c); £6.2 million from William Hill for failing to spot problem gambling and prevent money laundering

(Monaghan 2018) and £2.3 million from Ladbrokes Coral for accepting bets made with stolen money (Davies 2017b). In 2019 it emerged that Ladbrokes had paid almost £1 million to people a gambler had stolen from in order to support his betting, on the condition that they kept the matter private (Davies 2018d). The regulator has since warned companies about the use of non-disclosure agreements (Kollewe 2019). Not a single CEO lost their job as a result of these failures. In 2018 *Gaming Intelligence*, an industry magazine, awarded the title of Responsible Gambling Operator of the Year to: 'NO ONE' and noted the deterioration of public confidence in gambling which had taken place over the past year. Large fines illustrate that the regulator is behind the curve and playing catch-up, as in other financial markets, out-thought and outdone by people who are highly paid and highly motivated: they need not be unscrupulous, they are simply entrepreneurs and individualists reproducing the logic of neoliberalism.

Under these febrile conditions, a new approach to gambling is taking root in the UK, which focuses more on the damage it causes, and less on the opportunities it offers for entertainment, employment and tax revenue. This shift has been led by charities and lobbying groups, public health organisations, local authorities, people with direct experience of gambling harm and the families of young men who have committed suicide related to gambling. The gambling industry has contributed to the change by aggressively promoting their products and continuing to defend FOBTs even after it was clear that they were not only harmful but deeply unpopular. In response, the government has convened a group of experts and pledged to take a cross-department approach (Health, Education, DDCMS) to gambling in the future. Elsewhere in Parliament, the Labour Party is drafting a new gambling bill, and a special inquiry in the House of Lords reviewing the social and economic impact of gambling will report in 2020. In 2019 the Advertising Standards Association (ASA) introduced 'new rules to protect children and young people from irresponsible gambling ads' (ASA 2019). Under the guidance of MacArthur and Executive Director Tim Miller, the Gambling Commission has removed all references to 'responsible gambling' from its National Strategy to Reduce Gambling Harms, changed the name of the Responsible Gambling Strategy Board to the Advisory Board for Safer Gambling, and will consult on 'affordability' checks and limits for online gamblers (Crouch 2018b), the latter a potentially devastating development for online companies. The industry will consult their lawyers and weigh up how much to protest:

a decision which will partly be based on the virulence of the *Daily Mail* campaign.

The attempt to 'take the politics out of gambling' has failed: the pendulum appears to have swung, away from freedom, back towards control (Rose 2003). Some operators will simply carry on as before, trying to make as much money as possible before the music stops. Others are circling the wagons, making concessions (Davies 2019; Jack 2019) and exploring new ways to represent themselves. The ABB has been abolished, a casualty of the toxic debate on FOBTs (Gibbs 2019). A new organisation, an amalgamation of the old ABB and the Remote Gambling Association (RGA) has been christened the Betting and Gaming Council (BGC), and will be led by Brigid Simmons, former CEO of the British Beer and Pub Association. Renamed and refreshed, this organisation will respond to the new agenda in the same way as its predecessors, recognising the existence of gambling addiction, promising treatment for 'problem gamblers' and holding discussions around 'player' education. The true business of gambling: inventing and retaining products which increase house edge, reduce risk and are addictive is not only legal but also entirely legitimate within the current episteme, and will remain unchanged.

An experiment which began in the 1980s, to shift the burden of risk from the state to the citizen, has increased inequalities, and changed the ways in which we imagine wealth to be created and shared. Gambling has been at the heart of these shifts: in the City as it deregulated and embraced riskier, increasingly complex and opaque ways to make money, becoming less and less accountable as a result, and in government itself, which encouraged citizens to become self-sufficient individualists. It is no surprise that the gambling industry accepted the invitation by the government to recreate itself in the image of the wider market. From a sleazy business existing in the shadows, the gambling industry has partially and perhaps temporarily contrived to become an important part of the UK economy, and is, in those terms, a runaway success.

The story is far from over, and in fact a new chapter has already begun as UK companies use social capital generated in the UK (including the cachet of UK licences) combined with unprecedented knowledge of customers, products and marketing, to enter new jurisdictions including the US (Richards 2019).[3] By using fieldwork to explore the supply side of gambling and specifically the processes used to produce and defend particular products and ideas, I hope to have contributed to an international movement which shifts responsibility for the harm caused by gambling from individuals to the whole of society, including the gambling companies and governments which create the environments and narratives which enable them to flourish. The point of opening up the gambling industry in this way is to show that it is a machine, not an animal, and, as such, it can be dismantled and reprogrammed.

Notes

Introduction

1. The majority of funding that is dedicated to gambling research is linked, directly or indirectly, through taxation or voluntary contributions from the industry, to gambling profits. For this reason, I have applied to general research funds to support my work and argued, since 2013, that gambling research in the UK should be commissioned by the research councils (Cassidy et al. 2013). I have, in the past three years, accepted support for travel and accommodation from government departments and from organisations which ultimately derive their funding from government departments (including through hypothecated taxes on gambling), including the University of Helsinki Centre for Research on Addiction, Control and Governance; the Alberta Gambling Research Institute; the New Zealand Ministry of Health; the New Zealand Problem Gambling Foundation and the Gambling and Addictions Research Centre at Auckland University of Technology. In these cases, I have been satisfied that the 'cut outs' put in place between gambling profits and funding are sufficient to protect independence, although I am constantly assessing this position. The best guide to this conundrum is Adams (2016).
2. The research leading to these results has received funding from the European Research Council under the European Union's Seventh Framework Programme (FP/2007-2013) / ERC Grant Agreement number 263443.
3. The Indian Gaming Regulatory Act 1988 provided the legal basis for indigenous communities in the United States to offer gaming on their lands.
4. Even in the UK, where the industry is comprehensively regulated, problems have arisen, according to the respected market analysts GamblingData:

> There are many obstacles to be overcome when attempting to get a handle on the size of the UK online market. UK-listed entities, for instance, go some way in attempting to obscure the amounts they generate in net gaming revenue from any given territory, and their home market is no exception. Among the biggest players across the major products are privately-held entities which themselves are under no obligation to make geographic revenue shares available – or in some cases declare any revenue amounts at all. Meanwhile, the peculiarities of the UK's system of regulation means that its own Gambling Commission has found itself lacking data from the larger players. At best, it is thought the numbers put forward by the Commission for the size of the UK online market underestimate the actual total by at least two thirds. (GamblingData 2012: 8)

5. 'Grey' markets are defined as those where gambling is not explicitly banned, as it is in 'black' markets.
6. For example, John (Fire) Lame Deer told Richard Erdoes that, 'We Sioux are all natural gamblers' (Erdoes 1994: 131).

1   Gambling's new deal

1. As acknowledged in the *Gambling Review Report*, the total exceeds 100% as a result of rounding (Gambling Review Body 2001: 239).
2. The border between legal and illegal gambling is relatively visible in the UK, northern Europe, North America, Australia and New Zealand, although illegal practices like money laundering and loan sharking blur these distinctions. In Eastern Europe, Asia and Africa it is more porous. Some companies I worked with were willing to operate in places where gambling is explicitly banned – they enjoyed a relatively precarious existence subject to the whims of law enforcement and extradition treaties. Some established companies were willing to operate in both regulated and so-called 'grey' spaces, where gambling is not explicitly banned, in some cases using regional political entities to challenge the legality of restrictive regulation, as I will describe in chapter 8.
3. An idea attributed to Conservative politician Rab Butler, who drafted the act in 1960 (Oakley 2016).
4. The original adverts, designed by Saatchi and Saatchi, can be viewed on YouTube.
5. In fact, Sir Ivan Lawrence initiated the process of creating a national lottery when he won the draw to introduce a private members bill in 1991. Margaret Thatcher was 'very far from enthusiastic' according to Sir Ivan, afraid that, 'the feckless might be trapped into more fecklessness with the lottery'. The other sticking point was that, 'the Treasury had done a deal with the Football Pools' (*BBC News* 2011).
6. Online betting exchanges enable punters to bet directly with each other, without the intervention of a bookmaker. The world's largest, Betfair, was launched in 2000 and, in 2007, had 1 million clients and turnover of £1 million a week (see chapter 6). Betfair was able to offer up to 20% better odds and, unlike traditional bookmakers, makes its money by taking a commission from winning bets.
7. Seven out of the nine rejected recommendations, including the ability of local authorities to impose blanket bans on gambling premises, could be described as restrictive. The two remaining rejected recommendations were enabling of gambling opportunities (DCMS 2002).
8. In 2011 Tony Blair pointed out the discontinuity between his leadership and that of Gordon Brown: 'We didn't become old Labour exactly. But we lost the driving rhythm that made us different and successful. It was not a government of continuity from 1997 to 2010 pursing the same politics. It was 10 plus three' (Curtis 2011).

2   Raffles: gambling for good

1. Fourteen questions in the 2006/7 survey and eight in the 2009/10 survey.
2. All items were scored on a scale of 1 (strongly agree) to 5 (strongly disagree). Scores below 3 indicated a negative attitude towards gambling, above 3 a positive attitude. In 2006/7 all but two of the items produced an unfavourable score. The two items that scored positively were, 'People should have the right to gamble whenever they want' and 'It would be better if gambling was banned altogether'. In 2009/10 overall attitudes remained negative. Six of the eight questions produced negative responses, the two positive exceptions were the same as in 2006/7.
3. Officially, there are eight categories of raffle. Three require permission: 'small society lotteries' run by societies with non-commercial purposes, and with a limit of £20,000 in ticket sales, 'large society lotteries' which have a minimum of £20,000 in ticket sales and 'local authority lotteries' run by and for the local authority. Five categories do not require permission: 'private society lotteries' run to raise money for the society in question, 'work lotteries' played by a group of colleagues, 'residents' lotteries' played by people living at a particular address and 'customer lotteries' run by a business for its customers with prizes of £50 or less. Work lotteries, residents' lotteries and customer lotteries may not be run for profit so are not used for fundraising. The final category, 'incidental non-commercial lotteries' can be used to raise funds at non-commercial events, such as school fetes. All the sales and the draw must take place during the main event and prizes must not total more than £500. Raffles of this kind take place every day in the south-east of England.

3   The birth of the betting shop

1. Gross gambling yield (GGY) is defined by the Gambling Commission as 'the amount retained by operators after the payment of winnings but before the deduction of the costs of the operation'. In practice, what is being measured is debatable. I asked a senior executive to tell me how they calculated gross win and he told me, 'Can't tell you that one, only what is in the annual report. Most companies use Gross Win [GW] to measure machine profit although there are differences company to company as to what they deduct and that is a very closely guarded secret.'
2. The *Collins English Dictionary* defines 'totty' as 'people, esp. women, collectively considered as sexual objects'.
3. See, for instance:

    My Lords, will my noble friend take into account also that as a result of scratchcards 600 betting offices have notified the Horserace Betting Levy Board that they will have to close? Is she worried that if there are no licensed betting shops betting will go underground and probably be controlled by criminal gangs? (*Hansard* 1995)

4. I understand that this refers to a particular company which used red pens.

4   The rise of the machines

1. My first experience of slot machine gambling in the United States was at Kentucky Downs, or Duelling Grounds as we called it, a racetrack which introduced 'instant racing', a slot machine which is not technically a slot machine because it is running historical horse racing data rather than randomly generated numbers. The machines attracted players from nearby Nashville. At the time, Tennessee had no legal gambling other than a lottery. These kinds of interstate dilemmas are common and have acted as an accelerant where governments are struggling to find ways to tame deficits without increasing direct taxation.

2. Near misses are known to encourage repeat play (Clark et al. 2009), particularly among people identified as problem gamblers (Chase and Clark 2010). As a result, some operators have programmed machines to depict near misses more frequently than would occur by chance, a practice banned in some jurisdictions, including Australia (Queensland Government 2015). Losses disguised as wins 'inflate win estimates' (Barton et al. 2017). For more information about these features and how they affect EGM play see the recent literature review by Barton et al. (2017).

3. GamCare is the main charity responsible for the treatment of problem gamblers in the UK, which is funded by a voluntary levy from the industry.

4. 'Steppers' are traditional mechanical three-reel slots, which remain extremely popular and profitable, particularly among 'locals' playing in Las Vegas. Floor managers recognise the need to provide a good number of these machines on their floors for those customers who prefer the 'traditional' experience, with familiar symbols, paylines and user interface.

5. Quoted in *Hansard* 1968. See: https://api.parliament.uk/historic-hansard/commons/1968/feb/13/gaming-bill

6. The Campaign for Fairer Gambling is a not-for-profit entity set up and funded by Derek Webb, inventor of three-card poker, and his partner, Hannah O'Donnell (Ahmed 2017). The public face of the Campaign for Fairer Gambling is Matt Zarb Cousin, a young man who was also recovering from gambling addiction. Speaking from experience, he was a fresh and fearless voice among the usual group of compromised researchers and lobbyists. As the Campaign for Fairer Gambling became more influential and gained ground with journalists and policy makers the ABB went on the attack, claiming that Webb was motivated by commercial interests in the casino industry (Ramesh 2013), a claim that he has consistently denied (Webb 2017).

7. Arguable exceptions include Norway and New Zealand, where a public health approach to gambling has prioritised harm prevention and produced relatively effective interventions (Rossow and Hansen 2016).

8. A review of the international evidence by Williams et al. (2012) found that the least effective interventions are the most commonly implemented, a finding reinforced by a more recent review by Livingstone et al. (2019).

5   *The responsible gambling myth*

1. See, for example, the tips offered by ParentBet, a charity in Ontario set up to educate parents about youth gambling at: http://parentbet.net/how-can-gambling-be-healthy/: 'Gambling can be a "healthy" activity, in that it can be an enjoyable form of entertainment or socialization.'

2. For a fascinating, sobering description of how these principles operate in practice in clubs in suburban Melbourne see Rintoul and Deblaquiere (2019).

3. A 'Trixie' consists of 4 bets on 3 selections, a 'Yankee' of 11 bets on 4 selections, a 'Canadian' or 'Super Yankee' of 26 bets on 5 selections, a 'Heinz' of 57 bets on 6 selections and a 'Goliath' consists of 247 bets on 8 selections. The most popular of these multiple bets when I worked in betting shops were 'Lucky 15s' (15 bets on 4 selections) and 'Lucky 31s' (31 bets on 5 selections). These are highly profitable bets for bookmakers and promoted by offering a return at double the odds if only one selection wins, terms that many small-stakes punters find highly attractive, even though they are actually very poor value (Newall 2015). Selective or professional punters would not normally use multiples as they represent poor value for money relative to singles and doubles. The London market was traditionally dominated by singles and doubles, but this has changed completely since the introduction of machines and the rise of betting on soccer.

4. A 'slow count' is an attempt to place a bet after the 'off', the start of a race, thereby preserving the option of pulling out if a horse or dog is slow out of the traps. Deciding whether or not to accept a bet close to the off was left to the discretion of managers until EPOS took over, when it became an automated process.

5. During the popular Cheltenham Festival race meeting this shop can take up to 1100 slips each day. In the past five years it has made an annual profit of between £125,000 and £250,000. The volatility is partly due to overall good or bad years at important festivals such as Cheltenham and the movements of big punters, but also reflects a more general upward trend based on FOBT profits.

6. Measured over a period of three weeks.

7. Operators are keen to describe betting shops as 'community hubs', in fact when I told the Association of British Bookmakers that I had started working in betting shops they encouraged me strongly to write about their 'community feel'. At one meeting their representative told me:

> Betting shops are such interesting, social places aren't they? Now that would be really interesting. I should think that would be a perfect focus for an anthropologist. People would be really interested if you decide that you wanted to write about that, something that is not often written about. Not problem gambling, but the very social side of gambling, and how people use betting shops as community centres. We would support that very strongly.

8. In a survey of 100 punters a year after the smoking ban had been brought in, William Hill found that over 70% felt that the betting shop experience was

better post-smoking ban, with 56% saying that the ban made shops 'more welcoming'. Hill's also reported, 'a higher ratio of women in betting shops than ever before, and this trend looks set to continue into the future, despite the increasing appeal of online gambling' (*Gambling Online Magazine* 2008).

9. Jill is referring to the responsibility that managers have to transfer cash from the shop to the bank (Murphy 2012).

10. The *Panorama* crew visited 39 shops during filming and observed 23 acts of violence and anti-social behaviour.

6   The bookmakers' lament

1. The practices described in this chapter are not unique to Warringtons, nor were they thought unusual by people working there. The purpose of the chapter is not to criticise the behaviour of one firm, but rather to explore the betting industry as a whole, using this company as an example. The betting industry during this period exhibited a lack of differentiation, for reasons described in the chapter. Homogeneity was reinforced by the regular movement of staff between companies, sought not only for their skills and knowledge, but also for their up-to-date, commercially sensitive information.

2. Train was no stranger to cross-border gambling: he had started a remote betting service for German customers in 1983, taking advantage of the poor service and high margins offered by the state monopoly. Punters received a weekly coupon by post which they completed and returned to the UK. According to Train, business flourished until the Post Office was privatised and delivery times increased, forcing him to relocate to Austria. In the early 1990s he was interested in the potential of the internet but recalls that, 'everyone told me to leave it well alone. It would only ruin the reputation of my business.' He persevered, 'my view on life is that one shouldn't just accept things as they are, but start questioning and looking at things from different angles. I just ignored those who asked why anyone would ever want to place a bet on the Net' (*iGaming Business* 2008).

3. Satellite Information Services, providers of content in betting shops, partly owned by UK bookmakers and now called Sports Information Services.

4. For a comprehensive description of the betting exchange phenomenon and its implications for horse racing and betting see O'Connor (2017).

5. There were some disadvantages to the new system which put off some traditional punters: it could not easily accommodate multiple bets; it was an account-based system – many punters preferred the apparent anonymity of the betting shop; it required a computer and an internet connection (the speed of which could impact profitability); the interface was not intuitive unless you had worked as a financial trader and, finally, the switch to decimal odds was difficult for those who were accustomed to fractional odds of, for example, 33/1 or 6/4.

7   Online in Gibraltar

1. As online gambling shadows the spread of mobile technologies, the frontier takes new forms. A recent article, 'Africa: dig for opportunities and strike

gold' reports the findings of an 'expert panel' at a conference in London and suggests that, 'When it comes to Africa there is a whole continent of potential for those looking to boost their profit margins.' The author suggests that there is much to learn from existing markets: 'Plotting the opportunities in Africa is made easier if you see its countries as following a similar growth curve as that of Europe over the past 15 years' (Gannagé-Stewart 2018).

2. According to the Gambling Act, 'remote' gambling includes all kinds of gambling via remote communication, that is, via the internet, telephone, television, radio or any other electronic means.

3. In 2015, a survey of 225 countries showed that 39 (including China, Japan and Turkey) banned online gambling, while 61 offered licences. The majority (93) did not ban online gambling, but nor did they offer licences (KeytoCasino 2015).

4. Alderney and the Isle of Man were added to the list in 2007, Tasmania and Antigua and Barbuda in 2008. Applications from Curaçao, Kahnawake and Alexander First Nation were not granted (Kilsby 2008).

5. The additional surge during the World Cup prompted criticism in *The Times* where columnist Rachel Sylvester called on the Prime Minister to take action (2014). The gambling industry responded by forming the Senet Group, 'an independent body set up to raise standards in the sector, supporting the Gambling Commission's work to make services safer and fairer ensuring, in particular, that responsible gambling messages are put to players with frequency and prominence' (see http://senetgroup.org.uk/responsible-gambling-standards/).

6. In December 2014 the rules were changed so that operators offering services to UK customers must also be licensed and taxed there, marking the end of the experiment with an open market for online gambling. The Treasury estimated that the new rules would generate an additional £300 million each year (HM Treasury 2013). However, the change was justified primarily on the basis of consumer protection: to limit access to UK markets for any other reason would fall foul of European law.

7. A chargeback is a request to the debit or credit card provider to reverse a transaction.

8   The regulation game

1. The Gambelli case explains why, when the UK government introduced a point of consumption tax for online gambling, they did so on the basis of 'consumer protection'. To introduce the tax in order to rake back some of the revenue lost to companies based offshore, would invite the scrutiny of the ECJ.

2. 'The Wild West' refers to the online industry pre-regulation, 'the car crash that was PayPal and Visa' was the withdrawal of Paypal from payments for online gambling in 2003 (they have recently re-entered). '2005' refers (I think) to the Unlawful Internet Gaming Enforcement Act (United States Treasury Department 2006), which made online gambling illegal in the US, and forced publicly quoted companies to stop taking American players,

causing a massive drop in their value. 'Poker' refers to 15 April 2011, also known as 'Black Friday', when the United States Department of Justice issued an indictment against the three largest online poker websites in the country.

3. He is referring to a scandal which arose when a company licensed in his jurisdiction went bankrupt and was unable to pay its customers.

Conclusions

1. Research has shown that people suffering from mental illness are likely to be treated with less sympathy than those who are physically unwell (Weiner et al. 1988).
2. This example was brought to my attention by Charles Livingstone. For more information about this campaign see: https://www.towardszero.vic.gov.au/safe-people/why-safe-people-matter
3. For example, in 2018, William Hill's strategy was 'focused around three priorities': 'Driving digital growth in the UK and internationally; Growing a business of scale in the US; and Remodelling UK Retail' (William Hill 2018).

References

ABB (Association of British Bookmakers), 2013a. *The Truth about Betting Shops and Gaming Machines*, 12 August. London: ABB, www.abb.uk.com/the-truth-about-gaming-in-betting-shop/

ABB (Association of British Bookmakers), 2013b. *The ABB Code for Responsible Gambling and Player Protection in Licensed Betting Offices in Great Britain*. London: ABB.

Abt, W., J. Smith and E. Christiansen, 1985. *The Business of Risk: Commercial Gambling in Mainstream America*. Lawrence, KS: University Press of Kansas.

ACIL Allen Consulting, Deakin University, Central Queensland University and the Social Research Centre, 2017. *Fourth Social and Economic Impact Study of Gambling in Tasmania: Report 1*. Hobart: Tasmanian Department of Treasury and Finance.

Adams, P., 2007. *Gambling, Freedom and Democracy*. Routledge Studies in Social and Political Thought. London: Routledge.

Adams, P., 2016. *Moral Jeopardy: Risks of Accepting Money from the Alcohol, Tobacco and Gambling Industries*. Cambridge: Cambridge University Press.

AGA (American Gaming Association), 2017. *AGA Code of Conduct for Responsible Gaming*, www.americangaming.org/sites/default/files/AGA%20Code%20of%20Conduct%20for%20Responsible%20Gaming_Final%207.27.17.pdf

Ahmed, M., 2017. Unlikely duo behind the multimillion hit facing British bookmakers. *Financial Times*, 29 September, www.ft.com/content/a6b40dfe-a1fe-11e7-9e4f-7f5e6a7c98a2

Aitken, M., 2015. Heartbroken partner of gambling addict who took his own life calls for new curbs on betting terminals. *Daily Record*, 1 November, www.dailyrecord.co.uk/news/real-life/heartbroken-partner-gambling-addict-who-6740736

Amsel, P., 2018. Maine's biggest ever illegal bookmaker cops a plea. 25 May, https://calvinayre.com/2018/05/25/business/maine-biggest-illegal-bookmaker-guilty/

Anderson, P., A. de Bruijn, K. Angus, R. Gordon and G. Hastings, 2009. Impact of alcohol advertising and media exposure on adolescent alcohol use: a systematic review of longitudinal studies. *Alcohol Alcoholism* 44(3): 229–43.

Anonymous, 1947. *Mass Observation Report into Gambling*. Unpublished report, Mass Observation Archive, University of Sussex Special Collections, www.massobservation.amdigital.co.uk/Documents/Details/MASS-GAMBLING/FileReport-2560

Appel, H., 2004. Occupy Wall Street and the economic imagination. *Cultural Anthropology* 29(4): 602–25.

ASA (Advertising Standards Association), 2019. *Protecting Children and Young People – Gambling Guidance*, 13 February, www.asa.org.uk/resource/protecting-children-and-young-people-gambling-guidance.html

Atkinson, S., 2006. Gibraltar proves a winning bet. *BBC News*, 14 August, http://news.bbc.co.uk/1/hi/business/4776021.stm

Australian Associated Press, 2011. Gambling reforms un-Australian: industry. *Sydney Morning Herald*, 11 April, https://tinyurl.com/yyrrfbam

Australian Associated Press, 2014. Gambling: Australians bet more and lose more than anyone else. *Guardian*, 4 February, https://tinyurl.com/y2ltg9r9

Australian Government Department of Communications and the Arts, 2019. Interactive Gambling, www.communications.gov.au/what-we-do/internet/internet-governance/online-gambling

Babor, T., R. Caetano, S. Casswell, G. Edwards, N. Giesbrecht, K. Graham et al., 2010. *Alcohol – No Ordinary Commodity: Research and public policy*, 2nd edn. New York: Oxford University Press.

Badcock, J., 2017. Spain plans to end Gibraltar's 'privileged' existence as a 'tax haven' in Brexit negotiations. *Telegraph*, 3 May, www.telegraph.co.uk/news/2017/05/03/spain-plans-end-gibraltars-privileged-existence-tax-haven-brexit/

Banks, G., 2011. Presentation to South Australian Centre for Economic Studies, Corporate Seminar, Adelaide, 30 March, 6.

Barton, K.R., A. Yazdani, N. Ayer et al., 2017. The effect of losses disguised as wins and near misses in electronic gaming machines: a systematic review, *Journal of Gambling Studies* 33: 1261, https://doi.org/10.1007/s10899-017-9696-0

Baxter, D., M. Hilbrecht and C. Wheaton, 2019. A mapping review of research on gambling harm in three regulatory environments. *Harm Reduction Journal* 16: 12.

BBC News, 1999. UK Casinos gamble on new freedom. 23 August, http://news.bbc.co.uk/1/hi/uk/428516.stm

BBC News, 2004. Bingo scandal sees markets gyrate. 20 February, http://news.bbc.co.uk/1/hi/business/3508257.stm

BBC News, 2006. UK gaming rule bid 'not tax grab'. 31 October, http://news.bbc.co.uk/1/hi/uk_politics/6100012.stm

BBC News, 2007. Manchester wins super-casino race. 30 January, http://news.bbc.co.uk/1/hi/uk_politics/6312707.stm

BBC News, 2011. National Lottery: Sir Ivan Lawrence on Margaret Thatcher's doubts. 28 October, www.bbc.co.uk/news/uk-politics-15027222

BBC News, 2012. Undercover in Britain's bookies. 5 November, www.bbc.co.uk/news/uk-20182750

BBC News, 2017. Ladbrokes Coral bought by online rival GVC. 22 December, www.bbc.co.uk/news/business-42452945

BBC Sport, 2001. Brown scraps betting duty. 7 March, http://news.bbc.co.uk/sport1/hi/front_page/1207748.stm

Belger, T., 2016. Dad whose gambling-addicted son hanged himself calls for crackdown on fixed-odds betting terminals. *Liverpool Echo*, 20 February, www.liverpoolecho.co.uk/news/liverpool-news/dad-whose-gambling-addicted-son-10922618

Bennett, O., 2013. Fancy a flutter? The rise of the middle-class gambler. *Management Today*, www.managementtoday.co.uk/fancy-flutter-rise-middle-class-gambler/article/1182983

Beugge, C., 2013. Mike Tindall's racehorse: from £12,000 to £200,000. *Telegraph*, 12 February, www.telegraph.co.uk/finance/personalfinance/investing/9862223/How-to-invest-in-a-racehorse.html

Binde, P., 2005. Gambling across cultures. *International Gambling Studies* 5(1): 1–27.

Blackmore, R., 1891. *The Jockey Club and Its Founders: In Three Periods*. London: Smith, Elder.

Blaszczynski, A., R. Ladouceur and H. Shaffer, 2004. A science-based framework for responsible gambling: the Reno model. *Journal of Gambling Studies* 20(3): 301–17.

Bloomberg, 2016. Bloomberg industry market leaders. 10 February, www.bloomberg.com/graphics/industries/

Bolger, J., 2004. Need to know: global business briefing – economics. *The Times*, 5 March, www.thetimes.co.uk/article/need-to-know-global-business-briefing-k5jmzfxs78n

Born, M., 2003. Minister broadcasts her desire for competition. *The Telegraph*, 18 July, www.telegraph.co.uk/news/uknews/1436410/Minister-broadcasts-her-desire-for-competition.html

Bowers, S., 2003. Odds-on favourite. *Guardian*, 7 June, www.theguardian.com/business/2003/jun/07/9

Bowers, S., 2008. William Hill to buy in technical experts to save internet arm. *Guardian*, 11 January, www.theguardian.com/business/2008/jan/11/williamhill

Breen, H., 2008. Visitors to northern Australia: debating the history of Indigenous gambling. *International Gambling Studies* 8(2): 137–50.

Brown, M., 2001. Welcome to the ministry of fun, Tessa. *Guardian*, 11 June, www.theguardian.com/media/2001/jun/11/mondaymediasection.generalelection

Browne, M., E. Langham, V. Rawat, N. Greer, E. Li, J. Rose, M. et al., 2016. *Assessing Gambling-related Harm in Victoria: A Public Health Perspective*. Melbourne: Victorian Responsible Gambling Foundation.

Browne, M., M. Bellringer, N. Greer, K. Kolandai Matchett, V. Rawat, E. Langham et al., 2017. *Measuring the Burden of Gambling Harm in New Zealand*. Wellington, New Zealand: Ministry of Health.

Bullough, O., 2017. Defend Gibraltar? Better condemn it as a dodgy tax haven. *Guardian*, 9 April, www.theguardian.com/commentisfree/2017/apr/08/defend-gibraltar-condemn-it-as-dodgy-tax-haven

Burton, D., D. Knights, A. Leyshon, C. Alferoff and P. Signoretta, 2004. Making a market: the UK retail financial services industry and the rise of the complex sub-prime credit market. *Competition & Change* 8: 3–25.

Busby, M., 2018. Revealed: how bookies use AI to keep gamblers hooked. *Guardian*, 30 April, www.theguardian.com/technology/2018/apr/30/bookies-using-ai-to-keep-gamblers-hooked-insiders-say

Casino News Daily, 2018. Las Vegas, Macau Casino revenue comparison report (with Infographic), 21 February, https://tinyurl.com/y2yomvlc

Cassidy, R., 2002. *Sport of Kings: Kinship, Class and Thoroughbred Breeding in Newmarket*. Cambridge: Cambridge University Press.

Cassidy, R., 2012a. *Reassessing the Distinction between Gambling and Problem Gambling: An Anthropological Approach*. ESRC Impact Report, RES-164-25-0005. Swindon: ESRC.

Cassidy, R., 2012b. Horse versus machine: battles in the betting shop. *Journal of the Royal Anthropological Association* 18(2): 266–84.

Cassidy, R., 2014. 'A place for men to come and do their thing': constructing masculinities in betting shops in London. *British Journal of Sociology* 65(1): 170–91.

Cassidy, R., C. Loussouarn and A. Pisac, 2013. *Fair Game: Producing Gambling Research*. Goldsmiths, University of London, https://tinyurl.com/yyvgjorr

Castrén, S., M. Heiskanen and A. Salonen, 2018. Trends in gambling participation and gambling severity among Finnish men and women: cross-sectional population surveys in 2007, 2010 and 2015. *British Medical Journal Open* 8(8).

Chan, T., 2018. Japan's pinball gambling industry makes 30 times more cash each year than Las Vegas. *Independent*, 26 July, www.independent.co.uk/news/world/asia/pachinko-japan-pinball-gambling-revenue-money-las-vegas-a8464881.html

Chapman, B., 2018. Bet365 boss Denise Coates' pay rises to 'eye-watering' £265m. *Independent*, 21 November, www.independent.co.uk/news/business/news/bet365-denise-coates-boss-pay-265-million-pounds-salary-a8645351.html

Chase, H. and L. Clark, 2010. Gambling severity predicts midbrain response to near-miss outcomes. *Journal of Neuroscience* 30: 6180–7.

Chinn, C., 2004. *Better Betting with a Decent Feller: Bookmaking, Betting and the British Working Class, 1750–1990*. London: Aurum Press.

Clapson, M., 1989. *Popular Gambling and English Culture, c.1845 to 1961*. PhD thesis, University of Warwick.

Clark, L., A.J. Lawrence, F. Astley-Jones and N. Gray, 2009. Gambling near-misses enhance motivation to gamble and recruit win-related brain circuitry. *Neuron* 61(3): 481–90.

Clubs Australia, 2015. *Responsible Gambling*, www.clubsaustralia.com.au/advocacy/policy-centre/responsible-gambling

Cohen, M., 2015. As VIP play shrinks and shifts, Morgan Stanley upbeat on global gaming. *Forbes*, 7 April, https://tinyurl.com/yxqyzpoj

Collins, P., 2013. Tacky and demeaning: football must face the truth about its gambling addiction. *Daily Mail*, 14 December, www.dailymail.co.uk/sport/football/article-2523856/PATRICK-COLLINS-Football-face-truth-gambling-addiction.html

Conolly, A., E. Fuller, H. Jones et al., 2017. *Gambling Behaviour in Great Britain in 2015: Evidence from England, Scotland and Wales*. London: National Centre for Social Research.

Copley, C., 2015. Germany rallies around Volkswagen in diesel emissions scandal. *Reuters*, 15 October, https://uk.reuters.com/article/uk-volkswagen-emissions-germany-regulati/germany-rallies-around-volkswagen-in-diesel-emissions-scandal-idUKKCN0S91AS20151015

Cosgrave, J. and T. Klassen (eds), 2009. *Casino State: Legalized Gambling in Canada*. Toronto: University of Toronto Press.

Cox, J., 2018. £30 stake limit for fixed-odds betting terminals. *Independent*, 19 March, www.independent.co.uk/news/business/news/gambling-stake-limit-30-pounds-fixed-odds-betting-terminals-commission-recommendation-addiction-a8262801.html

Crawley, M., 2017. 4 surprising things about the Ontario government's finances. *CBC News*, 16 October, www.cbc.ca/news/canada/toronto/ontario-government-revenue-kathleen-wynne-tax-1.4300960

Cremin, J., 2003. Talking shop: why Gaskell and others of his ilk cannot be replaced. *Racing Post*, 28 May.

Crouch, T., 2018a. Tracey Crouch's statement on the government response to the consultation on proposals for changes to gaming machines and social responsibility measures. Oral statement to Parliament, www.gov.uk/government/speeches/tracey-crouchs-statement-on-the-government-response-to-the-consultation-on-proposals-for-changes-to-gaming-machines-and-social-responsibility-measure

Crouch, T., 2018b. Gambling: Written question – 142403, 9 May, www.parliament.uk/business/publications/written-questions-answers-statements/written-question/Commons/2018-05-09/142403/

Cummings, L., 2002. Is UK the new gambling capital? *BBC News*, 6 October, http://news.bbc.co.uk/1/hi/business/2278853.stm

Curtis, P., 2011. Tony Blair: New Labour died when I handed over to Gordon Brown. *Guardian*, 8 July, www.theguardian.com/politics/2011/jul/08/tony-blair-new-labour-gordon-brown

Davies, M. 2010. Is everything okay, Ralph? A view from Barnes village. 2 February, http://markxdavies.blogspot.com/2010/02/is-everything-ok-ralph.html

Davies, M. 2013. Global markets, changing technology: the future of the betting industry. In R. Cassidy (ed.), *The Cambridge Companion to Horseracing*. Cambridge: Cambridge University Press, pp. 177–90.

Davies, R. 2016a. Paddy Power's £280,000 penalty equal to three hours' trading. *Guardian*, 8 March, www.theguardian.com/business/2016/mar/08/paddy-power-pre-merger-revenues-hit-850m

Davies, R. 2016b. Gambling Commission orders Betfred to pay £800,000. *Guardian*, 14 June, www.theguardian.com/society/2016/jun/14/gambling-commission-orders-betfred-to-pay-800000-pounds

Davies, R. 2017a. Gambling firm 888 penalised record £7.8m for failing vulnerable customers. *Guardian*, 31 August, www.theguardian.com/society/2017/aug/31/gambling-firm-888-fined-online-bookmaker-problem-gamblers

Davies, R. 2017b. Ladbrokes Coral hit by £2.3m penalty over rogue bets. *Guardian*, 6 November, www.theguardian.com/business/2017/nov/06/ladbrokes-coral-hit-by-23m-penalty-over-rogue-bets

Davies, R. 2018a. Labour blasts government for delays to fixed-odds betting terminal curbs. *Guardian*, 15 June, www.theguardian.com/uk-news/2018/jun/15/labour-blasts-government-for-secret-delays-to-fixed-odds-betting-terminal-curbs

Davies, R. 2018b. FOBTs row: minister quit over claim pro-gambling MP secured delay. *Guardian*, 2 November, www.theguardian.com/uk-news/2018/nov/02/fobts-row-minister-quit-over-claim-pro-gambling-mp-secured-delay

Davies, R. 2018c. Sky Bet fined £1m for failing to protect vulnerable customers. *Guardian*, 28 March, www.theguardian.com/society/2018/mar/28/sky-bet-fined-vulnerable-customers-gambling-commission

Davies, R. 2018d. Ladbrokes wooed problem gambler – then paid victims £1m. *Guardian*, 17 December, www.theguardian.com/society/2018/dec/17/ladbrokes-wooed-problem-gambler-then-paid-victims-1m

Davies, R. 2019. UK gambling firms' offer to boost levy branded a bribe. *Guardian*, 20 June, www.theguardian.com/society/2019/jun/19/top-uk-gambling-firms-offer-increase-voluntary-levy-fund-treatment-problem-gamblers

Davies, R. and S. Marsh, 2018. UK gambling regulator calls on industry to stamp out sexism. *Guardian*, 5 February, www.theguardian.com/society/2018/feb/05/uk-gambling-regulator-calls-on-industry-to-stamp-out-sexism

DCMS (Department for Culture, Media, Digital and Sport) 2002. *A Safe Bet for Success – Modernising Britain's Gambling Law*, Cm. 5397, www.gov.uk/government/publications/modernising-britains-gambling-laws-draft-gambling-bill

DCMS (Department for Culture, Media, Digital and Sport) 2003. *The Future Regulation of Remote Gambling: A DCMS Position Paper*. London: DCMS.

DDCMS (Department for Digital, Culture, Media and Sport), 2018a. Government to cut fixed odds betting terminals maximum stake from £100 to £2. Press release, 17 May, www.gov.uk/government/news/government-to-cut-fixed-odds-betting-terminals-maximum-stake-from-100-to-2

DDCMS (Department for Digital, Culture, Media and Sport), 2018b. *Government Response to the Consultation on Proposals for Changes to Gaming Machines and Social Responsibility Measures*. May, https://assets.publishing.service.gov.uk/government/uploads/system/uploads/attachment_data/file/707815/Government_response_to_the_consultation_on_proposals_for_changes_to_gaming_machines_and_social_responsibility_measures.pdf

DDCMS (Department for Digital, Culture, Media and Sport), 2018c. Tracey Crouch's statement on the Government Response to the Consultation on proposals for changes to Gaming Machines and Social Responsibility Measures. 17 May, www.gov.uk/government/speeches/tracey-crouchs-statement-on-the-government-response-to-the-consultation-on proposals-for-changes-to-gaming-machines-and-social-responsibility-measure

Djohari, N., G. Weston, R. Cassidy, M. Wemyss and S. Thomas, 2019. Recall and awareness of gambling advertising and sponsorship in sport in the UK: a study of young people and adults. *Harm Reduction Journal* 16(24): 1–12.

Dodds, A., 2006. The core executive's approach to regulation: from 'better regulation' to 'risk-tolerant deregulation'. *Social Policy & Administration* 40(5): 526–42.

Donoughue, S., 2019. The system is broken. *Gambling Insider*, March/April: 46–7.

Douglas, T., 2004. Papers turn on gambling law change. *BBC News*, 28 October, http://news.bbc.co.uk/1/hi/entertainment/3963307.stm

Doward, J., 1999. A rock and a hard place for betting. *Observer*, 14 November, www.theguardian.com/business/1999/nov/14/gibraltar.internationalnews

Doward, J., 2000. A rock and a cheap flutter. *Observer*, 24 September, www.theguardian.com/technology/2000/sep/24/business.theobserver

Downs, C., 2010. Mecca and the birth of commercial bingo 1958–70: a case study. *Business History* 52(7): 1086–106.

Ebrahimi, H., 2012. Ladbrokes fires digital director Richard Ames over botched strategy. *Telegraph*, 30 July, www.telegraph.co.uk/finance/newsbysector/retailandconsumer/9436936/Ladbrokes-fires-digital-director-Richard-Ames-over-botched-strategy.html

ECJ (European Court of Justice), 1994. Case C-275/92, Her Majesty's Customs and Excise v. Gerhart Schindler and Jörg Schindler, ECR I-1039.

ECJ (European Court of Justice), 2003. Case C-243/01, Criminal Proceedings against Piergiorgio Gambelli and Others, ECR 1-13031.

Economist Daily Chart, 2017. The world's biggest gamblers: Australia was the first country to deregulate gambling, and it shows. 9 February, https://tinyurl.com/yy5u2vcx

EGR Magazine, 2012. Ralph Topping. *EGR Magazine*, September.

Elliott, L., 2001. How Thatcher stumbled on her Big Idea. *Guardian*, 20 March, www.theguardian.com/society/2001/mar/20/5

Ellson, A., 2018. World Cup kicks off a £2.5bn betting splurge. *The Times*, 25 June, www.thetimes.co.uk/article/world-cup-kicks-off-a-2-5bn-betting-splurge-qgx8prl5m

ERC (European Research Council), 2015, *Turning the Tables: Researching Gambling Research*. 12 March, https://erc.europa.eu/projects-figures/stories/turning-tables-researching-gambling-research

Erdoes, R., 1994. *Lame Deer, Seeker of Visions*. New York: Simon and Schuster.

Evans, C., 2014. Betting shops, single staffing. Westminster Hall Debate, 5 February, www.theyworkforyou.com/whall/?id=2014-02-05b.99.0

Evans, R., 2002. Bookmakers close ranks. *Telegraph*, 9 September, www.telegraph.co.uk/sport/horseracing/3034168/Bookmakers-close-ranks.html

Ewens, J., 2018. Industry urged to keep regulation from 'emotional' politicians. *Gambling Compliance*, 11 September, https://gamblingcompliance.com/premium-content/insights_analysis/industry-urged-keep-regulation-emotional-politicians

Filby, E., 2013. Margaret Thatcher: her unswerving faith shaped by her father. *Telegraph*, 14 April, http://tinyurl.com/dywheld

Findlay, J., 1986. *People of Chance: Gambling in American Society from Jamestown to Las Vegas*. New York: Oxford University Press.

Ford, J., 2019. The troubling legacy of Britain's gambling experiment. *Financial Times*, 19 July, www.ft.com/content/cde538be-a821-11e9-b6ee-3cdf3174eb89

Foucault, M., 1970. *The Order of Things*. London: Pantheon.

Freedland, J., Football is addicted to gambling – and it's harming children. *Guardian*, 13 February, www.theguardian.com/commentisfree/2019/feb/13/protect-children-gambling-ads-football-target

Gambling Commission, 2018a. *Gambling Participation in 2017: Behaviour, Awareness and Attitudes*, Annual Report, February, www.gamblingcommission.gov.uk/PDF/survey-data/Gambling-participation-in-2017-behaviour-awareness-and-attitudes.pdf

Gambling Commission, 2018b. *Young People and Gambling 2018*. Birmingham: Gambling Commission.

Gambling Commission, 2019a. *Industry Statistics, April 2016 to March 2018*. Birmingham: Gambling Commission.

Gambling Commission, 2019b. Gambling Commission Industry Statistics – May 2019. Birmingham: Gambling Commission, www.gamblingcommission.gov.uk/Docs/Gambling-industry-statistics.xlsx

Gambling Online Magazine, 2008. Bookies breathe easy despite smoking ban. 1 July, www.gamblingonlinemagazine.com/gambling-news-detail.php?articleID=703

Gambling Review Body, 2001. *Gambling Review Report* (Budd Report), Cm. 5206, July. London: Department for Culture, Media and Sport.

GamblingCompliance, 2018. *UK Online Gambling: Data Forecasting and Market Shares*. London.

GamblingData, 2011. *In-play Betting Report*. London: GamblingData.

GamblingData, 2012. *Regulated European Online Markets Data Report*. https://tinyurl.com/y46zg7bj

Gaming Intelligence, 2018. Responsible gambling operator of the year: NO ONE. 6 February, www.gamingintelligence.com/business/46172-responsible-gambling-operator-of-the-year-no-one

Gannagé-Stewart, H., 2018. Africa: dig for opportunities and strike gold. 9 May, www.igbaffiliate.com/articles/africa-dig-opportunities-and-strike-gold

Ge, C. ,2016. Wynn Macau, Sands China and Melco Crown Entertainment, three of Asia's biggest casino operators, all reported recovering businesses for high rollers in 2016. *South China Morning Post*, 20 July, https://tinyurl.com/yyudtmzw

Geertz, C., 1973. Deep play: notes on the Balinese cockfight. In C. Geertz (ed.), *The Interpretation of Cultures*. New York: Basic Books, pp. 412–53.

Gibbs, E., 2019a. Gambling trade associations in UK join forces. 25 February, https://calvinayre.com/2019/02/25/business/gambling-trade-associations-uk-join-forces/

Gibbs, E., 2019b. Two UK gaming groups to be dissolved as a new one emerges. 4 July, https://calvinayre.com/2019/07/04/business/two-uk-gaming-groups-to-be-dissolved-as-a-new-one-emerges/

Goffman, E., 1967. *Interaction Ritual: Essays on Face-to-face Interaction*. Oxford, UK: Aldine

Goodale, J.C., 1987. 'Gambling is hard work': card playing in Tiwi society. *Oceania* 58(1): 6–21.

Goodwin, B., M. Browne, M. Rockloff and J. Rose. 2017. A typical problem gambler affects six others. *International Gambling Studies* 17(2): 276–89,

Graeber, D., 2011. *Debt: The First 5,000 Years*. London: First Melville Books.

Grierson, J., 2016. Paddy Power founder lobbied against fixed-odds terminals. *Guardian*, 5 December, www.theguardian.com/society/2016/dec/05/paddy-power-founder-lobbied-against-fixed-odds-terminals

GVC, 2019. *Capital Markets Day*. 16 May. https://gvc-plc.com/wp-content/uploads/2019/05/2019-GVC-Capital-Markets-Day-Presentation.pdf

Habib, T., 2012. Welcome to Ghas Mandi: Asia's largest gambling den. *Pakistan Today*, 25 July, www.pakistantoday.com.pk/2012/07/25/welcome-to-ghas-mandi-asias-largest-gambling-den/

Haigh, P., 2002. Are you collaborating with this virtual abomination? *Racing Post*, 3 May.

Hancock, L. and G. Smith, 2017. Critiquing the Reno Model I-IV international influence on regulators and governments (2004–2015) – the distorted reality of 'responsible gambling'. *International Journal of Mental Health and Addiction*. Advance online publication, doi: 10.1007/s11469-017-9746-y

Hansard (1960) Betting and Gaming Bill. *Hansard* vol. 623, 11 May, https://hansard.parliament.uk/Commons/1960-05-11/debates/0c227af7-f68c-47d4-bcf7-125acb241071/BettingAndGamingBill

Hansard (1995) Lord Gisborough in HL Deb., 22 November. *Hansard* vol. 567, cols 298–300, https://publications.parliament.uk/pa/ld199596/ldhansrd/vo951122/text/51122-02.htm

Hansard (2013) Minister of State Hugh Robertson, Culture Media and Sport, oral answers to questions, 10 January. *Hansard* vol. 556, https://hansard.parliament.uk/Commons/2013-01-10/debates/13011036000009/CultureMediaAndSport

Hariyadi, M., 2018. Christian couple sentenced to flogging for gambling in Aceh. 28 February, www.asianews.it/news-en/Christian-couple-sentenced-to-flogging-for-gambling-in-Aceh-43223.html

Hastings, G., M. Stead, L. McDermott, A. Forsyth, A. MacKintosh, M. Rayner et al. 2003. *Review of Research on the Effects of Food Promotion to Children: Final Report and Appendices.* Food Standards Agency, www.food.gov.uk/multimedia/pdfs/foodpromotiontochildren1.pdf

Hastings, G., O. Brooks, M. Stead, K. Angus, T. Anker and T. Farrell, 2010. Failure of self-regulation of UK alcohol advertising. *British Medical Journal* 340. https://doi.org/10.1136/bmj.b5650

Hattersley, R., 2004. Betraying the values my party stood for. *Daily Mail*, 15 October, www.dailymail.co.uk/news/article-322008/Gambling-futures.html

Hey, S., 2001. When the bookies hit the jackpot, *Independent*, 27 April.

Hey, S., 2008. Our national love affair: a history of the betting shop. *Independent*, 5 April, www.independent.co.uk/sport/racing/our-national-love-affair-a-history-of-the-betting-shop-804966.html

HM Customs & Excise, 2003. *The Modernisation of Gambling Taxes: A Report on the Evaluation of the Gross Profits Tax on Betting.* London: The Stationery Office.

HM Treasury, 2013. Gambling tax: new rules and sanctions to prevent avoidance by gambling companies. News story, 16 August, www.gov.uk/government/news/gambling-tax-new-rules-and-sanctions-to-prevent-avoidance-by-gambling-companies

Ho, C., 2016. Senate Republicans revive legislation to ban online gambling. *Washington Post*, 28 September, https://tinyurl.com/y3fboctj

Ho, J., 2013. Macau at odds over responsible gambling. *South China Morning Post*, 24 May, www.scmp.com/news/hong-kong/article/1244405/macau-odds-over-responsible-gambling

Hodgins, D.C., J.N. Stea and J.E. Grant, 2011. Gambling disorders. *Lancet* 378: 1874–84.

Horowitz, R., 2013. *America's Right Anti-establishment Conservatism: From Goldwater to the Tea Party.* Cambridge: Polity.

House of Commons Culture, Media and Sport Committee, 2012a. *The Gambling Act 2005: A Bet Worth Taking?* First Report of Session 2012–13, vol. 1, https://publications.parliament.uk/pa/cm201213/cmselect/cmcumeds/421/421.pdf

House of Commons Culture, Media and Sport Committee, 2012b. Minutes of Evidence HC 421, https://publications.parliament.uk/pa/cm201213/cmselect/cmcumeds/421/120112.htm

House of Lords, 2004. Improving the framework of regulation. Chapter 8 in *Select Committee on Constitution Sixth Report*, https://publications.parliament.uk/pa/ld200304/ldselect/ldconst/68/6810.htm

Huggins, M., 2000. *Flat Racing and British Society 1790-1914: A Social and Economic History*. Sport in the Global Society. Portland, OR: Frank Cass.

Huggins, M., 2003. *Horseracing and the British 1919–1939*. Manchester: Manchester University Press.

Humphreys, B., B. Soebbing, H. Wynne, J. Turvey and Y. Lee, 2011. *University of Alberta SEIGA Research Team: Final Report to the Alberta Gaming Research Institute on the Socio-economic Impact of Gambling in Alberta*, https://dspace.ucalgary.ca/handle/1880/48545

Hurt, C., 2005. Regulating public morals and private markets: online securities trading, internet gambling and the speculation paradox. *Boston University Law Review* 86: 371–441.

iGaming Business, 2008. Intertops toasts 25 years of trustworthy gambling. *iGaming Business*, 26 March, www.igamingbusiness.com/intertops-toasts-25-years-trustworthy-gambling%C2%A0

Jack, S., 2019. Bookmakers pledge £100m to avoid gambling crackdown. *BBC News*, 19 June. www.bbc.co.uk/news/business-48690743

Jackson, L., 2015. Live betting explosion at Bet365. 6 July, www.online-betting.me.uk/news/bet365-reveal-80-of-sports-betting-revenue-comesfrom-live-in-play-betting.html

Janower, C., 1996. Gambling on the internet. *Computer Mediated Communication* 2(2), https://onlinelibrary.wiley.com/doi/full/10.1111/j.1083-6101.1996.tb00054.x#fn1

Jensen, C., 2017. Money over misery: restrictive gambling legislation in an era of liberalization. *Journal of European Public Policy* 24(1): 119–34.

Joint Committee on the Draft Gambling Bill, 2003–4. Session 2003–04, vol. 1, Stationery Office, p. 60, https://publications.parliament.uk/pa/jt200304/jtselect/jtgamb/63/6309.htm

Jones, B., 2018. The online gaming industry is going up, up and away. *Gambling Insider*, 20 August, www.gamblinginsider.com/in-depth/5770/the-online-gaming-industry-is-going-up-up-and-away

Jowell, T., 2002. Licensing and gambling reform. Talk to the British Institute of Sport and Leisure Annual Conference at the Royal Lancaster Hotel, 20 November, www.tourismalliance.com/downloads/Tessa%20Jowell%20Speech.doc

Judt, T., 1998. The Third Way is no route to paradise. *New York Times*, 27 September, www.nytimes.com/1998/09/27/opinion/the-third-way-is-no-route-to-paradise.html

Karlsson, A. and A. Håkansson, 2018. Gambling disorder, increased mortality, suicidality, and associated comorbidity: a longitudinal nationwide register study. *Journal of Behavioral Addictions* 7(4): 1091–9.

Katz, R., 2019. The Supreme Court has undone a century of American opposition to sports gambling. *The Nation*, 25 February, www.thenation.com/article/sports-gambling-supreme-court-betting/

Keneally, P., 2017. Australia gripped by poker machine addiction. *Guardian*, 14 December, www.theguardian.com/australia-news/2017/dec/14/australia-gripped-by-poker-machine-addiction-report-says

KeytoCasino, 2015. Online gambling access around the world. 11 May, www. keytocasino.com/en/article/online-gambling-access-around-the-world.html

Kilsby, J., 2008. Antigua added to UK gambling 'whitelist'. *GamblingCompliance*, 5 November, https://gamblingcompliance.com/premium-content/insights_ analysis/antigua-added-uk-gambling-%E2%80%98whitelist%E2%80%99

King, L., 2011. Side-stepping the censors: the failure of self-regulation for junk food advertising. *The Conversation*, 26 June, https://theconversation.com/ side-stepping-the-censors-the-failure-of-self-regulation-for-junk-food-advertising-2006

Kingma, S. 2008. The liberalization and (re)regulation of Dutch gambling markets: national consequences of the changing European context. *Regulation & Governance* 2(4): 445–58.

Kite, M., 2004. 'Opponents of new gambling law are snobs', says Tessa Jowell. *Telegraph*, 24 October, www.telegraph.co.uk/news/uknews/1474933/Opponents-of-new-gambling-law-are-snobs-says-Tessa-Jowell.html

Knights, D., 1997. Governmentality and financial services: welfare crises and the financially self-disciplined subject. In G. Morgan and D. Knights (eds), *Regulation and Deregulation in European Financial Services*. London: Macmillan, pp. 216–36.

Kohler, D., 2016. On the regressivity of gambling taxes in Switzerland. *Swiss Journal of Economics Statistics* 152: 193.

Kollewe, J., 2019. Gambling regulator warns firms over use of gagging orders. *Guardian*, 31 January, www.theguardian.com/society/2019/jan/31/gambling-regulator-warns-firms-over-use-of-gagging-orders

Krugman, P., 2009. Reagan did it. *New York Times*, 31 May, www.nytimes. com/2009/06/01/opinion/01krugman.html?_r=2&

Kyodo, 2016. Why Singapore is seen as the model for Japan's casino gamble. *South China Morning Post*, 19 December, www.scmp.com/news/asia/east-asia/article/2055702/why-singapore-seen-model-japans-casino-gamble

Ladbrokes, 2006. *Responsible Business: Performance Report 2006*. Harrow: Ladbrokes, www.ladbrokesplc.com/~/media/Files/L/Ladbrokes-V2/responsible-business-downloads/csr-report-2006.pdf

Ladbrokes, 2016. *Fair Play. Performance Update. Corporate Responsibility Report.* Harrow: Ladbrokes, https://gvc-plc.com/wp-content/uploads/2018/03/ladbrokes-coral-cr-report-2016.pdf

Lancet. 2017. Problem gambling is a public health concern. *Lancet*, 309(10098): 913.

Langham E., H. Thorne, M. Browne, P. Donaldson, J. Rose and M. Rockloff. 2016. Understanding gambling related harm: a proposed definition, conceptual framework, and taxonomy of harms. *BMC Public Health*. 2016;16:23.

Lazzarato, M. 2009. Neoliberalism in action: inequality, insecurity and the reconstitution of the social. *Theory, Culture & Society* 26: 109–33.

Littler, A., 2007. The regulation of gambling at European level: the balance to be found. *ERA Forum* 8(3): 357–71.

Livingstone, C., 2018. A case for clean conferences. *Drug and Alcohol Review* 37(5): 683–6.

Livingstone, C., A. Rintoul and L. Francis, 2014. What is the evidence for harm minimisation measures in gambling venues? *Evidence Base* 2: 1–24.

Livingstone, C., A. Rintoul, C. de Lacy-Vawdon, R. Borland, P. Dietze, T. Jenkinson et al. 2019. *Identifying Effective Policy Interventions to Prevent Gambling-related Harm*. Melbourne: Victorian Responsible Gambling Foundation.

Louie, S. 2014. Asian gambling addiction. *Psychology Today*, 10 July, www.psychologytoday.com/gb/blog/minority-report/201407/asian-gambling-addiction

Lund, E., 2018. The re-regulation of the Swedish gambling market explained. 1 August, www.gambling.com/news/the-re-regulation-of-the-swedish-gambling-market-explained-1512200

Lundh, A., J. Lexchin, B. Mintzes, J. Schroll and L. Bero, 2017. Industry sponsorship and research outcome. *Cochrane Database Systematic Review*, 16 February: 2.

Mackenzie, D., 2008. *An Engine Not a Camera: How Financial Models Shape Markets*. Cambridge, MA: MIT Press.

Markham, F., M. Young and B. Doran, 2016. The relationship between player losses and gambling-related harm: evidence from nationally representative cross-sectional surveys in four countries. *Addiction* 111: 320–30.

Massachusetts Gaming Commission, 2015. Expanded Gaming Act, http://massgaming.com/about/expanded-gaming-act/

MF, 2017. How bookmakers deal with winning customers. *The Economist*, 4 October, www.economist.com/the-economist-explains/2017/10/04/how-bookmakers-deal-with-winning-customers

Miers, D., 2004. *Regulating Commercial Gambling: Past, Present and Future*. Oxford Socio-Legal Studies. Oxford: Oxford University.

Miles, T., 2018. Antigua 'losing all hope' of U.S. payout in gambling dispute. 22 June, www.reuters.com/article/uk-usa-trade-antigua/antigua-losing-all-hope-of-u-s-payout-in-gambling-dispute-idUSKBN1JI0VZ

Ministry of Health, 2014. *Roles*. 19 March, www.health.govt.nz/our-work/mental-health-and-addictions/gambling/strategic-direction-overview/roles

Mitchell, T., 1991. The limits of the state: beyond statist approaches and their critics. *American Political Science Review* 85(1): 77–96.

Monaghan, A., 2018. William Hill fined £6.2m by Gambling Commission. *Guardian*, 20 February, www.theguardian.com/business/2018/feb/20/william-hill-fined-62m-by-gambling-commission

Morgan Stanley, 2015. *Morgan Stanley Global Gaming Report 2015*. http://docslide.us/data-analytics/morgan-stanley-global-gaming-report-2015.html

Murphy, S., 2012. When going to work is far from a safe bet. *Guardian*, 11 May, www.theguardian.com/money/2012/may/11/work-safety-betting-shop-staff

Nash, R., 2013. Sporting with kings. In R. Cassidy (ed.), *The Cambridge Companion to Horseracing*. Cambridge: Cambridge University Press, pp. 13–25.

New Zealand Ministry of Health. 2015. *Strategy to Prevent and Minimise Gambling Harm 2016/17 to 2018/19: Consultation Document*. Wellington: Ministry of Health.

Newall, P., 2015. How bookies make your money. *Judgment and Decision Making* 10(3): 225–31.

Newman, O., 1968. The sociology of the betting shop. *British Journal of Sociology* 19: 17–35.

Nicoll, F., 2013. Finopower: governing intersections between gambling and finance. *Communication and Critical/Cultural Studies* 10(4): 385–405.

Nicoll, F., 2019. *Gambling in Everyday Life: Spaces, Moments and Products of Enjoyment*. New York: Routledge.

Nolan, K., 2015. Neoliberal common sense and race-neutral discourses: a critique of 'evidence-based' policy-making in school policing. *Discourse: Studies in the Cultural Politics of Education* 36(6): 894–907.

Oakley, R., 2016. The turf: on the money. *The Spectator*, 25 June, www.questia.com/magazine/1P3-4097182881/the-turf-on-the-money

O'Connor, N., 2017. A short history of the betting exchange industry. www.bettingmarket.com/refraichiro10388.htm All Rights Reserved.

Orford, J., 2012. Gambling in Britain: the application of restraint erosion theory. *Addiction* 107: 2082–6.

Orford, J., H. Wardle and M.D. Griffiths, 2013. What proportion of gambling is problem gambling? Estimates from the 2010 British Gambling Prevalence Survey. *International Gambling Studies* 13: 4–18.

Patel, J., 2018. LeoVegas Italy MD exclusive: 'Ad ban is insane and goes against EU law'. *Gambling Insider*, 29 August, www.gamblinginsider.com/news/5809/leovegas-italy-md-exclusive-ad-ban-is-insane-and-goes-against-eu-law

Paton, D., D.S. Siegel and L. Vaughan Williams, 2002. A policy response to the e-commerce revolution: the case of betting taxation in the UK. *Economic Journal* 112(480): F296–F314.

Paton, D., D.S. Siegel and L. Vaughan Williams, 2004. Taxation and the demand for gambling: new evidence from the United Kingdom. *National Tax Journal* 57(4): 847–61.

Payne, T., 2019. Gamblers paid to keep betting: UK's top online betting firm Bet365 gives losers CASH so they carry on spending, undercover investigation finds. *Daily Mail*, 17 February, www.dailymail.co.uk/news/article-6715159/Addicts-paid-gambling-UKs-online-betting-firm-Bet365-gives-losers-cash.html

Peev, G., 2012. High stakes machines in bookies lead to violence, claims gambling boss who helped introduce them to high street. *Daily Mail*, 1 November.

Pempus, B., 2015. Morgan Stanley nearly cuts in half U.S. internet gambling market estimate. *Card Player*, 31 March, https://tinyurl.com/y3dzrdy6

Percy, J., 2011. Bookies need respect too. 10 November, www.progressonline.org.uk/2011/11/10/bookies-need-respect-too/

Pickles, A., 2014. Introduction: gambling as analytic in Melanesia. *Oceania* 84: 207–21.

Piketty, T., 2014. *Capital in the Twenty-first Century*, trans. A. Goldhammer. Boston, MA: Harvard University Press.

Pitt, A., 2012. A study of gamblers and gaming culture in London, c. 1780–1844. MA thesis, University of York.

Pitt, C., 2013. Reflections draw on global phenomenon. *BOS Magazine*, March/April, http://content.yudu.com/A23ur1/bosmagmarapr13/resources/19.htm

Pomfret, J., 2002. China's high rollers find a seat at table – in Vegas. *Washington Post*, 26 March, https://tinyurl.com/y20qe492

Preda, A. 2009. *Framing Finance: The Boundaries of Markets and Modern Capitalism*. Chicago and London: University of Chicago Press.

Press Association, 2012. Harman, Blunkett: Labour gambling move wrong. *The Christian Institute*, 6 August, http://tinyurl.com/khjppw4

Press Releases, 2017. The park is open. Microgaming celebrates Jurassic World on Day 1 of ICE 2017. 7 February, https://calvinayre.com/2017/02/07/press-releases/the-park-is-open-microgaming-celebrates-jurassic-world-on-day-1-of-ice-2017/

Productivity Commission, 2010. *Gambling: Productivity Commission Inquiry Report.* Report no. 50. Canberra: Productivity Commission.

Puri, S., 2014. *Speculation in Fixed Futures: An Ethnography of Betting in between Legal and Illegal Economies at the Delhi Racecourse.* Københavns Universitet, Det Humanistiske Fakultet.

Queensland Government, 2015. *Australian/New Zealand Gaming Machine National Standard* § 3.3, https://publications.qld.gov.au/dataset/a-nz-gaming-machine-national-standards/resource/5904c4d0-19ea-4769-ae25-fa2605a8c9f2

Quinn, B. and G. Wilson, 2007. Gordon Brown scraps super-casinos. *Daily Telegraph*, 12 July.

Racing Post Staff, 1998. Anthony O'Hara, nominee, Betting Office Manager of the Year, 30 November.

Ramesh, R., 2013. High-stakes gambling machines 'suck money from poorest communities'. *Guardian*, 4 January, www.theguardian.com/uk/2013/jan/04/fixed-odds-betting-terminals-poorest-communities

Reith, G., 2004. Gambling and the contradictions of consumption: a genealogy of the 'pathological' subject. *American Behavioural Scientist* 51(1): 33–55.

Rennie, D., 2001. Chinese drug addiction 'in the genes'. *Daily Telegraph*, 15 March, https://tinyurl.com/yxuungzs

Richards, R., 2019. William Hill, MGM resorts committed to U.S. sports betting, 7 July, https://ats.io/news/william-hill-mgm-resorts-committed-to-u-s-sports-betting/3587/

Riches, D., 1975. Cash, credit and gambling in a modern Eskimo economy: speculations on origins of spheres of economic exchange. *Man* 10(1): 21–33.

Rintoul, A. and J. Deblaquiere, 2019. *Gambling in Suburban Australia*, Research Report. Melbourne: Australian Institute of Family Studies.

Rock, G., 2001. Gambling a-gogo. *Guardian*, 29 April, www.theguardian.com/sport/2001/apr/29/comment.theobserver

Rose, N., 1999. *Powers of Freedom: Reframing Political Thought.* Cambridge: Cambridge University Press.

Rose, N., 2003. Gambling and the law: the new millennium. In: G. Reith (ed.), *Gambling: Who Wins? Who Loses?* New York: Prometheus, pp. 113–31.

Rossow, I. and M.B. Hansen, 2016. Gambling and gambling policy in Norway–an exceptional case. *Addiction* 111: 593–8.

Rowlatt, S., 1933. *Final Report of the Royal Commission on Lotteries and Betting 1932–3*, Cmd 4341. London: HMSO.

Rudgard, O., 2019. Social media giants face US grilling over failure to protect children. *Telegraph*, 10 July, www.telegraph.co.uk/technology/2019/07/10/social-media-giants-face-us-grilling-failure-protect-children/

Sahlins, M., 2008. *The Western Illusion of Human Nature.* Chicago: Prickly Paradigm Press.

Sallaz, J., 2009. *The Labor of Luck: Casino Capitalism in the United States and South Africa*. Berkeley: University of California Press.

SBC News, 2014. William Hill's single manning trial comes under scrutiny. 12 August, www.sbcnews.co.uk/retail/2014/08/12/uk-mps-attack-william-hills-retail-employee-policies/#ixzz3LPJCaUBl.

Schüll, N., 2005. Digital gambling: the coincidence of desire and design. *Annals of the American Academy of Political and Social Science* 597: 65–81.

Schüll, N., 2012. *Addiction by Design: Machine Gambling in Las Vegas*. Princeton, NJ: Princeton University Press.

Schüll, N., 2013. Turning the tables: the global gambling industry's crusade to sell slots in Macau. In R. Cassidy, A. Pisac and C. Loussouarn (eds), *Qualitative Research in Gambling*. New York: Routledge, pp. 92–106.

Schwartz, D., 2006. *Roll the Bones: The History of Gambling*. New York: Gotham.

Scott, A., 2015. Keeping Macau responsible. *World Gaming Magazine*, https://fba. um.edu.mo/keeping-macau-responsible/

Select Committee on the European Union, 2017. Uncorrected oral evidence: Brexit: Gibraltar. http://data.parliament.uk/writtenevidence/committee evidence.svc/evidencedocument/european-union-committee/brexit-gibraltar/ oral/46200.html

Sherwell, P. and P. Hennessy, 2006. Prescott did talk about casinos says Done. *Telegraph*, 16 July, www.telegraph.co.uk/news/uknews/1524035/Prescott-did-talk-about-casinos-says-Dome-firm.html

Shore, C. and S. Wright, 2015. Governing by numbers: audit culture, rankings and the new world order. *Social Anthropology* 23(1): 22–8.

Sidney, C., 1976. *The Art of Legging*. London: Maxline International.

Silver, A., 2014. Legalize and regulate sports betting. *New York Times*, 13 November, www.nytimes.com/2014/11/14/opinion/nba-commissioner-adam-silver-legalize-sports-betting.html

Singh, N., 2018. Thane anti-extortion cell nabs Sonu Jalan, India's leading cricket bookie. 29 May, www.dnaindia.com/india/report-thane-anti-extortion-cell-nabs-sonu-jalan-india-s-leading-cricket-bookie-2620071

Sky News, 2014. World Cup betting set to smash £1bn barrier. 11 July, http://news. sky.com/story/1299404/world-cup-betting-set-to-smash-1bn-barrier

Smith, K., 2013. *Beyond Evidence-based Policy in Public Health: The Interplay of Ideas*. Basingstoke: Palgrave Macmillan.

Smith, S.W., C.K. Atkin and J. Roznowski, 2006. Are 'drink responsibly' alcohol campaigns strategically ambiguous? *Health Communication* 20(1): 1–11.

Smurthwaite, T., 2000. How big a gamble is the zero-tax plan? Economists evaluate John Brown's call for punters' deductions to be abolished. *Racing Post*, 3 February, www.thefreelibrary.com/How+big+a+gamble+is+the+zero-tax+pla n%3F%3B+Economists+evaluate+John...-a060968396

Steinmetz, A., 1870. *The Gaming Table: Its Votaries and Victims, in All Times and Countries, Especially in England and in France*. London: Tinsley Brothers.

Steketee, M., 2016. Gambling pays off ... for Australian governments, *ABC News*, 16 July, www.abc.net.au/news/2015-07-17/steketee-gambling-pays-off-for-australian-governments/6625170

Stocks, T., 2015. Red roses and slain dragons. Presentation, 23 April, https://docplayer.net/5662945-Red-roses-and-slain-dragons-a-presentation-by-tim-stocks-chairman-james-stocks-co-and-partner-taylor-wessing-llp.html

Stradbrooke, S., 2013. Online gambling companies ponder future as UK gov't confirms 15% POC tax. 16 August, https://calvinayre.com/2013/08/16/business/uk-govt-confirms-online-gambling-point-of-consumption-tax/

Stradbrooke, S., 2016. Crown Resorts hires legal team to probe liability over China arrests. 25 November, https://calvinayre.com/2016/11/25/casino/crown-resorts-legal-review-liability-china-arrests/

Stradbrooke, S., 2018a. Italy's gambling ad ban won't apply to existing contracts. 2 July,https://calvinayre.com/2018/07/02/business/italy-gambling-ad-ban-carveout-existing-contracts/

Stradbrooke, S., 2018b. Vietnam identifies first casino to take part in locals gambling trial. 18 June, https://calvinayre.com/2018/06/18/casino/vietnam-first-casino-locals-gambling-trial/

Strathern, M. (ed.), 2000. *Audit Cultures: Anthropological Studies in Accountability, Ethics, and the Academy*. London: Routledge.

Sweney, M., 2013. TV gambling ads have risen 600% since law change. *Guardian*, 19 November, www.theguardian.com/media/2013/nov/19/tv-gambling-ads

Sylvester, R., 2014. Stop bombarding our kids with betting ads. *The Times*, 29 July.

Tattersalls, 2018. *October Yearling Sale Book 1*. www.tattersalls.com/october1-sale-overview.php

Tempest, M., 2004. MPs: 'Bill will increase problem gambling'. *Guardian*, 7 April.

Thomas, A., 2014. Is horse racing entering the final furlong? *Telegraph*, 23 August, www.telegraph.co.uk/finance/newsbysector/retailandconsumer/leisure/11052183/Is-horse-racing-entering-the-final-furlong.html

Thomas, P., 2002. The worst job I ever had – virtually, that is. *Racing Post*, 5 July.

Thomas, W., 1901. The gaming instinct. *American Journal of Sociology* 6: 750–63.

Thorley, C., A. Stirling and E. Huynh, 2016. *Cards on the Table: The Cost to Government Associated with People Who Are Problem Gamblers in Britain*. London: IPPR.

Tomiyama, A., 2017. Vietnam to legalize gambling by locals next month. *Nikkei*, 17 February, https://asia.nikkei.com/Economy/Vietnam-to-legalize-gambling-by-locals-next-month

Travis, A., 2001. Britain set to embrace 'Las Vegas' gambling. *Guardian*, 18 July, www.theguardian.com/uk/2001/jul/18/alantravis

Treanor, J., 2013. Farewell to the FSA – and the bleak legacy of the light-touch regulator. *Guardian*, 24 March, www.theguardian.com/business/2013/mar/24/farewell-fsa-bleak-legacy-light-touch-regulator

United States Treasury Department 2006. *Unlawful Internet Gambling Enforcement Act, Examination Handbook Section 770*. https://occ.gov/static/ots/exam-handbook/ots-exam-handbook-770p.pdf

Vockeroth, B., 2014. New centre to analyze problem gambling. University of British Columbia News, 12 November, https://news.ubc.ca/2014/11/12/new-centre-to-analyze-problem-gambling/

Walsh, D., 2003. Betting terminals odds on for clearance. *The Times*, 20 November, www.thetimes.co.uk/article/betting-terminals-odds-on-for-clearance-sc7wf3cq2zo

Wardle, H., C. Seabury, H. Ahmed, C. Payne, C. Bryon, J. Corbett et al., 2014. *Gambling Behaviour in England and Scotland: Findings from the Health Survey for England 2012 and Scottish Health Survey 2012*. London: The Gambling Commission.

Webb, D., 2017. Sponsored post: Derek Webb: The bookies' trade body desperately attacks the Centre for Social Justice over its FOBT report. *Conservative Home*, 23 August, www.conservativehome.com/sponsored/2017/08/sponsored-post-derek-webb-the-bookies-trade-body-desperately-attacks-the-centre-for-social-justice-over-its-fobt-report.html

Weiner, B., R. Perry and J. Magnusson, 1988. An attributional analysis of reactions to stigmas. *Journal of Personal and Social Psychology* 55(5): 738–48.

Weir, S., 1999. The City has taken over the quangos under New Labour. *Independent*, 23 November, www.independent.co.uk/arts-entertainment/the-city-has-taken-over-the-quangos-under-new-labour-1128029.html

Weissmann, J., 2014. Is illegal sports betting a $400 billion industry? *Slate*, 21 November, https://tinyurl.com/y7e8qqnv

Wiesmann, G., 2011. Betfair files German states monopoly complaint. *Financial Times*, 3 July, www.ft.com/content/acbcofbc-a598-11e0-83b2-00144feabdco

William Hill, 2018. *Capital Markets Day*, 6 November, www.williamhillplc.com/media/12685/capital-markets-rns-6-november-2018.pdf

William Hill, 2019. *Final Results 53 Weeks ended 1 January 2019*, 1 March, www.williamhillplc.com/media/12911/wmh-2018-full-year-results-presentation-1-mar-19.pdf

Williams, R.J. and R.T. Wood, 2016. What proportion of gambling revenue is derived from problem gamblers? Communication presented at the Alberta Gambling Research Institute Conference, Banff, https://prism.ucalgary.ca/bitstream/handle/1880/51141/Williams_AGRI2016_What_Proportion_of_Gambling_Revenue_is_Derived_from_PG.pdf;jsessionid=390CD0D05C2C9316A233B27C8AC68DF7?sequence=18

Williams, R.J., Y. Belanger and J. Arthur, 2011. *Gambling in Alberta: History, Current Status, and Socioeconomic Impacts*. Edmonton, AB: Report prepared for the Alberta Gambling Research Institute.

Williams, R.J., B.L. West and R.I. Simpson, 2012. *Prevention of Problem Gambling: A Comprehensive Review of the Evidence and Identified Best Practices*. Report prepared for the Ontario Problem Gambling Research Centre and the Ontario Ministry of Health and Long Term Care, www.uleth.ca/dspace/handle/10133/3121.

Williams, R.J., R.A. Volberg, R.M.G. Stevens, L.A. Williams and J.N. Arthur, 2017. *The Definition, Dimensionalization, and Assessment of Gambling Participation*. Report prepared for the Canadian Consortium for Gambling Research, 1 February.

Willink, H., 1951. *Report of the Royal Commission on Betting, Lotteries and Gaming, 1949-51*, Cmd 8190.

Wilson, T. and M. Saito, 2018. Foreign casino operators go all in as they vie for Osaka licence. Reuters, 20 August, https://tinyurl.com/y4s58fot

Witherow, T., 2018. Finance director, 35, stole £1million from his employer to fund gambling addiction after betting firms convinced him to spend £50k in ONE DAY by giving him free holidays. *Daily Mail*, 2 December, www.dailymail.co.uk/news/article-6452499/Finance-director-35-stole-1million-employer-fund-gambling-addiction.html

Wood, G., 1998. Racing: advance of the High Street bookie. *Independent*, 25 September, www.independent.co.uk/sport/racing-advance-of-the-high-street-bookie-1200462.html

Wood, G., 2013. Bookmakers' starting prices often costing punters an arm and a leg. *Guardian*, 3 February, www.theguardian.com/sport/blog/2013/feb/03/horse-racing

Wood, V., 2019. Brigid Simmons to step down from British Beer & Pub Association. *The Caterer*, 4 July, www.thecaterer.com/articles/555514/brigid-simmons-to-step-down-from-british-beer-pub-association

Woodburn, J., 1982. Egalitarian societies, *Man* NS 17(3): 431–51.

Woodcock, A., 2012. Labour's law on gambling ruined lives, says Harman. *The Scotsman*, 6 August, www.pressreader.com/uk/the-scotsman/20120805/282071979043363

Woodhouse, J., 2017. Fixed odds betting terminals. House of Commons Briefing Paper Number 06946, 24 February, http://cliftondavies.com/wp-content/uploads/2017/02/HoC-Library-Briefing-Paper-Fixed-Odds-Betting-Terminals.pdf

Woolley, R. and C.H. Livingstone, 2009. Into the zone: innovating in the Australian poker machine industry In S.F. Kingma (ed.), *Global Gambling: Cultural Perspectives on Gambling Organisations*. New York: Routledge, pp. 38–63.

Worhunsky P., M. Potenza and R. Rogers, 2017. Alterations in functional brain networks associated with loss-chasing in gambling disorder and cocaine-use disorder. *Drug and Alcohol Dependence* 178: 363–71.

Young, M. and F. Markham, 2017. Rehabilitating Reno: a commentary on Hancock and Smith. *International Journal of Mental Health Addiction*, 15(6): 1187–92.

Zaloom, C., 2006. *Out of the Pits: Traders and Technology from Chicago to London*. Chicago: University of Chicago Press.

Zelizer, V., 1979. *Morals and Markets: The Development of Life Insurance in the United States*. New York: Columbia University Press.

Zelizer, V., 1994. *The Social Meaning of Money: Pin Money, Paychecks, Poor Relief, and Other Currencies*. New York: Basic Books.

Zheng, V. and P. Wan, 2014. *Gambling Dynamism: The Macao Miracle*. Berlin: Springer.

Ziolkowski, S., 2017. *The World Count of Gaming Machines 2016*. Gaming Technologies Association, Australia, http://gamingta.com/wp-content/uploads/2017/05/World_Count_2016.pdf

Zuboff, S., 2019. *The Age of Surveillance Capitalism*. London: Profile.

Index

49s (numbers draw) 77
888 (online company) 131, 184
888 Ladies 150

academics, 170
  relationships with gambling
    industry 2, 167–8
account holders and holding 20, 138,
    143–4, 148–9
  bets between 122
  closing of winners' accounts 117–8,
    137
Adelson, Sheldon 10
advertising 42, 136, 184
  for gambling banned in UK 22
  role in addiction to gambling 15
  on television 142
Advertising Standards Association
    (ASA) 185
Advisory Board for Safer Gambling 185
Africa 193–4
Alberta, Canada 89–90, 92
alcohol industry 15, 16, 89, 92, 182
Alderney 131
algorithms 109, 125, 126, 139
ambient gambling 28, 74
American Gaming Association (AGA)
    179
amusements with prizes (AWP) 67,
    77, 80
analytics 138
Anschutz, Philip 36
anti-statist statism 174
anthropology: as approach to gambling
    studies 1, 5–6, 16–17, 18, 135,
    155–6
Antigua 129
arbitrage betting 109, 123, 159
artificial intelligence (AI) 133
Asia 139, 179
Asian gamblers: stereotype of 13

Association of British Bookmakers
    (ABB) 25, 33, 67, 80, 107, 186,
    191
  and responsible gambling 179
  policy on safety and security in
    betting shops 102, 104–5, 106–8
Association of Social Anthropologists 6
Atlantic City 153
Australia 2, 9, 13, 15, 74, 89, 91, 179
  government policies on gambling
    27, 130, 182, 191
  indigenous people 47
  Interactive Gambling Act (2001)
    130
  and 'problem gamblers' 76, 92
Australian Churches Gambling Task
    Force 12
automation 133, 139

baccarat 8–9
backgammon 159
Bali: cockfighting in 47
Banks, Gary 89
banks and banking: social role of 39
Barbuda 129
Belgium 158
Bet Acceptance Centre 112, 113,
    114–5, 121
bet365 122, 134, 136, 141
bet-in-play 109, 133, 136, 150–1, 184
'Bet-in Play Now' (advertisement) 134
Bet Regret 180
BetBrain 122
Betfair 26, 121–3, 131, 166, 189
  impact on bookmakers 121–6, 126
BetFred 59, 66, 103, 184
Better Regulation Task Force (BRTF)
    31–2
betting, definition of 125–6
  non-remote betting 58–9
  see also gambling

Betting and Gaming Bill (1960) 62, 65
Betting and Gaming Council 16, 186
betting industry 1, 2, 18–19
    decline of 126
    moves offshore 26
    reaction to National Lottery 25–6
    taxation on 26
    see also gambling industry
betting shops 1, 2, 18, 19, 24, 57, 58–9,
    63–5, 97, 102, 190
    ban on advertisements for 25
    changing role of workers in 70,
        105–6, 108
    codes of practice 93–4
    customers of 94–100, 106–7
    daily routine of 94–7, 106–8
    etiquette of customer behaviour in
        97, 100
    female staff in 65, 102–3
    and horseracing 66–8, 78
    impact of Betting and Gaming Bill
        on 65
    impact of deregulation on 18
    impact of FOBTs on 76, 106
    impact of smoking ban on 192–3
    licensing of (1961) 57, 62–3
    in London 94–7
    as masculine space 65, 97
    money in 97–8
    as part of leisure industry 18, 24, 63
    promoted as community hubs 192
    removal of restrictions on 67–8
    single manning in 106
    as social spaces 57
    television in 24, 63
    violence and robberies in 96, 102–6,
        107
    virtual horseracing in 70–2
    and women 57, 64, 100–2, 193
    workers in 63–4
Betting Show (1998) 78; (2006) 30
Betview Magazine 122
Big Bang 24
Big Data 126
bingo 65, 150
Black, Andrew 121
Blackmore, Richard 67

Blackpool 30
Blair, Tony 189
Blandford, Mark 27
Blunkett, David 22
bonus culture 137, 138
bonuses 134, 146, 148, 151
bookies *see* bookmakers
bookmakers and bookmaking 18, 24, 31
    animosity to casinos 33–4
    codes of practice 80, 81
    honesty of 60–1
    and horseracing 70
    impact of Betfair on 121–4
    impact of National Lottery on 25, 67
    lack of skill of 70
    reaction to BRTF report 32
    reaction to Budd Report 31
    reaction to National Lottery 25–6
    resistant to innovation 34–5, 141–2
    workers in 63–4, 83
    see also traditional bookmakers
Brazil 171
British Amusement Catering Trade
    Association 33–4
British Beer and Pub Association 16
British Betting Office Association 35
British Columbia, Canada 91–2
British Horseracing Board 66, 67
British Racing Authority 67
Brown, Gordon 30, 130, 189
Brunei 9, 153
Budd, Alan 27–8, 32
Budd Report *see Gambling Review
    Report*

Caborn, Richard 29–30
Callaghan, Jim 63
Campaign for Fairer Gambling 87, 88,
    90, 172, 191
Canada 9, 74, 76, 89–90, 91–2, 128
'Canadian' 192
capitalism 39, 85, 175
    see also neoliberalism
casino industry 33, 36, 38, 58–9
    animosity to bookmakers 33–4
casinos 7, 25, 29, 77, 80
    see also resort casinos

Championship League 150
Chandler, Victor 26, 131
'chasing soft money' 139
Cheltenham Festival 75, 192
Chicago Board of Trade 109
children 15, 28, 183–4
China 8, 9, 153
Chinese gamblers 13
Christian Socialists 58
city traders 123–4
Coates, Denise 134
clock bags 60
Clubs Australia 179
Coalition to Stop Internet Gambling
    (CSIG) 10
cockfighting 47
Code for Responsible Gambling and
    Player Protection in Licensed
    Betting Offices in
    Great Britain (ABB)107–8
commercial gambling 1, 3, 8, 17,
    global expansion of 1, 7, 11, 12–14
    synergy between late capitalism and
    17, 175
Committee on Culture, Media and
    Sports 12, 29–30
conferences 3, 9–10, 11, 20, 88–9 129,
    154, 155, 158
conflicts of interest
    between academics and industry 2,
    167–8
    between industry and funding of
    research 16–17, 88–9
    between government and industry
    166–8
    between public good and
    profitability 39, 87, 92–3, 163,
    164, 181, 182, 184
Conservative government (UK) 23, 25,
    27, 32, 87
Coral 59, 66, 78, 130
Costa Rica 128, 129
Cousin, Matt Zarb 191
Cremin, Jim 122
cricket 153
Cromwell, Oliver 58

cross-border gambling 110, 132, 156,
    193
Crouch, Tracey 76, 164
Curley, Barney 118

Daily Mail 29, 30, 33, 63, 175, 183, 184
demand principle 18, 27, 28
democratization of credit 36
Denmark 162
Department of Culture, Media and
    Sport (DCMS) 22, 29, 80
Derby (horse race) 58
Derby Day (William Powell Frith) 58
Deregulation and Contracting Out Act
    (1994) 27
Deregulation of Betting and Gaming
    Order (1966) 67
Di Baddest 10
Di Maio, Luigi 171
Dilston Races 58
direct to business service (B2B) 140
direct to customer service (B2C) 140,
    142
disordered gambling *see* 'problem
    gamblers'
dog racing 18, 68
Dogs Playing Poker (Coolidge) 12
Done, Peter and Fred 66
Donoughue, Steve 38, 182
drugs 82

e-Bay 141
e-gaming 111, 112
    see also online gambling
e-mail 141
Easyodds 122
Economic and Social Research Council
    6
Efford, Clive 87
electronic gaming machines (EGM) 8,
    73–5, 89–90, 150
electronic points of sale (EPS) 70, 96,
    115, 120–1
Endorphina 10
Epsom race course 58
Europe 130, 171
European Commission 157–8, 159

European Court of Justice (ECJ) 157, 158, 161–2
European Research Council (ERC) 6
European Union countries 154, 155, 158, 171–2
  laws on gambling 27, 156–8, 161–2,
Evans, Richard 122

Fair Play Performance Update (Ladbrokes) 175
Featurespace 88
fieldbooks 115, 118
fieldwork 3, 4, 6, 14, 19, 79, 111, 186–7
  in Gibraltar 131–2
financial services, deregulation of 24, 38, 172
Financial Services Act (1986) 24
fines and fining 184–5
Finland 92, 154
fixed-odds betting terminals (FOBTs) 18–19, 33, 42, 58, 63, 73, 76–86, 185
  codes of practice 80, 81, 180
  hostility to 82–4, 183
  impact on betting shops of 76–8
  links to problem gambling 86, 87, 89, 172
  reduction of maximum stake 76, 88, 89, 172
  success of 79–83
Fong, David 180
foot-and-mouth disease: impact on horse racing 26
football 136–7, 150, 184
France 156, 158
Frater, Steve 77, 78, 85
free bets 82, 134, 151
free market 17, 163, 170, 174
  impact on gambling industry of 28, 31, 163
  as separation of economy and society 30
  see also neoliberalism
Free Trade and Processing Act 129
fruit machines *see* slot machines
Future Regulation of Remote Gambling, The (DCMS) 29

Gala Coral 59, 131
Gabelli case 157, 194
GambleAware 6, 89, 180
gamblers
  attitude of industry to 82–4
  freedom of choice of 23–4, 170
  individual responsibility of 17, 38, 86, 87, 91, 145, 176–8
  monitoring of 115–7
  reaction to responsible gambling initiatives 180
  recruitment and retention of 11, 117, 136–7, 138, 139, 142, 151
  see also problem gamblers
gambling 1, 7, 21, 45, 125, 150–2
  addiction to 15, 74, 177–8, 179
  attitudes to 21, 39, 41–6, 183–5, 190
  biological and genetic factors attributed to 13, 179
  'common sense' approach to 160–1, 163, 166
  definitions of 43–6, 55
  expenditures on 28–9, 149–50
  as form of taxation 14
  funding of research into 187
  harm caused by 14–15, 39, 182–3
  as natural instinct 11–13
  objections to seen as class prejudice 38
  opinions on meaning of 43–6, 55
  promotion as part of leisure industry 168
  as public health issue 91–3
  research into 5, 182
  surveys on 41–2
  in UK 4, 15, 22, 156
  universality of 11–13
  and women 37, 60
  see also commercial gambling; online gambling; remote gambling; responsible gambling, etc.; Australia; Japan; United States etc.
Gambling Act
  (2005) 18, 33, 58, 63, 65, 129, 130, 163, 176
  (2007) 1, 111

Gambling Commission 15, 23, 42, 55, 130, 184, 185
  approval of by industry 163–4
  definition of gambling by 45
  dismissal of objections as middle-class 38
  ineffectiveness of 124
Gambling Compliance 11
gambling executives 2, 3–4, 17, 36
  women 134
gambling industry 2, 3, 14, 16, 128, 160
  attitudes of workers in 132, 134–5
  changing attitudes to 183–4
  codes of practice 93–4
  'common sense' approach to 160–1, 163, 166
  dependency on government 158, 172, 175
  deregulation of 18, 28, 30, 32, 34, 38–9, 173
  diversification of 112–3, 150
  exploitation of changes in regulation 85–6
  framing and reframing of 22, 176, 183
  funding of research into 16, 88, 187
  global expansion of 1, 7, 11, 12–14, 73
  global value of 7
  government polices on 4, 17–18, 29, 34, 91, 180, 185, 186
  government revenues from 89–90, 194
  laws on 23, 156–8
  Mass Observation report into (1947) 44
  productions of 15, 16, 174–5
  profits from 7, 26–7, 92
  promotion of responsible gambling 92, 175–6, 179
  reaction to BRTF report 32
  reaction to National Lottery 27
  reaction to opposition 37
  regulation of 4, 8, 28, 32, 85, 91, 130, 155–6, 164–8, 172
    see also 'light-touch' regulation
  relationships with politicians 168–72
  self-regulation of 32, 81, 97, 175
  sexism in 10, 37, 79–80
  transformation of 23, 24–5, 38–9, 150
  workers in 3, 159–60
  see also betting industry; commercial gambling; online gambling, etc.
gambling machines 9, 28, 33–4, 75
  see also fixed-odds betting terminals
Gambling Review Report 28, 30–1
gambling studies 15–16
Gambling With Lives 90
GamCare 79, 88, 144, 177, 191
games of chance 46–7
Gaming Act (1968) 23, 84
Gaming Board 23, 29, 80, 81
Gaming Intelligence (magazine) 185
Garn-St. Germain Depository Institutions Act (1982) 24
Geertz, Clifford 47
Germany 156–7, 166
Ghas Mandi 153
Gibraltar 19, 26, 127, 130–5, 143, 150, 181
  diversification towards independence 131
  social life of industry workers 134–5
  and World Cup (2014) 136
Gilmour's Act (1986) 23, 24
Global Draw 77, 78
global financial crisis (2008) 39, 174
Global Gaming Expo (G2E) 10
Glynn, Richard 88
Goa 153
'Goliath' 192
Goodale, Jane 47
Goulden, Neil 87
Graeber, David 39
Grand National 18, 75
Grandstand Racing 70
Greece 158, 159
Green Monkey (race horse) 68
Greenway, John 30
Gross Gambling Revenue (GGR) 7

Gross Gambling Yield (GGY) 58, 59, 190
Gross Win (GW) 190
Grubmuller, Walter 77, 78, 85
Guernsey 130
GVC 59, 138,139

Hadza people 46, 56
Haigh, Paul 71
Hammond, Philip 76
Harman, Harriet 22
Harrison, Sarah 184
Hattersley, Roy 29
Hawkswood, Clive, 129
Health Survey for England 42
'Heinz' 192
Henley Centre 25, 67
Ho, Stanley 8
Honkavaara, Finn Jukka 110
horse desk 113, 118, 124
horse racing 18, 26, 57–8, 60, 65,
    66–72, 78, 112, 126
  compilation of odds 113, 114
  economics of 68–9
  handicaps 119
  impact of National Lottery on 26, 67
  levy on 69
  number of events per day 68, 69, 70,
    112
  prize money 67
  on television 24
Hungary 156
'hypocrisy test' 157

Iacovou, Andrew 106
illegal gambling 15, 18, 24, 59–62,
    91, 189
in-play *see* bet-in-play
India 9, 127, 153
Indian Premier League 154
Indonesia 153
inequality, rise of 39, 186
'Infinity' (game) 81
innovation 34–5, 141–2
'Instant Racing' 74
Institute for Public Policy Research
    (IPPR) 15

Institute for the Study of Commercial
    Gambling (ISCG) 180
International Casino Exhibition (ICE)
    9–10
internet 19, 109–10
Internet Casinos Inc. 127–8
Intertops 110
Inuit people 46, 56
Ireland 159
Isle of Man 130, 194
Italy 157, 158, 159, 171–2

Jacobite Rebellion (1715) 58
Japan 9, 21–2, 73, 91, 179–80
Jockey Club 66–7
Joint Committee on the Draft
    Gambling Bill 29, 30
Jowell, Tessa 21, 23, 29, 38, 130
Judt, Tony 22
'Jurassic Park World' (game) 10

Kagarlitski, Joseph 66
Kentucky Downs (racetrack) 191

Labour Government *see* New Labour
Labour Party 185
Ladbrokes 27, 59, 66, 88, 122, 130,
    131, 185
  advertising 136
  move to online 110
  and responsible gambling 175
Las Vegas 8, 9, 10, 22, 12, 74, 75, 80,
    81, 153, 191
Lawrence, Sir Ivan 189
lawyers acting for gambling industry
    34, 85–6, 169–71
LeoVegas 171
Leyland, Paul 126
liabilities
  calculation of 113
  management of 116, 117, 118–9, 120,
    121
'light touch' regulation 17, 24, 129, 154,
    162–3, 136
Lindahl, Niklas 171–2
live betting 136
London Evening Standard 63, 185–6

losing players 139, 151
lotteries 7, 190
'Lucky 15s' 192
'Lucky 31s' 192
Lucky Day 140, 142–3, 145

McArthur, Neil 184, 185
McCririck, John 114
Macau 8–9, 10–11, 75, 90, 179, 180
    Venetian Macau resort 181
Macau Gaming Inspection and
    Co-ordination Bureau 180
Major, John 25, 27, 32
Manchester 30
market economy see free market
marketing 134, 137–40, 151
Mass Observation report (1947) 44
May, Theresa 86
Melanesia 12
Mellor, David 22
men 53–4, 134, 134, 145
    and betting shops 65, 97
Methodism 62
Miller, Tim 185
minimal risk wagering patterns 137
mobile casino gambling 19, 151
mobile first companies 140, 151
mobile phone gambling 136, 140,
    143–4, 150
modernity and modernisation:
    language of free market 11, 30,
    36, 38
money: in betting shops 97–8
Morgan, Piers 175
Morgan Stanley 7, 8
Morris, Tony 68
Murphy, Lee 76
Murray, Albert 85
Muslim countries 9, 153
Myers, Ryan 76

'Nanny State' 38, 39
National Basketball Association (NBA)
    8
National Casino Forum (NCF) 33
National Gambling Helpline 79
National Indian Lottery 127

National Lottery 25, 27, 38–9, 55, 58,
    189
    impact on horse racing 66–7
    objections to 25
National Strategy to Reduce Gambling
    Harms 185–6
near misses 191
neoliberalism 11, 17, 35, 174–5 176,
    185
New Labour 22, 27, 32, 39, 129
New York Times 8
New Zealand 14, 93, 164, 182, 191
    Gambling Act (2003) 93
Newman, Otto 65
Newmarket racecourse 1, 57, 67, 68
'Nobody Harmed' campaign 93
non-disclosure agreements 185
Norway 154, 162, 191
Novomatic 77
numbers draws 77–8

O'Donnell, Hannah 191
odds, compiling of 112–3, 114, 139
odds comparison sites 122
Oddschecker 122
Office of National Statistics 21
Office of Responsible Gambling
    (Australia) 91
off and on course markets 120, 123
offshore gambling industry 66, 127,
    128, 130, 160
online betting exchanges 189
online gambling 1, 7, 9, 19, 58–9, 73,
    85, 109, 119, 110, 127–30
    compared with banking practices
    128–9
    European definition of 156, 159
    government policies on 180
    impact of World Cup on 136
    licensing of 129
    regulation of 154–5
    threat to traditional bookmakers 35
    UK size of 11, 188
open-cry trading 109–10
Orford, Jim 41, 88
over-the-counter betting (OTC) 19, 111
    decline of 97, 112

'overrround' 120

pachinko 9, 21, 74, 75, 100
Paddy Power 184
Pakistan 9, 153
Panorama (tv programme) 104–5
ParentBet 192
Parliamentary All-Party Betting and
    Gaming Group 38
PartyGaming 131
PayPal 194
Penrose, John 34
permission to lay (PTL) 115, 116, 117,
    123
People of Chance (Findlay) 12
Piketty, Thomas 39
Pink Casino 150
'pink gambling' 150
Playtech 110
pokies 9, 74
politicians 4, 17, 36
    defence of gambling industry
        175–6
    opposition to deregulation 29
    relationships with gambling
        industry 168–72
pornography 128, 129
Premier League 136–7, 150, 151
Prescott, John 36
prices, setting of 111, 113–4, 116
private companies 7, 74
privatisation 38, 174
'problem gamblers' 32, 76, 84, 86,
        89–90, 145, 149, 176–8
    attitudes of industry to 37
    denial of link between gaming
        machines and 86, 172
    preventative measures for 182–3
    self-blame 177–8
    women 92

Racehorse Owners Association 68–9
racehorse ownership: economics of
    68–9
racecourses 57, 58
racing *see* horse racing
Racing Post 70–1, 101, 103, 111

raffles 18, 40–1, 42, 44–5, 46–56, 190
    appropriate behaviour at 51
    fundraising for good causes 49, 53
    prizes at 47–8, 49, 51–3
    redistributive function of 50
    and women 53–4
    see also trolley raffles
random number generators (RNG) 69,
    70, 74, 77
Reagan, Ronald 24, 174
redistributive games 46, 56
remote gambling 19, 58, 109, 130, 151,
    194
Remote Gambling Association 129,
    156, 186
Reno model 178–9, 182
research
    funded by gambling industry 16
    funding for 6–7, 187
    methodology 3, 4, 5–6, 16–17, 18
resort casinos 22, 29, 33
Responsibility in Gambling Trust
    (RIGT) 6, 87–8
Responsible Business Performance Report
    (2006) 175, 176
Responsible Gambling Strategy Board
    185
responsible gambling 91–4, 151–2,
    175–8, 180
    promoted by industry 19, 92–3,
        179–80
risk, distribution of 122
    management of 123, 151, 174
risk-based regulation 172
risk taking 11, 12, 128
'risk-tolerant' deregulation 32
Robertson, Hugh 87
Rose, Nikolas 39, 45
roulette 76, 78, 80, 81
Rowlatt, Sir Sidney 62
Royal Commission on Betting, Gaming
    and Lotteries (1951) 62
Royal Commission on Lotteries and
    Betting (1932) 59–60, 62
Runner Runner (film) 128
runners 60
Russia 156

Safe Bet for Success, A (report) 28–9
Safebet Alliance 107
Sainsbury, David 70
Sands Corporation 8, 10
Satellite Information Services 77, 193
Scandinavian countries 9, 156, 165–6
Schindler, Jörg and Gerhart 156
Schüll, Natasha 74
Schwartz, David 12
Schwind and Pendleton 66
Scottish Health Survey 42
seaside arcades: gambling machines
    in 28
Select Committee on Betting Duty
    (1932) 60
Senet Group 93, 194
'shadies and shrewdies' 114, 124, 126
Sharpe, Graham 27
Sikkim 153
Silver, Adam 8
Simmons, Brigid 16, 186
Singapore 22, 57, 91, 154
Sio-mok, Melina Leong 180–1
Sky tv 136–7, 137, 184
Skybet 150, 184
slot machines 9, 10, 73–4, 75, 81, 191
'slow count' 96, 192
smart phones 133, 136, 140, 142, 150
Sonu Jalam 153–4
Spain 132, 133, 156
Spoof (game) 80
Sporting Bet 27
sports betting 9, 10–11, 153
    and women 145
Sports Information Services 77, 193
sports odds, compiling of 112–3
Sportsbook Online Betting Service 110
Stan James (company) 133
Stanley Bet 157
Stapeley, Barry 77
Starnet 128
starting price system (SP) 119
state monopoly gambling 94
Stein, Cyril 66
'steppers': slot machines 81, 191
Straw, Jack 27
street bookies 60–1

suicides: gambling related 14, 76, 86,
    90, 177, 185
Sunday Times 183
'Super Yankee' 192
surveillance capitalism 85
Sweden 14, 154

Tattersalls 68
taxation 26, 27
    gambling as form of 14
    point of consumption tax 136, 155,
        194
    turnover tax 78
technology: impact on gambling 121,
    151
telephone betting 66, 131
television 173–4
    advertisements for gambling 134,
        142
    in betting shops 24, 63
    racing programmes 24
Thank You for Smoking (film) 171
Thatcher, Margaret 24, 25, 32, 174, 189
Timeform 113
Times, The 183
tissue prices 95, 113–4
tobacco industry 15, 16, 89, 92
Tokyo 75, 100
Topping, Ralph 122, 141
trading and traders 115, 118, 123–4,
    125
traditional bookmakers 18, 34–5,
    75–6, 97, 125–6, 140–1
    impact of Betfair on 123–4
    reaction to FOBTs 85
    reaction to online betting 111–2
Train, Detlef 110, 193
'Trixie' 192
trolley raffles 46–8, 51, 52
'Truth about betting shops and gaming
    machines' (ABB) 179
Turks and Caicos Islands 127
Twerk slot 10

uncertainty principle 43, 46, 48, 56
United Arab Emirates 9, 153

United States 7, 8, 11, 21, 73, 151,
     185–6, 191
  betting shops 57
  government policies on gambling
     27, 130
  imposition of limits on gambling
     153
  online gambling 10, 11, 129
  responsible gambling 179
  Unlawful Internet Gambling
     Enforcement Act (2006) 130,
     194–5
'unstimulated demand' principle 62

Venetian Macau resort 181
Victoria, Australia 15, 92, 182
Victoria Responsible Gambling
     Foundation (Australia) 92
video lottery terminals (VLT) 74
Vietnam 91, 154
VIPs 20, 133, 144, 145–8
virtual horse racing 70–2
virtual reality roulette 10
Vospers, Dennis 63

Webb, Derek 191
weight of money 114
'When the Fun Stops' campaign 93
'White Listed' countries 130
William Hill 26, 27, 35, 59, 66, 88, 101,
     104, 106, 122, 134, 195
  advertising 136
  fine imposed on 184

online gambling 110, 130, 131, 141
  and responsible gambling 93
Willink Commission 62
Windsor, Barbara 150
winning players
  closing of accounts of 117–8, 137
  commission charged on 122
Winstone, Ray 134, 150
women 37, 60, 65, 128, 134, 142,
     144–7, 150, 151
  and betting shops 57, 64, 100–2,
     193
  'problem gamblers' 92
  and raffles 53–4
  and sports betting 145
  working in betting shops 102–3
Women's Institutes 40
Woodburn, James 47
working classes 60, 61–2, 64, 65, 97,
     144
World Cup
  (2014) 136, 194
  (2018) 151
World Gaming Magazine 180
World Health Organisation 89
World Regulatory Briefing (2018) 154
World Trade Organisation 129
Wray, Ed 121

'Yankee' 192

Zaloom, Caitlin 109–10
Zone, The 74

The Pluto Press Newsletter

Hello friend of Pluto!

Want to stay on top of the best radical books
we publish?

Then sign up to be the first to hear about our
new books, as well as special events,
podcasts and videos.

You'll also get 50% off your first order with us
when you sign up.

Come and join us!

Go to bit.ly/PlutoNewsletter